EMPOWERING PRACTICE?

To Melissa,
   to remind you of your
   trip to Hampshire.

Remember you can come back....

   yours

   Pauly

Other titles from The Policy Press include:

Supporting women and challenging men: Lessons from the Domestic Violence Intervention Project (1998)
Sheila Burton, Linda Regan and Liz Kelly
Paperback   ISBN 1 86134 068 0   £11.95

Domestic violence: A national survey of court welfare and voluntary sector mediation practice (1997)
Marianne Hester, Chris Pearson and Lorraine Radford
Paperback   ISBN 1 86134 061 3   £11.95

From periphery to centre: Domestic violence in work with abused children (1998)
Marianne Hester and Chris Pearson
Paperback   ISBN 1 86134 115 6   £11.95

Helping families after divorce: Assistance by order? (1999)
Adrain James and Louise Sturgeon-Adams
Paperback   ISBN 1 86134 163 6   £10.95

All the above titles are available from
Biblios Publishers' Distribution Services Ltd
Star Road, Partridge Green, West Sussex RH13 8LD, UK
Telephone +44 (0)1403 710851, Fax +44 (0)1403 711143

EMPOWERING PRACTICE?

A critical appraisal of the family group conference approach

Carol Lupton and Paul Nixon

The POLICY PRESS

First published in Great Britain in 1999 by

The Policy Press
University of Bristol
34 Tyndall's Park Road
Bristol BS8 1PY
UK

Tel +44 (01)117 954 6800
Fax +44 (0)117 973 7308
e-mail tpp@bristol.ac.uk
http://www.bristol.ac.uk/Publications/TPP

British Library Cataloguing in Publication Data
A catalogue record for this book is available from the British Library

ISBN 1 86134 149 0

Carol Lupton is Director of the Social Services Research and Information Unit, University of Portsmouth. **Paul Nixon** is Commissioning Officer, Family Group Conferences, Social Services Department, Hampshire County Council.

Cover design by Qube Design Associates, Bristol.

Photograph used on front cover supplied by kind permission of www.johnbirdsall.co.uk.

Printed and bound in Great Britain by Hobbs the Printers Ltd, Southampton.

Contents

Preface

This book is about the family group conference (FGC) approach to decision making in child welfare and protection. One of the central aims of FGCs is to empower children and their families via a process which enables their effective participation in decision making and by outcomes over which they have more control. Given growing international interest in FGCs, it is important that their development is underpinned by good quality research. The central aim of the book is to assess critically the available evidence on the empowerment potential of the FGC approach.

However, empowerment is an extremely slippery concept. Because of its appeal across the political spectrum, it is particularly important to be clear about the specific expectations and assumptions by which empowerment initiatives are underpinned. This book is therefore also more broadly about the meaning of empowerment in the contemporary child welfare context. In the face of the general clamour for 'evidence-based practice' it addresses the difficult question of how empowerment can be operationalised and its achievement assessed.

Acknowledgements

To Hampshire County Council and Portsmouth City Council Social Services Departments for their active support of the research and to Paul Nixon and Martin Stevens for their unfailing enthusiasm. Thanks also to colleagues attending the first and second international symposia on family group conferences in Winchester for their ideas and advice.

And, as always, to Mark, Daniel, Jack and Tess.

Carol Lupton

Thanks to Phil Taverner for his humour and comradeship throughout the FGC work, to the FGC coordinators in Hampshire for their enthusiasm and commitment to practice, to Family Rights Group for all their advice and guidance, and to my family for their patience, support and encouragement.

Paul Nixon

Introduction

Given our power to legitimate, we need to be more critical and
less casual about what we advocate as empowering. (Rappaport,
1995, p 107)

The last two decades have seen increased political, legal and moral debate
about the rights and needs of children worldwide. While the issues are
complex, and absolute agreement remains elusive, a consensus may have
begun to emerge in the shape of the United Nations (UN) Convention
on the Rights of the Child. Representing the first detailed international
treaty providing minimum standards for children, by 1995 the Convention
had been ratified by 175 countries. Article 12 of the Convention affirms
the principle that children should have a greater say over matters affecting
them and their lives. The Convention also stresses the importance of
families, extended families and communities in children's lives (Article 5)
and parents' duty to exercise their influence and powers over children
responsibly and in the child's best interests. Precisely how these standards
are best achieved remains contentious, however.

Balancing the different, and sometimes conflicting, rights and
responsibilities of children, their families and the State has been an enduring
problem for childcare policy and practice and was a central concern of
the 1989 Children Act (England and Wales). The ambition of the Act was
that these respective rights and responsibilities would be balanced by a
more inclusive and collaborative approach to families, although still
ultimately secured though social work agency procedures and the courts.
While the Act anticipated that its philosophy of inclusion would be
implemented through working in partnership with families and their
communities, in practice this partnership has been hard to achieve. The
growing interest in family group conferences (FGCs) as a model for
partnership may reflect a continued frustration at the inability to work
collaboratively and to manage in practice the tension between the role of
the family and that of the State in the care of children.

This book is about the FGC approach to decision making in child
welfare. Developed originally in New Zealand in work with Maori and
Pacific Islanders, the approach attempts to build on family and community
strengths in planning for the care and protection of children. One of its
central claims is to empower the children and the family members involved,

both via a process which is more enabling of their effective participation and by outcomes over which they have more control. Despite growing international interest in the FGC approach, however, its development has to an only limited extent been underpinned by good quality research. Much of the FGC literature is explicitly promotional, designed to describe the approach and encourage its development. The central aim of this book is thus to assess critically and dispassionately the available research-based evidence on the potential of the FGC approach to promote the empowerment of children and families.

However, empowerment is an extremely slippery concept. Although now common currency in both political and professional discourse, the idea is subject to considerable theoretical and ideological imprecision. It also has the capacity to appeal to politicians on both sides of the political spectrum, resonating with contemporary centre/left interests in new forms of citizen participation and (old) new right concerns to develop the market-based rights of public services consumers. Given its hybrid political appeal, it is important to be clear, in the specific context of its use, about the particular expectations and assumptions by which any empowerment initiative is underpinned. As Rappaport (1995) argues, before we rush to legitimise empowering practices, we need to be somewhat 'less casual' about what it is we are advocating. This book is therefore also more broadly about the challenge of empowerment and what it can and cannot mean in the contemporary child welfare context. If the concept of empowerment is difficult to define and identify, it is even more difficult to measure. In the face of the general clamour for 'evidence-based practice' the book also considers the difficult question of how the ambition of empowerment can be operationalised and the extent of its achievement assessed.

The concern to empower children and families has important implications for the professionals who work within the childcare field. The aim of enhancing the power and control of families may or may not involve a diminution of the power of professionals, but it will certainly require them to adopt different ways of working. The development of empowerment as a form of professional practice is itself, however, characterised by tension and ambiguity. As Baistow (1994/95) has argued, the idea contains both liberatory and regulatory potential. At one extreme, professionally-led empowerment may be something that is done to people whether they like it or not. It may also be the case, as Burford and Pennell (1995) argue, that empowerment practice involves professionals insisting on standards that they themselves could not achieve. In turn, the ability of professionals to work in empowering ways may be constrained by the broader process of professional disempowerment which occurred during the 1980s and 1990s through increased political scrutiny and greater administrative control of social work practice. As well as its effects on the children and families involved, therefore, the book is also concerned with the implications for social work professionals of an approach which attempts to enhance the control and responsibility exercised by family members over decisions affecting their children.

Family group conferences are a new and developing idea. Even in New Zealand their role is established in law but evolving in practice. In both New Zealand and the United Kingdom the FGC approach has had to develop in a hostile political and economic climate. In both countries, the dominance of new right ideology over the decades of the 1980s and 1990s has served to reconfigure the relationship between the family and the State, the public and the private. Stressing the virtues of individual self-reliance, the role of the State in the provision of family support has been heavily circumscribed. At the same time, the ideology of individual responsibility has underpinned more coercive and controlling responses to those families which appear to be unable or unwilling to discharge their responsibilities effectively. As central policy shifts have served to heighten the impoverishment of many families, the resulting social problems have increasingly been blamed on the deviance of individual parents and the deterioration of family values.

In such a context, where inequality and poverty are increasing but the available resources are decreasing, the operation of FGCs may seem to serve a number of political objectives. As Tunstill (1997) has argued in respect of 'family support', the idea is Janus faced: "It has the ability to point both towards an optimum child care policy, but also towards a limited and conditional version, painted against the backdrop of a minimal state" (1997, p 47). In the specific political context of the UK at the end of the 1990s, there is a real danger that FGCs are dominated by an agenda of reduced state intervention in family life, rather than the objective of achieving better decisions for children. In this context 'family empowerment' may translate in practice to obligatory self-reliance rather than to greater control over services, choices and life chances. The final focus of the book is thus on the implications for its empowerment potential of the specific political and economic context in which the FGC approach is developed.

After briefly examining the definition of empowerment and the different political tendencies which have ensured its current prominence in policy discourse, the first chapter of the book examines some of the tensions and dilemmas which characterise the idea of empowerment as a form of professional practice. A central question is posed about the relationship between family and professional empowerment and whether enhancing the control of families necessarily can be seen to diminish that of the professionals. Chapter Two considers the issues of empowerment and 'partnership' in the specific context of children's services and examines historically the extent to which participatory ways of working have been developed in the UK. The main factors which can be seen to have constrained more participatory or 'partnership' approaches are identified and assessed. The background to the development of the FGC approach in New Zealand is then described in Chapter Three and the central principles underpinning its operation are discussed. Chapter Four describes the historical development of FGCs in England and Wales and considers the implications of their current role for childcare workers. The central tension surrounding the operation of FGCs are highlighted as are the factors considered likely to hinder or encourage their future development.

The remaining chapters focus on the available research evidence on the operation of FGCs. Chapter Five briefly describes the range of national jurisdictions in which the FGC approach has been developed and the different ways in which the approach has been configured. The issues emerging from the international research pertinent to the question of empowerment are then highlighted. Taking these issues, Chapter Six examines their relevance to the operation of FGCs in England and Wales. Focusing on the FGC *process*, existing evidence on the extent and nature of any professional manipulation, the effect of power imbalances within the family group and the satisfaction of the family participants are identified and assessed.

Chapters Seven and Eight are concerned with the rather more difficult question of the evidence on FGC *outcomes*. In Chapter Seven, Martin Stevens reminds us of the complex research issues involved in the evaluation of the outcomes of child welfare interventions and the attempt to operationalise and measure an objective such as family empowerment. We make no apologies for including this methodological 'time-out'. In a book centrally concerned with the assessment of 'what works', it is vital to remind ourselves that the empirical means by which such assessments are made are not self-evident nor uncontested. The growing policy interest in establishing the 'evidence-base' for social work practice tends to overlook, or underplay, the difficulties of establishing cause and effect in real world contexts. Martin Stevens' chapter provides a timely reminder of the nature of those difficulties as well as offering some insight into the ways in which they may be overcome. Developing from the arguments of Chapter Seven, Chapter Eight critically examines the available evidence on the longer-term outcomes of FGCs, considering whether it is robust enough to demonstrate the ability of the FGC approach to ensure the welfare and safety of the children involved.

The conclusion in Chapter Nine assesses the balance of evidence on the central questions of the extent to which FGCs operate to enhance the control of family members and of the conditions that need to obtain for empowerment to take place. It also returns to the important issue of the implications of the approach for the development of professional practice. In identifying some of the potential tensions and ambiguities that currently surround the operation of FGCs, the conclusion, and the book more generally, seeks to suggest ways in which these may be minimised or resolved in the future. The authors are aware of a view that the operation of family group conferencing has been subject to more determined research scrutiny than is typically accorded to areas of professionally dominated practice. The concern is that this is so because FGCs put families, rather than professionals, at the forefront of decision making. We would argue, however, that it is precisely because the FGC approach does place so much more responsibility on the shoulders of the families involved that we must ensure that its wider development is carefully underpinned by extensive, rigorous and, above all, dispassionate research-based evidence. It is to this broader endeavour that the book aims to contribute.

ONE

The dilemmas of empowerment

Introduction

> Fundamentally, [the Children, Young Persons and their Families
> Act] is a change of statute law that incorporates procedures for
> empowering the families ... of 'at risk' children, to be able to
> work out and implement their own plans for the enhancement
> of the welfare of their own children. (Wilcox et al, 1991, p 1)

As the above quotation indicates, one of the explicit aims of the legislation
behind the New Zealand family group conference (FGC) is the
'empowerment' of families within the childcare decision-making process.
Not only is it believed that the FGC approach will empower family
members by affording them greater control over decisions about the care
and protection of their children, but it is also assumed that the particular
way in which such decisions are made within the FGC approach will, in
itself, empower those who take part:

> The reciprocity evident in the family group conference process
> helps emphasise the point that people can benefit from the
> challenge and opportunity of helping others. Receiving help
> can actually weaken one's self esteem, but giving help as well as
> receiving it can empower people and strengthen their sense of
> self worth. (Hudson et al, 1996, p 3)

In this way the FGC approach can be seen to fit snugly with the growing
preoccupation of UK social policy discourse over the 1990s with citizen–
consumer involvement in public service development and provision.
Described variously as "... the buzz word of the 1980s" (Adams, 1990, p
42) or the "theme for the 1990s" (Clarke and Stewart, 1992, p 18), the
idea of 'user empowerment' rapidly achieved political prominence over
these years, securing official approval in the guidance to the National
Health Service and Community Care legislation: "the rationale for this
reorganisation is the empowerment of users and carers" (DoH/SSI, 1991,

p 7). The popularity of the idea of empowerment in large part resulted from its attractiveness to political groups of the Left and Right alike. In the context of social welfare, for example, it played a central role in the language of user groups pressing for more control over State services but was also a key theme in the literature of New Right theorists, concerned with freeing the individual from unnecessary interference by, or dependence upon, those services.

Not surprisingly perhaps, given its hybrid political ancestry, the idea of empowerment is overlain by contrasting and often conflicting aims and expectations. As a result, the burgeoning literature on the topic is characterised by considerable conceptual imprecision and not a little idealistic wishful thinking: "... [Its] use is largely linguistic and rhetorical, relying on taken-for-granted meanings that need more careful scrutiny" (Baistow, 1994/95, p 35). It is not the intention of this chapter to reiterate the debates of the empowerment literature, which have been set out adequately elsewhere (Richardson, 1983; Adams, 1990; Beresford and Croft, 1993; Servian, 1996), but rather to identify the key ambiguities surrounding the idea of empowerment and consider their implications for social work practice. After briefly examining the definition of empowerment, the chapter traces the political background to its emergence on the UK policy agenda, identifying the differing and possibly contradictory assumptions by which it is underpinned. The chapter concludes by considering some of the constraints and tensions surrounding the idea of empowerment as professional practice and explores the implications for professional power of a commitment to more empowering ways of working with service users.

The nature of empowerment

Despite, or possibly because of, the popularity of the idea of empowerment, there is little agreement about its definition. Servian (1996), for example, identifies at least nine different meanings of the term prevalent within the literature, ranging from the impact of technological change to the effect of spiritual enlightenment. Some argue that the idea is easier to define in terms of its absence. Thus Rappaport describes its lack as a state of : "... powerlessness, real or imagined; learned helplessness; alienation; loss of a sense of control over one's own life" (1984, p 3). There is broad agreement that empowerment is the reversal of this situation in which those without power (the powerless or the 'disempowered') achieve greater control over one or more aspects of their lives and an enhanced sense of personal or political gratification. Adams (1990, p 43), for example, provides a fairly generic definition of empowerment as:"...the process by which individuals, groups and/or communities become able to take control of their circumstances and achieve their own goals, thereby being able to work towards maximising the quality of their lives". Similarly, Holdsworth describes the aim of empowerment as being "... to enable the formerly powerless to exert at least some measure of control over their lives" (1991, p 12).

Deeper examination of the concept, however, reveals considerable disagreement about the nature of empowerment and the means by which it is obtained. In particular, and most fundamentally, the use of the concept is underpinned by very different views about the nature of 'power' and the relationship between those who possess it and those who do not. On the one hand, many approaches to empowerment can be seen to rest upon an assumption that the acquisition of power on the part of certain individuals or groups necessarily involves its absence or diminution on the part of others. This conceptualises power as a finite or 'zero-sum' quantity in which there is a direct and inverse relationship between the ability of A to control the behaviour of B and the ability of B to resist the wishes of A. Within the context of State social work, for example, such an approach assumes that, in so far as the disempowerment of clients or service users results from the exercise of power on the part of professionals, their empowerment requires that the power of those professionals is reduced. The arguments of some proponents of the FGC approach are clearly based on this assumption. Thus there is talk about the possibility of FGCs resulting in a "... more equal sharing of power, status and influence" (Ryburn and Atherton, 1996, p 22) with a concomitant reduction in the power of professionals "... the professional role is correspondingly redefined and circumscribed" (Ryburn, 1994, p 7).

Alternative conceptualisations of the idea of empowerment, however, may be based on a view of power as an expandable or 'variable sum' quantity, in which the acquisition of power by some may not necessarily involve its loss on the part of others. From this perspective, it is argued, even those with mutually opposing interests may find that there are contexts in which the empowerment of the other 'side' enhances their own power. Recognition of this fact, after all, has long been the basis of political conspiracies and alliances. It is also possible to imagine a situation in which the 'empowerment' of the powerless could be secured without any significant negative effects upon the power of the powerful. Thus

Craig and Mayo (1995) argue that the successful pursuit of collective goals such as economic regeneration can be seen to benefit all groups within society.

The idea of zero-sum power can be seen to ignore the fact that power relationships are not hermetically sealed but are socially constructed, determined in large part by the operation of forces external to them. If A is a black woman manager, for example, and B a white male employee, the ability of A to control the actions of B will derive not just from her occupational status, but also in part from the wider structures of race and sexual inequality which characterise the social systems in which they both live and work. In a similar way the relationship between professional social workers and their 'clients' or service users can be understood as affected, not just by the influence of professionally-based power, but also by the operation of a range of economic, ideological and political factors which determine or constrain the actions of both sides of the relationship. In so far as some of these factors, such as the impact of 'new managerialist' approaches, for example, or of increased financial constraint, may be seen to disempower the professional as much as the client, it is possible to envisage scenarios in which both 'sides' of the relationship could benefit or suffer equally. Given the extent to which many childcare professionals are themselves disempowered by the structures and systems within which they work, it may be the case that they have more to gain than lose from a situation in which children and their parents/carers are accorded more control over the decisions affecting their lives.

The political history of empowerment

To appreciate the tensions inherent in the contemporary use of the concept of empowerment, we need to examine the very different ideological tendencies by which its political ascendancy has been driven. To do so, it is necessary to begin with the perceived failure of the British welfare state to fulfil the political vision of its founders. Marking the end of piecemeal and paternalistic forms of charitable assistance, the formation of the welfare state was to represent a new contract between the State and its citizens, providing them with a comprehensive and universal system of public support 'from cradle to the grave'. Original expectations that the welfare role of the State would diminish in the face of the improved health and economic security of the population, however, soon proved to have been misplaced. Instead, increased demand for health and welfare services as a result of demographic and technological change and the enhanced expectations of a more affluent public, meant that the range and volume of the State's activities were to expand dramatically over the post-war years. In the face of evidence about the wasteful, inefficient and costly nature of these activities, concern began to grow about the price the welfare state was exacting from the nation. This concern was given particular urgency by the international oil crisis and accompanying economic depression of the early 1970s.

In response, ways of ending the 'provider dominance' of the State began actively to be sought at central political level. There was a growing interest in the possibilities of voluntary effort, with David Owen as Minister for Health in the 1964 Labour government writing of the need to establish a 'partnership' between statutory and non-statutory providers of services. In the face of what was seen to be an increasingly passive and demanding citizenry, there was also a concern to encourage greater public involvement in local service development. The late 1960s saw a series of reports – the Skeffington Report (1969) on local planning, the Plowden Report (1969) on schooling and the Seebohm Report (1968) on the personal social services – which, in their different ways, all made the case for greater community and public participation. As Brenton (1985) has argued, the growing political consensus over these years about the importance of 'voluntary action' or 'partnership' was driven not so much by the ideological commitment to welfare pluralism as from the attempt to make a virtue out of the political necessity of cutting social expenditure. Nevertheless, it can be seen to represent a significant shift in the attitude of central governments towards the involvement of the non-statutory sector, which laid the foundation for subsequent moves towards a 'mixed economy 'of welfare provision.

At the local level, the experience of the paternalistic and unresponsive nature of State welfare services fuelled the rise during the 1960s and 1970s of new groups and organisations committed to many different forms of self-help and collective action. Many of these groups were defined in terms of their consumption (or not) of particular State services: tenants' associations, squatters' groups, patient associations and so on. Others focused on specific mental or physical conditions – such as the Epilepsy Action Group or the National Schizophrenia Fellowship – or campaigned around a particular social problem or issue, such as the Pre-school Playgroups Association or the Child Poverty Action Group. Although in the main committed (or consigned) to the use of State services, these groups were opposed to the manner of their provision and/or the

extent of their availability and accessibility; a political position which
some groups described at the time as being "in and against the state"
(London Edinburgh Weekend Return Group, 1979):

> **The alternative organisations, groups and movements that grew**
> **up in the 1960s and 70s were in many ways the by-product of the**
> **public welfare system; as much a reaction to the deficiencies,**
> **size and inaccessibility of the state welfare apparatus as the result**
> **of pressure to participate and protest engendered by the wider**
> **process of cultural and social change. (Brenton, 1985, p 36)**

One of the central problems with State-provided services was seen to be
the way in which they encouraged passivity and dependency on the part
of those receiving services. Users of services were viewed in terms of
their perceived needs or 'deficits' but were largely excluded from the
professionally-dominated process of defining these needs. Ignoring the
wider personal and social contexts in which their 'clients' lived, professional
interventions were focused on the individual, typically isolating and
pathologising the problem being treated. Little recognition was given to
the social construction of these needs – the fact that they were often the
product of "socially imposed constraints" (Oliver, 1990) rather than simply
the result of the physical or mental conditions of the individuals concerned.
The biophysical disempowerment of many service users was thus
compounded by diminished access to social goods such as employment,
affordable housing and a decent standard of education. In addition to the
objective of participating in, or 'reclaiming', the process of defining need,
therefore, the emergent service user groups also pressed for a broader
political shift from the role of client or patient, as passive recipient of help,
to the more active role of citizen, with rights to the means to participate
fully in social and economic life.

Many groups also campaigned for the creation of alternative forms of
service provision controlled by users and/or local people themselves. The
late 1960s and early 1970s thus also saw the emergence of a range of
'autonomous' service providers – such as women's aid refuges, rape crisis
lines, advice centres, housing cooperatives – which operated on very
different philosophical and organisational assumptions to those of
traditional State services. Typically based on the principles of self-help
and collective action, these new providers were committed not only to
the provision of assistance but, as importantly, to the particular means by
which this assistance was provided. Thus Kelly describes the aim of the

UK Women's Aid movement as not only providing a place of safety but also offering women using the service "... a different way of understanding what happened to them and the possibility of not being the 'victim' or 'client'. We talked about self-help, working with women, rather than for them" (1991, p 35). By demonstrating the possibility of acting on the world to change it, participation in these new forms of provision was seen to provide a personally empowering experience for those involved.

Central to the work of many of these groups and movements was the shift in focus from the needs or behaviours of individuals to more collective forms of identity and action. The social and physical 'disempowerment' of individuals was seen to stem not from their personal circumstances/ attributes, but from the operation of wider systems of race, sex, class and other forms of structural inequality:"... the powerlessness and loss which results from ... material and ideological oppression" (Mitchell, 1989, p 22). Many of the service-orientated and self-help groups were thus also linked to the broader agendas and activities of the 'new social movements' emerging at the same time in the UK. These larger-scale movements were defined in terms of the "politics of identity" (Williams, 1992, p 16) – women's groups, gay and lesbian movements, Black groups and the disabled persons' movement – and/or by a commitment to community, environmental or peace activism. Inspiration was also drawn from the activities of the anti-poverty and urban renewal movements emerging across the USA in the late 1960s and early 1970s (Brenton, 1985). Thus the routes to personal and political empowerment were, for some, linked to a commitment to wider sociopolitical change:

> **The new social movements are consciously engaged in critical evaluation of capitalist society and in the creation of alternative models of social organisation at local, national and international levels, as well as trying to reconstruct the world ideologically and create alternative forms of social provision. (Oliver, 1990, p 113)**

A similar concern with the oppressive and overarching powers of the central state informed the writings of the new liberals or New Right. Achieving political ascendancy in the UK with the election of Margaret Thatcher in 1979, these theorists argued that the growth of the welfare state was parasitical and destructive, spreading "... like bindweed at the expense of the ... wealth creating sector, strangling and threatening to destroy what it grew up on" (Keith Joseph, cited in Cutler and Waine,

1994, p 105). Due to the proliferation of publicly-provided services which eroded individual responsibility, moreover, the 'nanny' state was held to blame for the powerlessness and dependency of certain social groups.

The New Right prescription for 'empowerment' was, however, very different from that of the user/popular democratic movements, although it involved a similar attempt to rework the nature of the relationship between the individual and the State. In contrast to the dependency created by the welfare state's "citizenship of entitlement" (Ignatieff, 1989, p 63), the citizens of New Right theory were to be enabled to become independent beings; their right to security and support being replaced by rights to self-sufficiency and self-determination: "... the well-being of individuals is best promoted when they are helped to be independent, to use their talents to take care of themselves and their families, and to achieve things on their own" (Moore, 1987, p 5). In particular, those using public services would be empowered by being given the same rights as their counterparts in the private market, the key dimensions of which were defined as access to better information about, choice between, and redress from service providers.

Public empowerment in New Right thinking was thus seen to derive not from any right to support or assistance, but from the more negative right to be free from unnecessary dependence on, or interference by, the State. Its context was typically that of the use of a specific set of services or products, and its duration was correspondingly limited: empowerment became a one-off, finite experience rather than a longer-term process of personal growth and development. Its value moreover was not intrinsic (complaining is good for you) but rather instrumental, perceived in terms of the ends it serves: the ability to receive better information, voice concerns, achieve redress or to exit to other providers. Market-based empowerment was, above all, a very personal affair, limited to the preferences and actions of individual consumers, rather than the needs of groups, communities or the public at large.

The political popularity of New Right ideas about the welfare state was to grow during the 1980s and early 1990s. This was due in large part to the fact that they resonated with the everyday experience of ordinary people, as tenants of council housing, as recipients of State benefits or as residents of State-run residential homes, of services that were patronising, inflexible and of limited quality. The vesting of the public service user with the same rights as those of their private market counterpart fed into the growing demand for users to be treated with respect and to obtain redress against poor quality or inadequate services. A particularly popular theme of the New Right approach was its claim to empower the people against the state. Clarke (1996) describes the way in which public dissatisfaction was captured by New Right ideological imagery:

> One by one, arrogant doctors, liberal social workers, child-centred teachers and Marxist sociologists found themselves arraigned in the court of public opinion alongside 'loony-left councillors and 'bloody-minded public sector trade unionists'. (Clarke, 1996, p 6)

Power and the professionals

Although promoting very different visions of public empowerment, both popular democratic and New Right approaches contained an explicit critique of the 'disempowering' role of welfare professionals. From the New Right perspective, these privileged provider groups were seen to be the main cause of the overloaded State; their occupational raison d'être being to serve their own interests rather than those of the public. Welfare bureaucrats, professionals and service users were viewed as forming an 'iron triangle' with mutually reinforcing interests in the institutionalisation of dependency (Green, 1987). Social workers were considered particularly to blame for the rising costs of welfare expenditure by shoring up dysfunctional and potentially dangerous families:

> ... the operation of 'welfarism' in the hands of the new experts, of which social work was perhaps *the* prime example, encouraged soft, permissive attitudes to deviance, fecklessness and the actual and potentially violent – the traditional dangerous classes. (Parton, 1994, p 23)

For New Right theorists, the solution to the power of professionals was again the operation of the public sector market. The enhanced rights of the (deserving) welfare consumer, faced with an increased choice of providers, would force professionals to be more directly accountable to those who use their services. Developments such as the Citizen's Charters in the early 1990s were explicitly presented as an opportunity to use the power of the consumer as a wedge against that of professional groups (Stewart and Walsh, 1992).

For those involved in the new user and social movements, attitudes towards the role of professionals were more mixed and reflected the very different political stances deriving from the 'variable' and the 'zero-sum' conceptualisations of power. Some groups shared the New Right view of professionals as part of the problem, seeing them as playing a central role in maintaining the powerlessness of those with whom they work. In this view, the professionals' ability to impose their definitions of need and appropriate solutions derived from the use of their professional power to exclude service users from the decision-making process:

> ... by taking active measures to prevent users occupying influential and authoritative positions; failing to act to remove barriers and obstacles to participation; and/or creating a reality in which it is normal for users to be passive and quiescent. (Braye and Preston-Shoot, 1995, p 100)

From this perspective, the empowerment of service users is seen to be possible only at the expense of those who possess professional or organisational power. Langan and Lee, for example, argue that the process of user empowerment necessarily involves the transfer of power from professionals into the hands of those who are "... systematically deprived of it within the framework of the welfare state" (1989, p 9). For some, moreover, this transfer of power is unlikely to occur voluntarily and must be actively taken away from those who hold it:

> Empowerment happens not just because people want to give away power, but because oppressed people engage in wresting it away from them. (Braye and Preston-Shoot, 1995, p 100)

In contrast, rather than being identified as part of the problem, others argue for professionals (alternatively, or in addition) to be seen as part of the potential solution; serving in certain contexts as allies, advocates and/or mediators for service users. Hallett (1987), for example, argues the importance of professionals as conduits to relevant research-based knowledge and information:

> It is wasteful and inefficient wilfully to undervalue the expertise, accumulated wisdom and knowledge available from social research to which professionals customarily have access. (Hallett, 1987, p 20)

As well as the advantages of professional knowledge and training, many in the user movement acknowledged the important role of the professional as a 'go-between' providing an essential link between laypersons and the complex internal world of welfare organisations. In this capacity professionals can assist user groups to operate more effectively by virtue of their knowledge of the appropriate structures, personnel and debates. As Croft and Beresford concede:"Some of the best and most valued work of both statutory and voluntary organisations has been in the field of professional advocacy" (1988, p 16). Moreover, others argue, it is important to recognise that on many issues there may be important areas of commonality between the interests of professionals and those who use their services. As Richardson comments, it is not appropriate to see the issue as being one of opposing sides:

> ... to designate the participatory process as a simple power struggle between two opposing sides is to misunderstand the essential nature of the interests involved. While the aims of consumers and other decision-makers are unlikely to be strictly congruent, they are also rarely strictly conflicting.... There is, in short, a partial battle and a partial meeting ground.... (Richardson, 1983, p 80)

Paralleling the rise of user movements was a growing concern on the part of social work professionals to develop a practice that at the very least did not further disempower its clients and, at best, actively worked to enhance their sense of power and control. Responses to this concern, however, similarly differed according to the degree of power transference that was seen to be necessary or possible between social workers and those with whom they work. The result was a range of professional approaches to user empowerment, from the more liberal, 'working in partnership' variants (Fisher et al, 1989; Biehal and Sainsbury, 1991; Marsh and Fisher, 1992) to the more radical 'anti-oppressive practice' stance of writers like Ward and Mullender (1991); Dominelli (1996); Langan and Lee (1989) and Philipson (1992).

Writing from within the 'partnership' school, Biehal and Sainsbury argue that social workers committed to empowerment must recognise and work within the fact of existing power imbalances between social workers and their clients. The partnership between social workers and users is thus seen to be inherently unequal, not least because many of the latter do not freely chose to enter the relationship. The role of the empowering social worker is to work towards maximising the control and self-determination of clients within the constraints of this unavoidably unequal relationship: "... it is possible to think of partnership practice as ... pushing the concept of clients' rights to the limits of what can be currently achieved within the framework of local authority social work and the broader structures of power and inequality in Britain" (1991, p 253). Although professionals must work wherever possible to maximise the rights of their clients, some rights may be beyond the power of social workers to ensure and some may have to be limited (Biehal and Sainsbury, 1991):

> **No social work practice can be perfect, and the partnership practice model can never be perfectly implemented. So, in speaking of clients' rights, we need to be clear that we are proposing standards of social work which cannot be achieved in full: social workers should not be condemned for occasional failures to safeguard their clients' rights. (Biehal and Sainsbury, 1991, p 255)**

In contrast, the more radical critique focuses on the oppressive nature of professional social work and perceives the possibility of a more profound shift in the balance of power that obtains between social workers and those with whom they work (Corrigan and Leonard, 1978; London Weekend Return Group, 1979; Dominelli and McLeod, 1989; Ahmed, 1990). Such writers argue that the 'choice' apparently provided to service users within the idea of 'partnership practice' is illusory (Dominelli, 1996). By failing to challenge the power structures on which the client/ professional relationship is based, such practice ultimately leaves the control over the terms and conditions of that partnership to the professionals:

> **Emerging professional principles for partnership practice (Marsh and Fisher, 1992) promote user choice without clarifying how professionally led consumerism empowers users, and argue that statutory mandates can form the basis of partnership without addressing the criticism that this is not partnership but participation in a preset agenda. (Braye and Preston-Shoot, 1995, p 102)**

For writers such as this, the notion of empowerment is meaningless unless it attempts to confront and combat the wider structures and processes which reproduce inequality: the point is not just to recognise the wider effects of discrimination and oppression, but to try and change them. Professionals, it is argued, need to work more actively to empower those they work with by confronting the forces of oppression, including their own oppressive attitudes, in their everyday practice. Empowerment is more than just 'enabling' clients to have their say, the commitment to empowerment needs to be accompanied by "... a commitment to combating and challenging injustice and oppression, which shows itself in action as well as words" (Ward and Mullender, 1991, p 22). At times this will mean assisting service users to confront managers or managerialist practices and supporting them in "... grass roots empowerment, consumer orientated perspectives and collective forms of working" (Dominelli, 1996, p 156). In turn this will require anti-oppressive working with service users underpinned by "anti-racist, feminist and related struggles" (Ward and Mullender, 1991, p 28), which reject the "splintering of the public and private, of person and society" (Ward and Mullender, 1991, p 29). The partnership approaches, it is argued, have reinforced the process of the individualisation of social problems and failed to address the collective forms of deprivation (Dominelli, 1996); progress towards real change requires that work with individual clients is linked to broader political and collective struggles. Thus, for Brake and Bailey, the 'essence' of empowerment is a professional practice which sets out to "... bring together clients with common needs and problems to engage in collective action on their behalf" (quoted in Ward and Mullender, 1991, p 29).

Empowerment as professional practice

Empowerment for whom?

Whatever the variant, the notion of empowerment as professional practice can be seen to raise some important practical and ethical dilemmas. The first of these stems from the central question, not of how empowerment is to be achieved (although we will return to this later), but with (or on) whom it is attempted. At its broadest, the idea of public empowerment is beset by tensions between the different roles of 'consumer', 'client', 'citizen' and 'community' which comprise 'the public' as an individual or collective presence. The empowerment of one section of the public may not be in the broader interests of other groups nor of the public as a whole. Thus the empowerment of the public as market-based individual consumers may not serve the interests of the public as citizens or the public as community. Such tensions were intentionally heightened by New Right driven policies in which the 'empowerment' of the public as taxpayers (those who pay for but who may not use welfare services) was explicitly promoted at the expense of the public as welfare recipients (those who use but may not be seen to have paid for such services) (Clarke, 1996).

As Braye and Preston-Shoot (1995) argue, the concept of empowerment assumes a consensus between different groups which may be unlikely to obtain in reality. In the specific context of the welfare services characterised by the growing imbalance of supply and demand, for example, the empowerment of one client/service user group may be at the expense of the empowerment of others. Even within a single user group, it is clear that there may be a number of different 'stakeholders' with different needs and expectations, to whom it may be impossible equally to respond. It is possible in some cases moreover that the empowerment or self-empowerment of one group or individual may serve directly to discriminate against or 'disempower' other vulnerable groups. Thus Page (1992) questions what the response should be of practitioners committed to anti-oppressive work with white youths who identify their collective interests as being best served by discriminatory employment or housing policies. Criticising the stance of Ward and Mullender, he argues:

A key problem facing facilitators who work in this area is deciding how to respond to the group's right to autonomy on the grounds of gender or race if these then throw up demands which appear incompatible with the need to ensure that the 'various forms of oppression are ... understood and confronted together'. (Page, 1992, p 90)

In the absence of clear political or professional consensus surrounding specific areas of empowerment practice, Page argues, it is difficult to know how practitioners are to avoid utilising some form of implicit, and individually specific, "hierarchy of acceptable oppressions" (1992, p 90) to judge who is and who is not most eligible for empowerment.

As we shall discuss in the next chapter, this issue may be especially problematic in work with children and families, where the tension between the interests of children and the rights of parents may be particularly strong. In respect of child protection, for example, Boushel and Lebacq (1992) identify as a 'fundamental dilemma' the question of how to protect a child from abuse, while upholding the rights of their parents/carers.

Those who argue that it is the child themself whose empowerment needs must prevail may underestimate the interconnectedness of these needs with the empowerment of others, such as parents/carers or, indeed, in the context of inter-agency decision making, the power of particular professional groups. As Baistow points out: "... empowerment is not independent of our relationships with those who provide care, or with the community in which we live" (1994/95, p 44).

To empower or not to empower?

One of the main tensions for professionals attempting to work in empowering ways concerns the willingness of service users to become empowered. In many cases it is clear that the initial motivation and enthusiasm for empowering activities has come not from users themselves, but from professionals concerned that this would be good for them. To an extent, however, the idea of professionally-led empowerment can be seen as a contradiction in terms. Thus Baistow (1994/95) argues that, by becoming something which is done to you by others rather than something which you do for yourself, the concept of empowerment has lost its original 'reflexivity'. As such it reinforces the (disempowering) perception that those who are to be empowered are passive and lacking in self-determination (Baistow, 1994/95; Smith, 1997). It also assumes that professionals know best, not just about the fact that people need to be empowered, but also about the particular dimensions of their lives for which empowerment is needed as well as about the particular ways in which that empowerment will be achieved. This, however, may underestimate the difficulties of defining others' needs in respect of empowerment and in assessing the extent to which these needs have been met (see Chapter Seven). Thus a local manager in an investigation of consumerism undertaken by Lupton and Hall commented "... you can make all kinds of assumptions that people feel better, are participating, but in the end, as in access to records, you can still find that people are pretty alienated and don't know what the service is about" (Lupton and Hall, 1993, p 10).

Others argue that the fact of professionals taking the lead may not necessarily present a problem, if the opportunities for self-help and greater responsibility are welcomed by those involved. Thus Adams (1990) in his discussion of self-help and empowerment argues that it is a legitimate approach for professionals, given their greater access to appropriate resources, to light the empowerment 'touch paper' and stand back:

> **The concept of empowerment through integral self-help implies the paradox that professionals exercise power in their commitment to providing the initial resources and the stimulus of suggesting directions in which the activities move, but at the same time try to stand back and let the self-helpers put their own definition on what happens. (Adams, 1990, p 45)**

A central dilemma, however, does arise when those so targeted do not appear to want to be empowered. Some people may perceive that they do not have the energy or inclination to get involved in activities designed to provide for their empowerment and may prefer to let others (particularly professionals) do things do them. As another respondent in Lupton and Hall's consumerism study commented: "It's a bit like going to catch a train and being asked to drive it. Do clients want to drive or do they want to be taken?" (manager, adult services, quoted in Lupton and Hall, 1993, p 10). The apparent disinclination for empowerment may be particularly the case on the part of more vulnerable service users. As several writers have pointed out, it may be extremely difficult to take up the opportunity of empowerment if one has been disempowered all one's life (Ward and Mullender, 1991; Braye and Preston-Shoot, 1995). Long-term service use can result in the phenomenon of "learned helplessness" (Seligman, 1972) in the face of professional decision making, resulting in an acquired inability to make choices for oneself. Thus another respondent in Lupton and Hall's research described what he saw to be the attitude of some older clients: "They tend to beat themselves into a submissive acceptance of what we give them. They're unable to say want the want, It's an 'I'm old, I don't count' attitude" (older person's team manager, quoted in Lupton and Hall, 1993, p 10).

In some cases, particularly in respect of health services, users may feel they wish to cede the responsibility for decision making to those they perceive as the 'experts'. This may be due not only to the large measure of trust still invested in professionals – and the belief that the professional knows best – but may also be the result of a desire to avoid 'regret' over the unsuccessful outcomes of choices made (Shackley and Ryan, 1994). In other cases, reluctance to accept the offer of greater empowerment may stem from the, possibly realistic, perception that the inequality of power is real and that being seen to speak out and against those with power may result in the loss or deterioration of services: "The bottom line is that people in residential units don't have much power: when you are that dependent you need to be careful what you say" (residential home manager, quoted in Lupton and Hall, 1993, p 8). This issue presents a particular dilemma for the professional committed to empowering practice. While on the one hand it is important to respect people's rights not to be empowered by others, on the other hand it is clear that such a situation can be seen to reflect, and in turn help fulfil, the traditional unequal relationship of helper and helped. For those not committed to the idea of empowerment, the belief in the apathy of service users may be taken to justify more traditional, paternalistic, ways of working.

It is clear moreover that empowerment – understood as greater self-control or self-reliance – may be done to/expected of some service users whether they like it or not; in certain cases 'being empowered' may not be an option. New Right and increasingly New Labour visions of empowerment in some contexts contain within them the requirement that citizens/consumers take steps towards greater personal responsibility if they are to qualify for, or prevent disqualification from, certain forms of welfare provision. Thus the 'responsible patient' role promulgated within the NHS (NHSE, 1996; DoH, 1996) potentially, at least, establishes the link between official expectations about appropriate behaviour and eligibility for treatment; those who recklessly over-eat/smoke/drink in the face of health advice to the contrary may increasingly start to find that certain treatments are withheld or delayed. Similarly the 'responsible parent' of New Labour's crime and disorder policies may find that refusal to be empowered to become a better parent (through attendance at parenting classes, for example) may result in financial or other penalties. As Baistow (1994/95) has argued, there is a sense in which, in these ways, empowerment is becoming the "... ethical obligation of the new citizenry" which it may be increasingly difficult to eschew:

> **Empowerment is not only good for you; it seems to be becoming essential for a better life. Therefore if you are unable to do it for yourself you may need professional assistance in doing so. Furthermore, you may need professional help to recognise that you are in need of this type of professional assistance. (Baistow, 1994, p 37)**

The resolution of these and other issues surrounding empowerment practice will of course depend on the particular client/user group involved and on the context of the work. Strategies for the empowerment of very elderly people, for example, may be of a very different nature to those relevant to work with older teenagers. In particular, there will be a central difference between those situations in which the involvement of the service user is voluntary and those – such as child protection or mental health – where professional intervention is neither invited nor desired. Some have argued that, in child protection for example, the statutory responsibilities of the social worker and the inter-agency procedures make it difficult to imagine under what conditions the family members could be empowered. Others have rejoined that such reservations are misplaced and have served unfairly to restrict the participation of parents/carers in decisions about their children. Boushel and Lebacq, for example, argue that successful empowerment work in child protection can be undertaken, particularly by supporting the avoidance and survival strategies of the child and their non-abusive parent/carer:

> **An emphasis on empowerment does offer ... the possibility of interventions that are experienced as less discriminatory and that validate and support the positive factors in the lives of children and their carers. (Boushel and Lebacq, 1992, p 49)**

Practical constraints

In addition to the philosophical and ethical issues discussed above, it is clear that the tensions within the development of empowerment as professional practice also stem from more practical constraints imposed by the political, organisational and social contexts in which professional social work is undertaken. The first and most important of these is the only limited extent to which any professional intervention impacts on the lives of most service users and their families/carers. Particularly in children and families' work, the inevitably transient and, some would argue, relatively ineffectual (Ryburn, 1991c; Howe, 1994; Parton, 1994) nature of professional interventions would seem to limit the possibility for the radical and transformative social change desired by those promoting anti-oppressive practice. As Smith (1997) has argued, although social work can reflect an awareness of structurally maintained inequality, its ability to confront this state of affairs is constrained by the nature and extent of the interpersonal interaction between social worker and client. The expectation that this interchange will provide an opportunity to identify and confront the forces of oppression appears to be naive and, in the face of the likelihood that many service users will be unaware of or uninterested in such issues, not a little arrogant. Pinderhughes' view that the role of the empowering social worker involves "... teaching them [clients] about power dynamics and the systems in which they live" (1983, p 335) may be seen in this way. Even the less radical 'partnership practice' approaches may be based on a certain over optimism about their likely impact in the face of the multiplicity of other factors influencing the complex and changing lives of those with whom professionals work (Lupton and Stevens, 1997).

Page (1992) argues that Ward and Mullender and others underestimate the practical difficulties that may be involved in challenging the broader structures of oppression in specific situations and argues that criticism of professionals for failing to do so may be misplaced. Responding to a specific example given by Ward and Mullender of non anti-oppressive practice, in which a social worker refers a woman to a battered women's refuge "... as if it were just another residential alternative" rather than a place which actively aims to change her life (1991, p 27), Page asks:

> **Is it so unacceptable for a hard pressed, ideologically indecisive social worker to refer a victim of violence ... to a refuge on purely pragmatic grounds (ie, a place of safety) given the dearth of suitable alternatives? (Page, 1992, p 91)**

It may also be the case that the options of finding a safe place and of changing one's life are not mutually exclusive; the former, indeed, may be seen as an essential precondition of the latter. It could also be argued that, if she is not to be further disempowered, the way in which a women defines her stay in a refuge must be left to her, not the ideologically decisive social worker, to decide.

Alongside the necessarily limited scope for sociopolitical or behavioural change in time-limited interpersonal encounters, it is clear that the potential for empowerment, of whatever variant, may also be constrained by a range of organisational and professional factors over which the individual professional has little or no control. First among these must be the limitations imposed by the cold financial climate in which social work continues to operate. Many of the 'terms and conditions' of empowering or partnership working laid out by those such as Biehal and Sainsbury (1991) arguably involve little in the way of additional resources, but they are likely to incur considerable time costs. The objectives of ensuring that clients are provided with all the relevant information, "... including everything that is said or written about them", and are enabled "... to share in exploring problems, goals, tasks and criteria of successful outcome" (1991, p 255), may prove unrealistic in the context, for example, of an over-stretched childcare team facing high levels of staff illness and turnover and carrying an extensive backlog of cases.

It is important to acknowledge, moreover, that there may be other resources involved in 'doing' empowerment properly (particularly in respect of adequate administrative support) and these may be difficult to secure in a context of continued financial constraint. In particular, unless we perceive social workers as somehow natural or 'instinctive empowerers', the importance of proper training and staff development to support those trying/keen to work in more empowering ways will be of central importance. Without adequate resources and organisational support, it is possible that many empowerment initiatives will fail, thus not only undermining their specific objectives but also, more worryingly, reinforcing precisely the sense of powerlessness they were designed to confront (Lupton and Sheppard, 1999).

In addition to the problems of time and resource limitations, there are other constraints potentially imposed by the organisational contexts in which social workers operate and from which they secure their livelihood and possibilities of career development. Such contexts may not be supportive, or may actually be undermining, of the objectives of 'partnership' or 'anti-oppressive' practice. This may not be an explicit or conscious attempt to restrict these ways of working, but rather the operation of what Barker and Peck have termed the "power of orthodoxy and convention" (1987). Recognition must be made of the relative powerlessness of the individual empowering a practitioner within an organisation whose structures, senior staff and overall culture are resistant to change or innovation (Higgins, 1992; Braye and Preston-Shoot, 1995). Such problems may be compounded in collaborative work which involves other agencies or professional groups less committed to the ideal or practice of user empowerment (Lupton et al, 1998; Lupton and Khan, 1998) and in a context of high public visibility and/or legislative constraint or ambiguity. It is difficult for professionals to empower others if they do not themselves feel valued or empowered within their institutions.

Other potential constraints include professional fears about loss of expertise/control, and concern about the ability of service users to make the right choices and exercise power responsibly. Such concerns have provided an important rein on more empowering or participatory approaches, particularly in the child welfare context. Ryburn (1991b) argues that professionals relinquishing the belief that they know best is a necessary precondition of effective empowerment:

> **It may be comforting for us to believe that, through a process of thorough assessment, grounded in expertise and training, we can know what will be best for children and their families. There is no evidence to support it. Indeed the history of social work with children and families is littered with the never-consulted causalities of a belief that we necessarily knew best. (Ryburn, 1991b, p 73)**

It would be completely to devalue the repository of skills, knowledge and experience that comprises the social work profession, however, for there not to be situations where, to some extent at least, the professionals may indeed know best. Not only is such a position ultimately 'disempowering' of social workers themselves, feeding as it does into the negative public evaluation of the profession but, ultimately, it may also serve to undermine the possibility of empowering work with clients. As we have argued, effective challenge to the specific and wider oppressions that serve to disempower clients may need to harness rather than deny the particular knowledge and skills possessed by professionals.

Finally, and most importantly, there is the problem of the expectations that can be placed on the social work profession as an agent of empowerment, given its own professional 'learned helplessness'. Driven in part by public moral panics about social workers that were variously too slow to intervene or too quick to take action, and in part by growing evidence of the ineffectiveness of social work interventions (Fischer, 1978; Gaylin et al, 1978) the 1980s saw the profession sink into a deepening crisis of self-confidence (Webb, 1992; Parton, 1994; Cooper, 1995). Cooper et al (1995) argue that, while it was difficult to see the full impact of these changes at the time they were happening, "... in retrospect, it is clear that the primary force acting on the social work profession then, and since, has been anxiety" (1995, p 111). Particularly, but not only, within child protection, this public and professional anxiety resulted in increased external regulation and control; the attempt to constrain the operation of professional judgement and discretion by an increased emphasis on formal structures and "procedural correctness" (Parton, 1995, p 87). One result of this very public crisis of confidence was the undermining of the status of social work relative to that of other professional groups enabling its 'annexation' by medical and legal professional approaches (Cannan, 1994/95; Howe, 1994; Braye and Preston-Shoot, 1995). The dominance of the legal model, in particular, Parton argues, has seriously undermined the ability of the profession to work in a more enabling or empowering way with children and families (Parton, 1991).

The erosion of professional autonomy and status may have also been compounded by the creation of social and healthcare 'markets', with the emergence of the deprofessionalised care manager role, and by the growth of new managerialist approaches within the public sector with their emphasis on performance management and measurement (Pollitt, 1990; Parton, 1994; Lupton et al, 1998). This process, it is argued, has involved the dominance of a new 'instrumental reason' concerned with the identification of the most efficient means to identified ends. This is seen to have supplanted or 'colonised' the 'communicative reason' believed previously to have characterised the caring, emotional elements of social work activity. The result is the "... distortion of the face to face interaction which lies at the heart of human caring" (Blaug, 1995, p 429). The fragmenting impact of new managerialist approaches on professional practice, some contend moreover, has been exacerbated by the emphasis given by the then Central Council for the Education and Training of Social Work (CCETSW) to the development of the 'competencies' approach (Cannan, 1994/95; Blaug, 1995; Dominelli, 1996) which is seen further to disaggregate and compartmentalise the individual components of the social work task. Such a process, it is argued, has undermined the necessary theoretical coherence underpinning professional practice, leaving: "... a hole at the centre of the enterprise" (Parton, 1994, p 30). The result has been a 'commodification' or 'proletarianisation' of professional work (Dominelli, 1996, p 163):

> **The social worker's practices are more likely to be task orientated and performance related, quantifiable and measurable, product-minded and subject to quality controls. Procedure manuals and lists of competencies define more and more what the social workers should do and how they must do it. Professional discretion disappears under a growing mountain of departmentally generated policy and formulae. (Howe, 1994, p 529)**

Conclusion

While it is clearly important for social work professionals to be committed to the idea of empowering (or not further disempowering) those with whom they work, it is important to be realistic about what can and cannot be achieved by single professionals working with individual or groups of service users in specific situations. Growing expectations are being placed on social work in this respect, from government, user and self-help movements and from within the profession itself but, as Braye and Preston-Shoot (1995) argue, it is important to recognise the limits of professional helpfulness. Whether delivered via 'partnership working' or self-directed groupwork, it is clear from the above that there may be very specific 'terms and conditions' under which professionals are able to encourage or enable user empowerment. These may not be the same as those that obtain in user or community-led empowerment activities. Clarity around the parameters of professionally-led empowerment is vital if service users are not to be encouraged unrealistically to raise their expectations and if hard-pressed social workers working in cash-limited organisations are not to be criticised unfairly for failing to change the world.

First among constraining conditions is the difficulty of establishing precisely what the concept of empowerment entails, given the different and often contradictory political objectives by which it is underpinned. It is clearly a concept which means all things to all people and its achievement may similarly be in the eye of the beholder. This conceptual confusion is not assisted by the fact that much of the debate takes place in abstract, almost rhetorical, terms which give little clue as to the particular ways in which, and extent to which, empowerment can be put into everyday practice.

In addition, we have argued that there may be inherent dilemmas in the idea of empowerment as professional practice. In so far as the initial decision to pursue empowerment, the identification of the subjects of empowerment and the selection of methods used is professionally-led, the whole enterprise may, potentially at least, serve to diminish rather than enhance the extent to which service users feel empowered. Actual people may have perfectly legitimate and rational reasons for not wanting to participate in activities devised for their empowerment. It is clear, moreover, that empowerment as professional practice will involve choices about which people/groups are/deserve to be empowered and will operationalise value judgements about the nature and extent of their empowerment. In the context of the contemporary welfare state, with its

New Right and, under Labour, new Puritan emphasis on self-reliance and responsibility, the process of empowerment may contain "regulatory as well as liberatory potential" (Baistow, 1994/95, p 35).

As well as having to deal with the conceptual and ethical problems involved, the empowering professional faces other more practical constraints. Limitations of time and resources, the pressures of organisational resistance and inertia and the proliferation of 'compulsory guidance' may all conspire to frustrate even the most committed of professionals. Add to this the only limited impact of most forms of professional intervention on the lives of those it is designed to help, and the broader disempowerment of the profession itself, and it seems clear that the expectations surrounding empowerment work may significantly exceed the capacity of social work professionals to deliver. This may be particularly the case where those expectations involve individual professionals challenging and confronting the wider structures of oppression. In the context of social work in the 1990s, individual social workers may have to consider carefully the practicability of the admonition that the focus of their intervention includes "... change at a structural level, identifying with the cultural, social and economic experiences of a community, not just ameliorating individual distress" (Milroy and Hennelley, 1989, quoted in Braye and Preston-Shoot, 1995, p 120).

In the end, of course, practical and conceptual constraints notwithstanding, it may be that the biggest barrier to more empowering ways of working is that of professional resistance. This will be considered in greater detail in the next chapter, but it is important here to acknowledge that much of this resistance stems from the fear that, by empowering those with whom they work, professionals will have to limit or surrender their own power and control. Such a view, however, based as it is on the zero-sum perception of power, fails to recognise the possibility that working in more empowering ways may enhance the power of professionals as well as that of service users. In so far as it perceives the professional/user power relationship in detachment from the wider political, social and economic processes which surround it, such a view may fail to consider the implication of the fact that the power of social work professionals has itself been systematically undermined over recent years. In such a context, alliances between service users and professionals may be seen to serve the wider interests of both sides of the partnership. It is to a consideration of the relationship between 'client' and professional power, in the specific context of children and family services, that the next chapter now turns.

TWO

Partnership and empowerment in children's services

Introduction

"There's no partnership. There's them and there's us, and they've got the power." (quoted in Lewis, 1995, p 29)

Most of the decisions about the care and protection of children take place, most of the time, in their own families. However, in spite (or perhaps because) of this fact, the history of family involvement in such decisions in the context of social services is one of restricted participation. While the concepts 'partnership' and 'empowerment' have increasingly occupied the language of child welfare social work, they have rarely led to tangible policies/practices that are experienced as 'empowering' by the children and families involved. Despite the rhetoric, when things are seen to have gone seriously wrong in families, the remedies are perceived to lie in the hands of the professionals. As late as the 1980s, the National Society for the Prevention of Cruelty to Children (NSPCC) opposed the full participation of children and parents in child protection conferences on the grounds that it would subvert the professionals' ability to problem solve expediently (Dale et al, 1986) and the Department of Health remained clear in its early draft of inter-agency arrangements for child protection, *Working together,* that there was no place for parents, let alone children, at child protection conferences (Horne, 1990).

Then the crisis in Cleveland erupted and the Report of the subsequent Inquiry raised concerns about social workers paying too little attention to the views and rights of the parents involved (Secretary of State for Social Services, 1988) and objectifying the roles of 'abused', abuser', 'abusing family' and so on. It was felt that, in responding to the concerns about abuse, professionals were in danger of losing sight of the real needs of the children they were trying to help. Children should be seen as people in their own right, not as an "object of concern" (Secretary of State for Social Services, 1988, p 245). While acknowledging the potential tension between the rights of parents and those of their children, the Report emphasised the right of both to be consulted and informed and the importance of recognising family strengths as well as weaknesses. By the time the final draft of *Working together* was produced, it was emphatic about the need to include families:

> **... it cannot be emphasised too strongly that the involvement of children and adults in child protection conference will not be effective unless they are fully involved from the outset in all stages of the child protection process, and unless from the time of referral there is as much openness and honesty as possible between families and professionals. (Home Office, 1991, p 43)**

The objective of improving participation thus stemmed, at least in part, from the failure to achieve good outcomes when families were not included in decision making. By 1995 the Department of Health produced *The challenge of partnership* (DoH, 1995c) which concerned itself with the question not of *whether* parents/carers should be involved, but of *how* they could be engaged further in child protection processes (Thoburn et al, 1995). This document argued that participatory approaches were more likely to lead to effective services and would ensure that the unique knowledge families have about themselves was fully utilised. Notably, it stated that families members have 'rights as citizens' to hear what is said about them and to:"... contribute to important decisions about their lives and those of their children" (DoH, 1995c, p 10).

This chapter will assess the extent to which this 'challenge' of partnership has been met in contemporary social work practice. After briefly considering the issues surrounding the idea of partnership in the child welfare context, the chapter examines the key tendencies characterising the development of childcare social work prior to the 1989 Children Act. The political crisis of confidence that led to the Children Act is described and the impact of the legislation, with its underlying principle of 'partnership', is assessed. Throughout the chapter the central factors inhibiting the development of more collaborative relationships between families and professionals will be highlighted.

Partnership, participation and empowerment

> **Partnership has become a watchword under the Children Act ...
> yet there is no consensus on precisely what this means in practice,
> whether it is desirable and, indeed, whether it can be achieved.
> (Kaganas, 1993, p 1)**

As indicated in the last chapter, one of the main mechanisms for the empowerment of service users is seen to be the adoption of a 'partnership' approach by professionals. Like empowerment itself, partnership is another concept of 'high social desirability', effectively straddling both Left and Right political positions. The idea of greater participation, for example, has played an important part in new managerialist concerns to increase the effectiveness and productivity of the workforce, but has also had a central role in Centre/Left debates about social inclusion and decentralisation of political power. It is manifest in the declared objectives of a wide range of political and economic policies from Citizen's Charters to shareholding democracies. Linked with the general drive for greater transparency and accountability on the part of public sector services and for a better choice and quality of services, 'partnership' is universally perceived as a 'good thing' (Rojeck et al, 1988).

The broad acceptance of partnership in the context of social welfare, however, is based on a central paradox. As Newman (1993) argues, its acceptance is almost unquestioned as a principle of good practice, without much critical thought or consideration. "In the context of social welfare services, partnership along with its active ingredient empowerment, has become so deeply embedded as a principle of good practice that any debate about its usefulness is rare" (1993, p 4). Despite the apparent consensus surrounding the partnership approach, it remains ill-defined and rarely practised. The uneven practical development of the idea of partnership may derive from the lack of certainty surrounding its definition; it may also, however, result from the fact that the perceived consensus about its benefits stems from political belief rather than empirical evidence.

In particular, while the idea of partnership has achieved considerable currency in contemporary social work, it is not clear, as Kaganas argues, precisely what it means in the child welfare context. To a child's parents, for example, the rhetoric of partnership may suggest a relationship of equals; to the professionals it may be interpreted as requiring only that parents are informed about any decisions regarding their children. The conceptual ambiguity which surrounds the term may indeed explain its absence from the primary legislation. While the volumes of official guidance and regulations accompanying the 1989 Children Act do make extensive use of the language of partnership, albeit as a principle rather than a right, its extent and nature remains confused. As the Department of Health has acknowledged: "There are wide ranging views and debates about how and when it is appropriate to work in partnership with families ... there is also a diversity of opinion about what constitutes partnership and what is meant by families in this context" (DoH, 1995c, p 7).

In its most general sense, partnership can be described as a 'shared activity' or 'joint business' in the pursuit of mutually agreed goals. Many social work commentaries have attempted to distil this fairly broad definition into a common set of practice principles surrounding 'partnership working' (Marsh, 1990; Family Rights Group, 1993: DoH, 1991c; Gibbons, 1992; DoH, 1995c) which can be identified as evident or not in the worker/client relationship. Tunnard (1991) for example, describes some of the key characteristics of effective partnerships as being: "... respect for one another, rights to information, accountability, competence and value accorded to individual input". In short, a situation in which "... each partner is seen as having something to contribute, power is shared, decisions are made jointly" (1991, p 1).

Such a view acknowledges that, while powers may be shared, they are not necessarily equal and that opportunities for exercising control or choice will fluctuate between different participants. The nature of any partnership therefore is unlikely to remain static, but will tend rather to evolve and change as the situation develops over time. As discussed in the previous chapter, it may be misleading to conceptualise power as a fixed 'zero-sum' quantity, shifting towards one group or individual at the expense of others. Attempts to improve participation in decision making may thus not be a question of balancing separate and conflicting rights and interests, but of developing a more inclusive process which identifies common goals, collective responsibilities and mutual understanding. As Schofield and Thoburn argue:

> **Enhancing the participation rights of all parties adds to the quality of the debate, which becomes better informed, but also to the quality of the experience of that debate for those whose lives may be permanently affected by the outcome. Participation is not a finite cake to be divided up. (Schofield and Thoburn, 1996, p 16)**

In the main, partnership discourse has tended to focus on the relationship between the social worker (characterised as 'the State') and the parents, understood in terms of representing 'the family', or even symbolising 'the community'. This may have served to oversimplify or polarise a potentially very diverse set of relationships. In particular, it may tend to conceptualise the situation as one in which the interests of 'parents' as an homogeneous group are set against those of State professionals/bureaucrats – also perceived in a monolithic way. Such a view ignores the important differences within the family group and, in particular, the distinctive role played by children, the wider family or the community and may also underestimate the extent of divergence within and between different professional groups.

The nature of the relationship between 'partnership' (as process) and 'empowerment' (as outcome) may also be more complex than commonly assumed. While it may be that greater involvement in decision–making processes results in the empowerment of children and families, this is not necessarily the case. Much will depend on the quality of that involvement and on the extent to which desired outcomes are achieved. It may be misleading therefore to view ideas such as participation, partnership and empowerment as successive stages on a ladder-like continuum, with each following logically in a particular context from the other. As we have argued in the previous chapter, depending on the practical and professional constraints involved, and the preferences of service users themselves, it may in some cases be important explicitly to 'uncouple' these different dimensions of the client/worker relationship.

Partnership – the early years

The development of the idea of partnership in child welfare has to some extent relied on professional aspirations to 'good practice' but has also critically been shaped by changing assumptions about the relationship between children, the family and the State. The arrival of the 1948 Children Act heralded the creation of local authority children's services departments that were to end the divisive administrative approach of the Poor Law and the Public Assistance Act. The new legislation, introduced at a time of real optimism about the welfare state, gave social workers more discretion and control over the services they provided. The Act was primarily designed to improve quality and standards for children in public care but there was a strong desire to develop preventative and supportive work, to keep children within their families and divert them from care in the first place (Packman, 1993). There was a consensus that the needs of the family and the role of the State were closely related and together could provide a framework for the well-being of children. As Parton comments:

> **A central plank in the post war reconstruction was the belief that a positive and supportive approach to the family was required so that the state and the family should work in partnership to ensure that children were provided with the appropriate conditions in which to develop. (Parton, 1991, p 21)**

These 'appropriate conditions' would be achieved through a helping and benign relationship between the family and the State whose separate interests were seen as almost entirely compatible. It was assumed that family problems could be tackled through a nurturing casework relationship and that social work methods of advice and counselling would help families in difficulty to 'normalise' their behaviour. The family was seen as a universal good and individual families were perceived to share collective identity and interests built on consensus rather than conflict.

In practice, attempts to support families were constrained by the lack of coordination between different agencies such as health, education and housing at both national and local levels, and also by a lack of a clear statutory duty on local authorities to help families before their situation broke down. In particular, although marked by a reduction in the use of institutional care, the years following the 1948 Act witnessed a commensurate growth in the use of foster care by strangers: by 1960 foster placements had risen from one third to one half of all children in care (Packman, 1993). Attempts at working in partnership meant that many children were placed in care under 'voluntary' arrangements with their parents' consent. In practice this apparently more consensual approach remained largely driven by professional judgements and pressures. As Parton (1991) comments:

> **... whatever the professional rhetoric may have suggested, it is unlikely that many children or parents would have experienced the service as working in partnership or (even) consultation. It is just as likely that the power and authority for the service went unchallenged though desperation, fear or deference to those who knew better. (Parton, 1991, p 21)**

It was not until the advent of the 1963 Children and Young Persons Act that the first real legislative steps were taken towards a more community-based service which aimed to diminish the need for children to be taken into care or brought before the juvenile court. The Inglesby Report (Home Office, 1960) had recommended a wide range of preventative measures which, although not fully embraced by the 1963 Act, had considerable influence on the nature of family work that subsequently evolved within local authorities. Children's departments could now begin officially to use resources on preventative work with families and collaborate with other agencies. The social work role at this time was far closer to that of family caseworker and the general optimism about the welfare state which prevailed throughout the 1950s and 1960s was most strongly reflected in the belief that its institutions and professionals could change families for the better. Therapeutic interventions, based on the emerging body of professional knowledge and methods, were at the core of social work and, even when coercive elements were employed, these were seen primarily in terms of achieving a more substantive therapeutic goal (Parton, 1991). Essentially, the interventions of social workers were conveyed through a paternalistic and benign relationship where participation centred on implementing what the social worker knew was best.

The Seebohm Report in 1968 sought further to extend the optimism underpinning social work by promoting the idea of community-based and family-orientated services that would be available to all and would "enable the greatest possible number of individuals to act reciprocally, giving and receiving services for the well being of the whole community" (Seebohm Report, 1968, para 2.11). To achieve this, social services departments would need to gain knowledge of their local communities, identify voluntary resources and develop skills to encourage citizen participation through local community-based forums. Their location within the local authorities, however, following the 1970 Local Authority Social Services Act, was to undermine rather than enhance the possibilities of a more participatory and inclusive approach on the part of social services departments. As Braye and Preston-Shoot argue, the provision of services through large, hierarchical and centralised bureaucratic systems, tended to militate against user or community involvement: "... top down bureaucracy can demonstrate a cohesion which leaves little space for negotiation or innovation and users' voices are lost beneath mounds of policy guidance and codes of practice" (1995, p 109)

Moreover, the official encouragement to preventative work was not accompanied by additional resources; indeed, it was hoped that successful preventative work would save money (Fox Harding, 1991, p 14). As a result, the 'community empowerment' vision of the Seebohm Report, involving: "A more radical notion of prevention ... stressing the significance of natural communities as definers of need, potential givers of help and essential goods and critics of statutory services" (Packman, 1993, p 227) was largely left to the voluntary organisations to implement.

Growing doubts started to emerge during the 1970s and early 1980s about the effectiveness of childcare social work which suggested that the optimism of the 1950s and 1960s may have been misplaced. Despite the language of prevention, the numbers of children in public care, and the length of time they remained there, continued to rise steadily throughout the 1970s (Packman et al, 1986). There was also an increased use of compulsory powers by social services departments rather than voluntary arrangements, in particular of the 'parental rights' resolutions, where a local authority could assume full parental rights through purely administrative processes. Harding (1989) notes that this power of administrative 'fiat' was a relic of the Poor Law and was linked with an increased emphasis on 'permanency planning' and greater professional control over child placement.

These years also witnessed growing public concern about the misuse of powers such as the parental rights resolutions. The (then) National Council for One Parent Families (NCOPF, 1982), for example, argued that parents were not being kept informed about, and had no way of influencing, the decision making of professionals. Similarly, the overuse of 'place of safety orders' by social workers, often employed as a means of initiating care proceedings without any involvement of families, was criticised as at best a misinterpretation of the law and at worse an abuse of the powers provided by the state (Packman et al, 1986). As a result of such concerns, a number of pressure groups developed at this time on behalf of children and families involved in the welfare system, including the Family Rights Group, the Voice of the Children in Care, the Children's Legal Centre and the National Association of Young People in Care. All highlighted a growing dissatisfaction with what was seen to be the disempowering nature of the decision making of large social work departments.

A crisis of confidence

Government concern about the effectiveness of childcare work also grew over the 1970s and 1980s, stimulated in large part by a wave of child abuse investigations, public enquiries and negative media attention. This concern was brought sharply into focus by the death of Maria Colwell, and the subsequent public inquiry (Secretary of State for Social Services, 1974) was to mark the beginning of much greater political, public and professional scrutiny of child abuse procedures and practice (Parton, 1979). The reaction of the social work profession was an increased use of local authorities' powers of compulsion and the proliferation of procedures and safeguards surrounding the detection and management of child abuse. In the face of increased political scrutiny and control over their actions, professional control over family life became, in turn, more overt:

> **More was seen of the controlling state than in the previous decade; the family-orientated support work of the 1950s and 1960s was giving way to a greater readiness to focus on the child as a separate individual, and to act coercively if need be, on her behalf. (Fox Harding, 1991, p 91)**

The net effect of this changed emphasis was to prove corrosive to relationships between professional and families, insofar as it placed them in potentially antagonistic positions. The relationship became characterised by spiralling mistrust: as anxieties about making mistakes drove social workers to become more suspicious and intrusive, so public concern grew about the increased power of professionals. In such a context, attempts at developing mutual understanding and partnership work were likely to be highly circumscribed (Jones and Novak, 1993). Thus was the benign and optimistic view of social work that prevailed in the 1950s and 1960s revealed too frequently over the subsequent two decades (in which the child protection discourse would dominate) to have been insubstantially based: "... a temporary coincidence of interests, rather than the expression of a structural totality" (Cooper, 1994, p 62).

The greater readiness of social workers to use their legal powers was allied to the need for professionals to gain greater control over child placements. The 'permanency' principle increasingly favoured the use of adoption and the permanent separation of children from their families. If both parents were deemed unable to care for the child, a permanent substitute carer was the primary aim of the social worker. The courts were used to secure placements and adoption was seen as the zenith in a hierarchy of permanent substitute placement options (Ryburn, 1994b). The emphasis, in the face of apparent 'parental failure', was to substitute rather than supplement families, with those parents identified as in some way 'unsatisfactory' being more likely to lose their children. This emphasis on protecting children from their parents and on substitute or 'stranger care' as a viable alternative was to characterise social work practice for the next 15 years.

A number of childcare research studies and reviews were conducted in the 1980s that were to influence, to some extent, the formation of the 1989 Children Act. These studies revealed that the reasons for children coming into the care system often related as much to material deprivation, poverty and lack of family support as they did to wilful abuse and neglect by parents (Holman, 1993; DHSS, 1985a; Packman et al, 1986; Bebbington and Miles, 1989). The greater readiness to remove children or instigate compulsory measures, however, was making it less likely that families would receive the support they needed to keep their children with them. The research revealed that many parents felt they were not getting the necessary help they needed and were distressed when foster carers appeared to receive more material assistance than they did. With the level of support provided to substitute carers, many parents claimed, they could have been enabled to care for their children themselves (Colton et al, 1995).

These studies were also repeatedly showing that, once children came into the care of the local authority, the role and influence of parents over their lives was greatly reduced or terminated (Social Services Committee, 1984; DHSS, 1985a). Much criticism was also directed at the lack of parental involvement in decision making (Prosser, 1978; Millham et al, 1986). Fisher et al (1986), for example, revealed that few parents of children in public care (let alone the children themselves) had much say about the foster placement and that social workers consistently underrated the continued responsibility and concern that parents felt for their children. Many still wished to fulfil their parental responsibilities even when the children were involved under compulsory powers. The fact that parents felt sad, angry, guilty and alarmed about their children's situation and the associated causal factors was seldom addressed by social workers (Rowe et al, 1984; Packman et al, 1986).

This lack of involvement ensured that parents frequently lost, and indeed were sometimes encouraged to lose, contact with their children (Rowe et al, 1984). The consequence for their children was often the reduction or end of any connection, not just with their parents, but with their wider family groups and communities (Aldgate, 1976; DHSS, 1985a). Those who remained in care became subject to permanency planning or adoption (Ormrod, 1983) or simply drifted, 'lost in care' (Millham et al, 1986). Those who left care were often ill-prepared for their return to family and community life (Triseliotis, 1980; Lupton, 1985). In contrast, research was revealing that, when it did occur, continuity of relationships between fostered children and their natural parents provided major benefits for the child (Rowe et al, 1984). Wedge and Mantle (1991) indicated the importance of sibling contact and other studies, such as that undertaken by Millham et al (1986), suggested that extended relatives such as grandparents, uncles and aunts were an underused source of potentially positive relationships for children that could be important to their emotional development.

The reluctance to work in 'partnership' with families around their children's care meant that parents/carers typically viewed decision making as opaque and unaccountable. Sinclair (1984), for example, discovered that 50% of all statutory reviews of children living in foster care lasted 10 minutes or less and that parents or future carers seldom attended. Berridge and Cleaver (1987) revealed that most foster carers held no animosity to parents, and that the lack of parental participation in reviews and decisions was likely to have stemmed from the attitudes of social workers and their desire to be in charge of the decision making. Greater parental involvement may also have been inhibited by attempts to 'protect' placements from the potentially negative influence of families who were seen to have 'failed' to care for their children.

The optimism of the 1989 Children Act

The government reviews of childcare research and law (Social Services Committee, 1984; DHSS, 1985a, 1985b) informed the drafting of the new childcare legislation although, as already indicated, the political momentum for change derived from the series of child abuse inquiries (Parton, 1995, 1997; Cooper, 1995). The arrival of the 1989 Children Act was widely welcomed and was seen to be relatively free of political dogma (Ball, 1996). Its main objective was to re-evaluate the relationships between the family and the State, and it was the issue of child protection that was most to influence this process. The Children Act rested on the belief that children are generally best cared for in their families, with both parents playing a full and active part. The legislation sought to minimise, where possible, the use of legal proceedings in family life and attempted to reconcile the different roles of the State and the family as well as the respective rights of children and their families, to "strike a balance between the rights of children to express their views on decisions made about their lives, the rights of parents to exercise their responsibilities towards the child and the duty of the state to intervene where the child's welfare requires it" (DoH, 1991a, p 1).

It has been argued that the Children Act sought, in this way, to construct a 'new consensus' on the different interests of children, families and the State and that finding the right balance between these contrasting rights and responsibilities lies at its heart (Parton, 1991). The tension between family rights/responsibilities and State intervention is most evident in child protection where the point of balance has been determined by contrasting political pressures from public inquiries that castigated social workers for lack of action and inertia on the one hand (London Boroughs of Brent, 1985, Greenwich, 1987 and Lambeth, 1987), or for over-intrusive, heavy-handed intervention on the other (Secretary of State for Social Services, 1988). In seeking to achieve better protection for children as well as greater rights for parents, it may appear that the new legislation was, from the start, attempting a difficult, some might say impossible, task. Writers such as Fox Harding (1991), however, argue that, rather than focus on potential areas of conflict, the 'bi-directional policy' of the Children Act could be viewed in more positive terms:

> ... from another viewpoint, however, what the legislation and policy is all about here is balance. While there are some conflicting objectives, it is argued, a better balance can be achieved. Thus it is reasonable, and not inconsistent, for the Children Act to attempt to proceed in two directions at once, adding to the power of parents here and strengthening the courts and authorities there. (Fox Harding, 1991, p 231)

The opening paragraphs of the Children Act set out the over-arching principle by which the government ratified the UN Convention on the Rights of the Child: the welfare of the child is to be the paramount consideration. Children and their feelings should occupy a more central place in decision making and be located at the top of the 'welfare checklist' that guides the court in any legal proceedings (DoH, 1991a). Underpinning this principle was the new concept of 'parental responsibility' for, rather than rights over, their children. The particular choice of words emphasised the duty to care for the child and raise them to "... moral, physical and emotional health" (1991a, p 2). This is the fundamental task of parenthood and the only justification for the authority parenthood confers (DoH, 1989) and will diminish, relatively and correspondingly, as children achieve a greater age and understanding and are able to make their own decisions.

The emphasis on the responsibilities of parents towards their children also requires a rethinking of children as having some autonomy from their parents. As Lyon and Parton (1995) argue, the move towards the language of responsibility: "... implies a reconceptualisation of children as persons to whom duties are owed, rather than as possessions over which power is exercised. This reconstitutes children as persons in their own right and thereby requires a greater effort to be made to involve children in decisions affecting them" (1995, p 41). However, it has also been argued that, without external supervision or control, there is no guarantee that parents will act responsibly and that the centrality accorded to parental responsibility has undermined the ability of the State to plan effectively for children at risk of harm (Eekelaar, 1991). Bainham (1990) further argues that the focus on parental choice and responsibility means that the welfare principles in the Act may be hijacked by non-interventionism.

The Children Act, however, not only sought to re-evaluate the relationship between the State and the family, but also to influence the way professionals worked with parents and children; to reframe the way they 'thought' about families and their responsibilities. Thus, the Department of Health called for: "... very fundamental changes in thinking and in policy and practice" (DoH, 1989, p 1) if the legislation was to be implemented effectively. Social workers would need to focus on "... participation, choice, openness, parental responsibility and every child's need for both security and family links" (DoH, 1989, p 1). The State has a duty to provide services, particularly under Section 17 and Part 3 of the Act, that will support and strengthen families and help children assessed as being 'in need'. The Act recognises the view that there is no perfect way to bring up children and that ideals of family life will vary according to culture, class and community (DoH, 1989). Race, religion, culture, class and language are all identified within the legislation as significant factors in decisions affecting children and there is acceptance that children's needs cannot be viewed in isolation from their cultural heritage and context. For the first time in primary legislation the need to consider these factors in decisions made about children looked after by local authorities was emphasised (1989 Children Act, Section 22 (5) (c)).

As we have seen, the Children Act envisaged a more residual role for the State in the care of children and sought to enhance children's and parents' rights where children were 'looked after' by local authorities. In particular, it aimed to make services more integral with family care and decision making so that the 'accommodation' (Section 20 of the 1989 Children Act) of a child would primarily be to provide short-term care aimed at easing pressure on families and thereby preventing permanent family break-up (DHSS, 1985a). Accommodation was therefore to be understood in the context of the underlying ambition of the legislation to keep children in their families where possible. Previous concerns about children's experiences in public care, discussed earlier, were to be addressed through requirements for much clearer decision-making processes and accountability with an emphasis on better consultation, planning and avoiding the 'drift' in care. The emphasis on cooperation, choice and voluntary arrangements as opposed to sanctions imposed through the courts, was encapsulated in the 'no order' principle in Part III of the legislation. Even with extensive intrusion into a family's life, for example, via the granting of a care order to the local authority, parental responsibility was to be maintained and social workers had to continue to involve parents and children in decisions.

The aftermath of the Children Act

Despite the optimism of the Children Act, however, the goal of greater family and community involvement was to remain elusive. While the legislation assumed that the balance of competing interests would be struck through negotiation, collaboration and partnership, in practice its achievement continued to rely on legal and procedural mechanisms to regulate both the family and the State. The precise point of balance between family autonomy and State intervention was established via a discourse of responsibilities and rights rather than via a more participatory decision-making process. Over the years following the Children Act, the evidence grew that, in policy and in practice, the aims of partnership, participation and family support remained substantially unrealised (Audit Commission, 1994; DoH, 1995a; Gibbons et al, 1995; Thoburn et al, 1995; ADSS, 1996). Grimshaw (1996), for example, noted improved, but still limited, child and family participation in planning and statutory reviews and other research indicated that there was little or no choice of placement for the children themselves or their parents (Cliffe and Berridge, 1991;

Triseliotis et al, 1995). In a study of 220 child protection cases, involving 370 family members across seven English social services departments, Thoburn et al (1995) found only 3% of family members could be seen to be involved as 'partners' and a further 13% as 'participating' in the decision-making process.

Notwithstanding the strong official encouragement given to a collaborative, community-based approach to social work in the Seebohm Report, reiterated by the Barclay Report (NISW, 1982) nearly 20 years later, there was little sign in subsequent years that such an approach had established itself in mainstream work with children and families (Jack, 1997). In particular, despite the emphasis on more inclusive services, research continued to show Black children being over-represented in admissions to the public care system, and problems with the engagement and assessment of families from Black and ethnic minority communities (Swarup, 1992; Barn, 1993). Sinclair et al (1995) for example, found that, while there had been some progress in developing services for African-Caribbean families, there were still considerable barriers to developing inclusive and sensitive services for the Asian community, the largest minority population in England and Wales.

While the Children Act may have started gradually to change practice in a more positive direction, it is argued that more significant change has been inhibited by political, financial, and organisational constraints operating at both local and national levels. Holman (1993), for example, identifies three main factors which he feels served to restrict the development of community-based partnerships and which may also be seen to have inhibited attempts to work more collaboratively with individual service users. First, the pre-eminence of child protection work to the exclusion of other forms of social work; second, attempts at the professionalisation of social work through the development of a specialist body of knowledge and skills that did not accord with the philosophy and methods of community work; and third, the infusion of New Right ideology into social work management, based on a residual role for the State in policing 'dangerous' families while leaving the majority to their privacy. In addition to such factors, constraints over more 'participatory' methods of working may also be seen to result from growing professional concern about losing control over situations for whose outcomes they would ultimately – and very publicly – be held responsible. Together these factors may be seen to have reformulated and redirected, rather than reduced, the nature of professional power and control.

Reconfiguring professional control

As we have indicated, the last two decades have seen a growing recognition of the problem of child abuse and the need to do something about it (NSPCC, 1996). Compulsory intervention into families by the State, in order to protect children, places duties on social workers to make inquiries as to whether children are at risk of 'significant harm' (Section 47 of the 1989 Children Act). There are, however, significant difficulties in defining 'harm' and there is evidence that the threshold for intervention has been gradually lowered over the last century (DoH, 1995a). Furthermore, definitions of abuse differ across cultures, ethnic and religious groups and by geographic location. Identification of 'harm' also varies considerably between and within local authorities using the same legislative criteria (DoH, 1995b). Responding effectively to child abuse has proved extremely complex and, in an area that is highly ambiguous and uncertain, social workers have been drawn towards more reactive and conservative practices. The public vilification of social workers who have made the wrong decision on the removal or non-removal of children, moreover, has driven practices and policies toward the use of more defensive and controlling methods that are the antithesis of more participatory approaches.

As we have seen, many have argued that the intention of the Children Act to ensure that the philosophy of participation centrally underpinned work with families has been undermined by policies and practices focused on the management of child abuse (King and Piper, 1990; Cooper, 1995; Boushel and Farmer, 1996). The growing public recognition of the problem of child abuse has led to greater demands upon the child protection system, with an increasing emphasis on procedures, bureaucratic responses and forensic approaches which have absorbed large amounts of precious resources. The child protection discourse, moreover, has tended to recast the relationship between families and professionals as one of clearly demarcated camps separated by a space that is legally defined and maintained (Cooper, 1995). Far from the earlier belief that the interests of the State and the family would be shared, practice was now based on the assumptions that the interests and intentions of these different parties was likely, crucially, to diverge. The resolution of the management of child abuse became polarised and adversarial, marked by a series of tensions: between child welfare and legal paradigms, between intervention and non-intervention, between child protection and family support, between professionals and families and between professional control and participation or family 'empowerment' (Cooper, 1995).

Social workers involved in child protection work, trying to establish the right balance of responsibilities between the State and family in the care and protection of children, found themselves operating within a system where the police, solicitors and the court played an increasingly central role in decision making. This served to focus attention on the need for evidence and legal rights to intervention or non-intervention, rather than on the needs of children and how they could best be met. As King and Trowell observe:

> ... to reduce the complexities to rights and their infringement may be the only way that the legal process can give the impression of dealing effectively with such conflicts. The suspicion remains, however, that the rights rhetoric is covering up vast areas of human experience which the law is ill-equipped to tackle. (King and Trowell, 1992, p 113)

In the face of this 'legal colonisation', and in a context of restricted resources, the child protection system has sought to focus on identifying 'high risk' situations. This in turn, it is argued, has encouraged a reductionist view of social problems that seeks to detect and predict the pathology of individual parents. In such a context, social work practice is limited to minimal intrusion in the lives of most families with services being framed in residual and largely negative terms (Jack and Stepney, 1995). In these ways, the problem of child abuse has effectively been redefined as the problem of 'dangerous families', the product of dysfunctional family interactions and/or the individual pathology of the abuser or even the abused:

> Thus, failure in parenting is frequently characterised as individual pathology or moral failure, rather than related to the experience of poverty and discrimination, or the impact of rapid social change and economic decline. (ADSS, 1996, p 4)

As Boushel and Farmer (1996) argue, this model of State intervention singles out particular families rather than addressing the general problem of social need: "... it is evident that most effort is made to protect children from family members and to protect society from delinquent children. Very much less effort is expended on trying to improve the circumstances which most profoundly affect children's development, such as poverty, poor housing, poor education" (Boushel and Farmer, 1996, p 95). Yet social, political and economic policies over the last two decades have placed increasing stress on some families and deepened social divisions. In 1995, for example, the Rowntree Foundation's study of income and wealth reported that the pace at which inequality had increased was greater in Britain than in any other industrialised country, with the exception of New Zealand. The result has been a significant increase in the number of children living in poverty in the UK (Kempson, 1996). Family poverty is a major risk factor in children's lives, adversely affecting their health, development and potential for achievement (Kumar, 1993; Oppenhiem and Harper, 1996):

> ... inexorably correlated with premature delivery, postnatal infant and childhood mortality, malnutrition and ill-health, childhood neglect; educational failure, truancy; delinquency, school age pregnancy and the birth of babies who are victims of premature delivery, postnatal, infant and childhood mortality.... (quoted in report of the Commission on Children and Violence – Gulbenkien Foundation, 1995, p 113)

Family experiences of poverty are characterised by social isolation, unemployment, lack of opportunity or self-determination, chronic stress, inadequate housing and ill-health. Cleaver and Freeman's (1995) study found that, of families caught up in the child protection system, over two thirds lived 'on the margins of society' and faced severe problems, more extreme than the abuse allegations with which they were confronted. Single mothers are among the groups particularly affected by the increase in relative poverty (SACHR, 1994). Cleaver and Freeman (1995), for example, found that the majority of children identified as 'at risk' lived with a single mother or within a reconstituted family. Despite this, single mothers were considered particularly to blame for the perceived breakdown of family life and, even under the new Labour government, were to experience punitive changes in welfare benefit legislation. This official tendency to 'blame the (female) victim' was reflected in social work practice. Operating on the basis of a model of the nuclear family, the focus of social work intervention was typically on the shortcomings of the women/ mothers involved (Hill and Aldgate, 1996, p 13). Farmer and Owen, for example, found that professionals reacted more punitively to women if they were perceived in any way to be the cause of the risk to the child and, in the majority of cases where the male presented the primary risk, interventions nevertheless tended to centre on the role of the woman in the household.

One of the main constraints on the provision of more supportive services derived from the growing overload on the child protection system. The publication of a series of Department of Health-funded studies into child protection (DoH, 1995a) raised real concerns that the system was drawing too many cases into the child protection net only to drop them off at a later stage with no services or support. Social work agencies were investigating children's needs through child protection procedures, with only a very small percentage (15%) being placed on the child protection register and many families receiving no help at all at the end of the process (Gibbons et al, 1995; DoH, 1995a). Little qualitative difference, moreover, was found between those cases ending up on the child protection register and those dropped off at an earlier stage (Giller et al, 1992). The common result of abuse investigations, however, was to weaken already vulnerable families further, with parents feeling disempowered, anxious and lacking in self-esteem (Cleaver and Freeman, 1995). As Rickford (1994) explains:

> **Far from filtering out the 'dangerous cases' the child protection system is a lottery which sucks in thousands of families struggling to bring up their children in appalling circumstances and offers them nothing except the added stress and stigma of an investigation. (quoted in Lupton et al, 1995, p 8)**

Conclusion

The term 'partnership' is gaining increasing currency within contemporary social work discourse and indeed holds a central position in the philosophy of the 1989 Children Act. This chapter has discussed the nature of participatory approaches in children's services and examined the extent to which they have been developed in England and Wales in the post-war years. Its central argument is that the extent to which families are able to participate in decisions about them and their children is determined by the changing assumptions surrounding the relationship between the family and the State.

While the early days of the welfare state were characterised by considerable optimism about the coincidence of interest between the needs of the family and the State, and thus about the ability of a benign and paternalistic social work practice to ameliorate family problems, such optimism proved difficult to sustain. The growth of the administrative and legal powers of social work departments resulted in the increased alienation and antipathy of the families with whom the professionals worked. Furthermore, there was scant evidence that their interventions were producing the desired results. A widespread crisis of confidence emerged over the ability of the State to provide safe and stable accommodation for those children and young people in its care. Coupled with growing political and public alarm over social workers' identification and management of child abuse, local authority social services departments were placed increasingly on the defensive, seeking ways of tackling the risks, while minimising the degree of intrusion into families' lives.

The growing tide of public discontent, fuelled in part by the emergence of national pressure groups working on behalf of families, in part by the mounting research evidence on the relative ineffectiveness of social work practice, and in part by the crisis in Cleveland following a series of child abuse inquiries, culminated in the 1989 Children Act. This legislation attempted to construct a new 'consensus' on the nature of the relationship between the family and the State which sought to balance the need to protect children with that of respecting the rights and responsibilities of their adult carers. Central to this balance was the principle of 'partnership'. The available research evidence, however, suggests that the relationship between families and professionals is generally very far removed from one of 'partnership'. The proliferation of systems and procedures designed to manage risk in the face of increased political scrutiny, has proved to be a significant block to family inclusion and participation. As a result, the tensions between the interests of children, their families and the State which the Children Act sought to alleviate have remained and may actually have been heightened by more coercive and legalistic approaches. In a climate of diminishing resources and growing social inequality, social work is increasingly being driven towards a more defensive and reactive form of practice.

Despite the exhortations of *The challenge of partnership* (DoH, 1995c), and the more general move towards enhancing the rights of the citizen–consumer, the evidence suggests that the extent of families' participation in or influence over social work decision making remains essentially limited. What *The challenge of partnership* fundamentally fails to address is the variety of ways in which the operation of organisational systems and professional cultures serve to inhibit partnerships with families. That official expectations around family functioning continue to imply the need for professional control is revealed in the Department of Health's description of the impact of 'partnership': "Professional practice which reduces a family's sense of powerlessness, and helps them to feel and function more competently, is likely to improve the well-being of both parents and children" (DoH, 1995c, p 10). In the next chapter we consider the impact of legislation similar to the Children Act but more radical in its ambition of including children and families in the way desired, but not yet realised, in England and Wales.

THREE

Lessons from New Zealand

Introduction

> One culture can learn much from another about childhood,
> parenting, education and family life. Diversity of culture is
> enriching and different cultural and ethnic values and family
> forms are sources of strength. (Race Equality Unit, 1990, p 2)

At the same time as the 1989 Children Act was being drafted in England
and Wales, similar legislation was being finalised in New Zealand. Both
enshrined much the same principles, but the 1989 New Zealand Children,
Young Persons and their Families Act (CYPFA), provided a far more
radical mechanism for enacting those principles than the UK Children
Act. Both Acts were heralded at the time as a challenge to the old order
and sought fundamentally to re-evaluate the relationship between the
family and the State. Thus, in the UK, the arrival of the Children Act was
described by Lord Mackay, then Lord Chancellor, as: "... the most
comprehensive and far-reaching reform of child law which has come
before Parliament in living memory" (*Hansard*, 1998, vol 502, col 488). In
New Zealand, the report strongly influencing the legislative reform –
Puao-Te-Ata-Tu – was described by Anne Hercus, Minister for Social
Welfare, as: "The most significant document ever presented to the
Department and Social Welfare" (quoted in Wilcox et al, 1991, p 3).

In particular, both Acts sought to keep children with their family of
origin where possible and placed emphasis on supporting rather than
replacing existing families. Both envisaged a central role for families as
carers and decision makers. However, while the theme of partnership
within the Children Act was implicit, contained not in the body of the
law itself but in the volumes of guidance and regulations by which it was
accompanied, the New Zealand law involved a far more central
requirement, explicit within the primary legislation, to work collaboratively
with the families involved. The practical manifestation of this requirement
was the family group conference (FGC). This chapter will examine the
sociopolitical factors surrounding the CYPFA and consider its main

objectives. The nature of FGCs, and the central values and assumptions by which they are underpinned, will be described and assessed and some of central issues and debates raised by their operation in the New Zealand context will be discussed.

The origin of family group conferences

The development of family group conferences resulted from the complex interplay of a range of influences and factors. In part, their emergence can be understood in the context of issues and debates common to child welfare discourse throughout the world; concerns, for example, about family responsibility, children's rights, cultural diversity and the respective roles of family, State and community (Hassall, 1996). In part, however, FGCs were the result of forces unique to the New Zealand context, in particular to the politically cohesive and influential nature of the indigenous Maori and Pacific Island communities. Ironically, the origins of what was to emerge as a radical alternative to traditional social work methods can be traced back to ancient traditions of family and community decision making.

Barbour argues that the advent of FGCs was, in some way, inevitable in New Zealand: "... a predictable, if not virtually inescapable" outcome of the converging effects of historical change, political struggle and developments in social work theory and practice (Barbour, 1991, p 16). For 60 years the New Zealand Department of Social Welfare had implemented interventionist strategies that were built on *Pakeha* (white European) models of family and social values underpinned by a dictum of professionals "knowing-best" (Ryburn and Atherton, 1996). It is argued that a parallel can be drawn between the colonisation of New Zealand by the British Empire and the 'colonisation' of social work theory and practice by ideas originating from the UK and later North America (Wilcox et al, 1991). For many years these ideas influenced the thinking and practices of social workers more extensively than those based on indigenous ways of working. In New Zealand, as in the UK, the role of the State in family life had, over the 20th century, increasingly moved away from a largely 'residual' model to one where it began to assume greater responsibilities for its citizens. Although seemingly confronting many of the social inequalities their people faced, the corollary of the growth of State social services was that the traditions of the Maori were effectively submerged by polices and processes based on *Pakeha* (white European) values.

In the latter half of the 20th century, and in common with most other post-industrial nations, the growing demand for welfare services in New Zealand led to increasing strain on State resources, sparking a Right Wing backlash against excessive taxation and the unaccountable practices of State bureaucrats. Concerns about the over-dependency of citizens on State welfare services resulted in increased political pressure for a reduction in the role and cost of the State and for the stimulation of greater individual and family self-reliance. Accompanying such pressures were important, and not unconnected, political and ideological shifts in respect of the role of the family in social life. At the same time as the State was withdrawing to a more residual role, New Zealand saw the emergence of a national pro-family policy, concerned with tackling, politically if not economically, the perceived disintegration of family life. Central to this policy approach was an emphasis on the importance of the family group in the care and welfare of its members.

Alongside and underlining this policy shift was a growing body of evidence from research and practice that change was needed in respect of children in public care. Public unease about a child welfare model that created family dependency was accompanied by growing concern about the institutionalisation of children, the quality of foster care and the effect of State intervention on young offenders (Caton, 1990). Failure to involve extended families in decision making to protect children was highlighted as a particular issue (Pilalis et al, 1988) and pressures began to mount for a move away from an expert model of social work to a more 'consumer'-orientated approach (Wilcox et al, 1991). The political momentum for greater openness and a dissatisfaction with the adversarial nature of court proceedings led to the establishment of a family court in 1978 and concerns about the mono-cultural and middle-class basis of social work resulted in the setting up, in 1983, of the Advisory Committee on 'Youth and Law in our Multicultural Society' to examine ways to improve the cultural sensitivity of the law. In their different ways, these developments all contributed to the growing momentum for change in national childcare legislation.

Origins of the Children, Young People and their Families Act

The emergence of child abuse in the 1970s as a growing social problem prompted the National Advisory Council on Child Abuse to propose a major rewrite of the childcare legislation. The International Year of the Child in 1979 saw the development of the New Zealand Committee for Children and the establishment of a new National Advisory Committee on the Prevention of Child Abuse. Set up by the Minister of Social Welfare in 1981, the Advisory Committee was strongly influenced by multi-disciplinary models of decision making imported from abroad (Schmitt, 1978). Its report recommended the replacement of the 1974 Children and Young Persons Act and legal recognition of the new multi-disciplinary child protection teams which had evolved in some parts of the country. Examining cases brought to the attention of social services, these teams were typically made up from people with expertise in a range of different aspects of child protection work, professionals, community bodies and other interested groups. They acted as consultative bodies and attempted to assist the decision making of the Department of Social Welfare; their success, however, was dependent on the nature of their relationship with the local departmental offices (Hassall, 1996, p 21).

In 1982 the Human Rights Commission Report looked at allegations of ill-treatment of young Maoris in institutions and concluded that there was significant cause for concern. If these institutions were to reflect the cultural needs of their young people, it was recognised that consultations with Maori representatives needed to take place. In 1984, a Maori Advisory Unit was established to look at the needs of Maori people in respect of public services. A year later it concluded that there was evidence of structural racism: "The Department was racist in the institutional sense; it was a typical, hierarchical bureaucracy, the rules of which reflected the values of the dominant Pakeha society" (MAU, 1985, p 16). This conclusion supported that of a parallel report from the Women's Anti-Racist Action Group which had argued that there was a clear need for a new approach to State services and structures (WARAG, 1984). Amidst widespread media coverage and growing political pressure to respond, the Minister of Social Welfare decided to set up a ministerial committee to advise on a Maori perspective for the Department of Social Welfare.

Puao-Te-Ata-Tu *(day break)*

At the same time as State organisations were trying to develop the best model to respond to mounting concerns about child abuse (Geddis, 1979), the Maori community was increasingly making its long-standing complaints known to the Department of Social Welfare. As discussed earlier, the professional organisation of decision-making meetings involved nothing approaching a partnership model. By the early 1980s child protection teams were typically dominated by professionals with little capacity or inclination to involve families in the decision-making process. The outcome of such meetings was the marked over-representation of children from Maori communities in public care, on the caseloads of predominantly non-Maori social workers and placed with white European carers. Interventions were based on white European (*Pakeha*) values and assumptions and it was felt that far too little was being done to strengthen or support the role of the *whanau* (extended family), *hapu* (clans) and *iwi* (tribe).

In July 1985 the Minister of Social Welfare charged the Ministerial Advisory Committee on a Maori Perspective to investigate and report on the operations of the Department of Social Welfare. The Committee was to produce a report on the most appropriate means to achieve an approach that would meet the needs of Maoris in policy, planning and service delivery. The Committee was chaired by John Rangihau and produced a report entitled *Puao-Te-Ata-Tu* (meaning 'day break') containing 13 separate recommendations for fundamental changes in policy and practice. These recommendations covered areas such as accountability, deficiencies in the law and practice, institutional behaviour, the importance of strengthening families, extended families, clans and tribes, recruitment and staffing, improving training and communication, departmental coordination, and a comprehensive approach to tackling wider social, economic and cultural issues (Department of Social Welfare, 1988). With specific reference to the existing 1974 Children and Young Persons Act, the Committee argued for "substantial ideological change" if the needs of Maori were to be met. In particular, it contended, the assumptions about the role of the family, the position of the child and responsibilities of the State required re-evaluation.

The relationship between Maori and the State was first formally expressed in the 1840 Treaty at Waitangi. This political statement promised a partnership between the Crown (British Government) and the indigenous community, with the Maori having control over their own people. Although there is dispute over the extent to which the agreement was subsequently honoured, Wilcox et al (1991) argue that this Treaty was central to the autonomy of the Maori in family decision making:

The Treaty of Waitangi, Article 2 (Maori version), in recognising the concept of '*tino rangatiratanga*' or authority (*mana*) of Maori

people over its resources (including people) clearly indicates for Maori, their right to make decisions over matters involving members of their families. (Wilcox et al, 1991, p 6)

In particular, while Article 2 of the Treaty provided for the State to intervene at the 'last resort' in matters of the care and protection of children, this only applied to *Pakeha* children. For Maori children, that right was to belong to the *whanau* (extended family) and *hapu* (sub-tribe) (Jackson, 1989). The working party envisaged that the adoption of the original principles of the Treaty was necessary to overcome the monocultural nature of the Bill. Rather than conducting a piecemeal analysis, therefore, the 1986 working party on the Children and Young Persons Bill undertook a more fundamental review of the current legislation:

... reviewed the basic assumptions and intentions underlying the Bill and endeavoured to develop proposals which were responsive to public concerns as to how those assumptions have been expressed. Particular attention was paid to the need to reflect in legislation the principles and spirit of the Treaty of Waitangi. (quoted in Cleaver, 1995, p 7)

The Committee considered how best to consult with the Maori community about its experience of social welfare services. It chose to travel around the country and meet people in the Maori setting taking an oral approach to the work, believing this to be the traditional approach of Maori people. In so doing the Committee heard strong messages of frustration, alienation and an angry sense of powerlessness although not matched with a sense of hopelessness. The depth of feeling they heard was described as a "... litany of sound – *Ngeri* – recited with the fury of a tempest on every *marae*, and from *marae* to *marae*":

"In two years, expected to clean up a 150-year-old mess...."

"... view clients as irresponsible and somehow deserving of their poverty, powerlessness and deprivation...."

"... white males at the top and middle...."

"An institution of social control...."

"...nurtures dependence and self-hatred rather than independence and self-love...."

"Give us the money and let us do it...."

"... violence done to tribal structures; violence done to cultural values...."

"Don't meet Maori people in their own world...."

"Pakeha control of Maori...."

"People have been institutionalised and rendered helpless...." (quoted in Department of Social Welfare, 1988, p 21)

The Committee concluded that the difficulties experienced by Maori people with the Department of Social Welfare were reflections of their socioeconomic status – the fact that: "The history of New Zealand since colonisation has been the history of institutional decisions being made for, rather than by, Maori people" (Department of Social Welfare, 1988, p 18) – and that the issue of racism was central. The most insidious and destructive form of racism, the Committee argued, was that of institutional racism, in which: "Participation by minorities is conditional on their subjugating their own values and systems to those of 'the system' of the power culture" (Department of Social Welfare, 1988, p 19). The Committee viewed bi-culturalism as the appropriate policy direction for better race relations in New Zealand; a sharing of responsibility and authority via a social and cultural 'partnership' rather than a separatist approach. It argued that Maori people should be directly involved in social welfare policy, planning and service delivery and given the resources to control their own programmes: "... the transference of authority over the use of resources closer to the consumer" (Department of Social Welfare, 1988, p 24).

In respect of child welfare, the Committee report recognised the importance of the cultural assumption that children and their needs are part of the wider family and community network: "The Maori child is not to be viewed in isolation, or even as part of nuclear family, but as a member of a wider kin group or hapu community that has traditionally exercised responsibility for the child's care and placement" (Department of Social Welfare, 1988, p 29). The technique, in the Committee's opinion, must be to "reaffirm the *hapu* bonds and capitalise on the traditional strengths of the wider group" (Department of Social Welfare, 1988, p 29). The view of the Committee was that the wider family and clan had been excluded from the decisions about the care of a child unnecessarily, due to an "... exaggerated emphasis on 'confidentiality'" (Department of Social Welfare, 1988, p 29). Its conclusions emphasised the need for 'preventative initiatives' to restrengthen family and community bonds and responsibilities to facilitate the Maori goal of caring for their own children and for the judicial determination of problems involving children to take place only as a last resort (Department of Social Welfare, 1988). It was recognised that significant resources would need to be channelled to support proposals for positive Maori involvement.

The 1989 Children, Young Persons and their Families Act

The family group conference, while never described nor envisaged practically in *Puao-Te-Ata-Tu,* occupies a central place in the Children, Young Persons and their Families Act. The inclusion of the word 'family' in the Act, differing significantly from the title of the earlier Children and Young Persons Bill, underlined the intention to strengthen and maintain family groups (Connolly, 1994). In providing a single and unified model to involve families in the decision-making process, it went much further than the UK Children Act in terms of its implications for social work practice:

> **The prescriptiveness of the New Zealand Act creates a difference that makes a difference. In practice, it means that the spirit of partnership implicit in the Children Act is significantly more explicit in the New Zealand legislation. (Ryburn, 1994a, p 7)**

However, the development of FGCs in fact sprang from a *lack* of any prescription for the way in which the principles and broad recommendations within *Puao-Te-Ata-Tu* should be implemented: "Management at a local level were not given any clear prescription for how the recommendations might be implemented in practice but were asked to see that it was done. It was therefore left to local initiatives to operationalise the recommendations of '*Puao-Te-Ata-Tu*'" (Wilcox et al, 1991, p 3). Wilcox et al argue that the strength of the report lay in the fact that it eschewed any particular practice method and thus forced staff to look at the issues, their existing practice and values rather than just imposing new methods on families. In particular, professionals were required to think about the attitudes they had to handing power and decision making back to the families with whom they worked.

The original draft of the 1986 Children and Young Persons Bill was reviewed by the new Minister for Social Welfare after one year and two key changes were recommended. The first was the need for a cultural perspective which demonstrated respect for cultural identify and status and an "Emphasis away from intrusive and disempowering interventions". The second was the requirement to involve parents, family groups, *whanau*, *hapu*, *iwi* in finding solutions to problems in families (Hassall,1996, p 25). The first draft of the Bill was seen to have lacked cultural sensitivity, made little provision for prevention or family support and to have been overly long and complex. Its original proposals were based on two pilot schemes that left decision making in the hands of professionals with families only involved in an ad hoc way. The child protection teams envisaged were viewed as bureaucratic, top-heavy and lacking in accountability.

Following *Puao-Te-Ata-Tu* and the pressure for change, a newly drafted Bill was presented to Parliament in 1989. This replaced the previously central child protection teams with a decision-making model that legally ensured family involvement. This model was the family group conference. The central place of the FGC evolved from a range of factors and influences but was helped by the fact that it easily substituted the original role envisaged for the child protection teams. The fact that practitioners on the ground were trying to develop more inclusive methods and encourage family decision making meant that, in areas of progressive practice like Lower Hutt, models of family decision making were already emerging that could replace the old, professionally-dominated, 'paternalistic' ways (Wilcox et al, 1991).

The Act came into force on 1 November 1989 after a development period of six years (Tapp, 1990), although the actual reform process was longer, stretching over 13 years (Geddis, 1993). The legislation was both novel, in that it recast the pre-existing relationship of the State and the family, where professionals regulated the boundaries between the rights of the parents and those of their children (Tapp, 1990, p 82) and at the same time traditional in so far as it was derived from ancient methods of tribal and community decision making and informal systems of social control (Wilcox et al, 1991; Hassall, 1996). As with its UK counterpart, the New Zealand legislation rested on the central assumption that children are generally best cared for by their families and that, in most cases, there is a consensus between the family and the State over what is best for the child. Thus, the Minister of Social Welfare presenting the Bill argued that children's needs should not be seen in isolation from those of their families and that enabling and helping the latter would ultimately benefit their children: "The Bill recognises that the well-being of children and young persons is bound in with the welfare of their families" (quoted in Tapp, 1990, p 32).

In providing a legal mandate to family decision making, the attempt was made to redress, in a very practical way, assumptions about how decisions for children should be best made. In this way the FGC approach involved a: "... move away from the traditional paternalistic system of welfare in which the child is rescued by the bureaucracy, [to one] in which the family is seen as the carer/protector and is supported to undertake this role" (Connnolly, 1994, p 90). Even so, at the final drafting of the Bill, there were questions from the Maori community about the right of the State to intervene in Maori decision making for their kin. The power of veto over family plans could be seen as the State intervening only at the last resort, but could also be seen to undermine the integrity of Maori traditions and culture. This situation contrasted with that in other jurisdictions, such as parts of North America, for example, where the law had no influence over tribal structures and processes.

The FGC approach

The FGC approach attempts to enable family groups to take collective responsibility for decisions regarding the care and protection of their children. In being prescriptive about the FGC process, the CYPFA seeks to enshrine the principle of family responsibility in all decision making for children and young people. Section 5 of the legislation states that: "... wherever possible, a child's or young person's family, whanau, hapu, iwi and family group should participate in the making of decisions affecting that child", and accordingly "... wherever possible, regard should be had to the views of that family" (Tapp, 1990, p 32). Furthermore, as with the UK Children Act, there is also an assumption that a child's connections with their family should be protected where possible: "... the relationship between a child and his or her family should be maintained and strengthened" (Tapp, 1990, p 32). Maxwell and Morris (1993) argue that the importance of the FGC process derives from the extent to which it can ensure the following: a shift to partnership–based interventions, rather than unilateral action by the State; the recognition of culturally diverse processes and values; the involvement of victims and others affected by the decisions in planning for the future of the child(ren).

The FGC approach has been described in detail elsewhere (see Wilcox et al, 1991; Paterson and Harvey, 1991; Barbour, 1991; Maxwell and Morris, 1992; Geddis, 1993; Fraser and Norton, 1996) and it is not proposed to repeat these descriptions here. The four main stages of the process can be outlined as follows, however (see Morris, 1996, p 4):

- In conjunction with the family, an independent coordinator plans for the FGC including preparing family members for the meeting, arranging practical matters such as the venue and refreshments and deciding who is to be invited.
- At the FGC professionals share information with the family about their concerns, their responsibilities and the services they can offer.
- The family has a private time to discuss the issues and develop its plan for the care and/or protection of the child.
- The family, professionals and the coordinator meet again to agree a plan and negotiate services, including any contingency plans and/or plans to meet again.

Perhaps the most important characteristics of the FGC for the purposes of this discussion is the changed role of the professionals: they are there to provide information about the problems as they see them and the support and resources their agencies may be able to provide, not to offer their opinions about the appropriate action to be taken. The family members make the plan for the care and protection of the child after the professional 'information-givers' have left. The professionals are charged with agreeing the family plan, however unconventional, unless they have strong reasons for believing it will place the child at risk. As Ryburn has argued, the FGC model thus significantly redefines the role of the professional: "[the Act] gives a fundamentally clearer and more important role to family groups in making their decision about care and protection and as a result the professional role is correspondingly redefined and circumscribed" (Ryburn, 1994a, p 7).

FGCs – dilemmas in practice

As with the UK Children Act, the New Zealand legislation attempted to achieve a balance between the interests of child protection and those of family protection. The New Zealand legislation, however, placed more explicit emphasis than the UK Act on the role of the family in the care and protection of the child. To this end, the CYPFA states that "... children must be protected from harm, their rights upheld, and their welfare promoted" (Atkins, 1991, p 389) and also that: "... the primary role in caring for and protecting a child lies with the child's family" (Atkin, 1991, p 389). The assumption is that 'protection' and 'promotion of welfare' will fundamentally be the families' responsibility, with the role of the State being secondary or residual. Thus the Act continues: "A child's family should be supported, assisted and protected as much as possible" and "Intervention into family life should be the minimum necessary to ensure a child's safety and protection" (Section 13 of the 1989 CYPFA). The central difference between the UK and the New Zealand legislation thus lies in the assumption of the latter that the needs of children and of their families are similar, if not the same, rather than separate domains with competing interests, that the law must monitor and control:

> **The Act reflects a balancing of competing interests, with the safety of the child being only part of that balancing process. The interests of the family ... will, it is hoped, coincide with the need to make the child safe. (Atkin, 1991, p 393)**

In making this assumption, the New Zealand legislation adopts a more 'collectivist' view of family life in which the needs of individual members will be met through the sharing of mutual responsibilities and interests. As Hassall writes: "Families are de facto decision-making bodies. It is inherent in the idea of family that members will act jointly rather than as individuals in some matters" (Hassall, 1996, p 17).

One of the main issues raised by the operation of the FGCs in New Zealand, however, is the potential tension between the rights and interests of the child and those of their wider family/tribal group. Although the CYPFA clearly states that, in the case of a conflict of interest, the interests of the child will be the deciding factor, some have questioned the extent to which the desire to enable families may result in the child's interests becoming secondary, or even lost, to those of more powerful adults. Furthermore, others have argued, the assumption of minimum intervention in family life may not always sit easily with the requirement to protect children or to provide help and services to particular family members whose needs may be different from or in conflict with the wider family group (Tapp, 1990; Geddis, 1993). Particularly in the context of violent families, Tapp (1990) argues, the family group perspective may serve to tip the balance of power too heavily in favour of the family group and the State may be seen to have withdrawn too far: "The Act classifies family violence by adults against children far towards the private end of the continuum" (1990, p 144). Private discussions in particular may appear to leave the child in a potentially vulnerable position, given the oppressive and coercive nature of some family relationships. Such discussion may: "Tip the scales dangerously ... [and] put into the hands of the family who abused the child the final responsibility for making decisions regarding the child's future protection and well-being" (Geddis, 1993, p 142).

Against this, others argue that families do not in general collectively abuse children. While a particular member or members of a family may abuse, the presence of a wider family group will include individuals who have not abused the child and can act for that child. As Wilcox et al (1991, p 9) have argued: "... most abuse occurs by family members on their own children. We also believe the paradox that the best protection is offered by the family, in its widest sense". Nevertheless, as a result of concerns about the appropriate point at which the 'balance' was struck, additional steps were taken subsequent to the CYPFA legislation to ensure that the child's interest remained centre-stage at all times. In spite of the provisions of Section 6 (relating to the interests of the child), the Mason Report (1992) reviewing the legislation commented on the perceived weakness of the paramountcy principle and recommended amendments to the Act that would reaffirm this principle, stating explicitly that the child's interests shall at all times be treated as the first and paramount consideration. The government accepted this recommendation and drafted amendments to the Act "... to confirm the priority of the paramountcy principle" (quoted in Allan, 1992, p 19) while noting that balancing the interests of the child against the importance of the family remains a "... contentious issue" (Allan, 1992, p 19).

The New Zealand CYPFA made strong assumptions about the legitimacy of extended family groups being involved in decision making. While from a Maori perspective this may have been culturally appropriate it raises questions about its relevance to other cultural groups in New Zealand. Thus Atkin (1989) queries the applicability or the FGC model for the (majority) non-Maori child for whom the concept of *whanau* as the 'family of belonging' may have little meaning: "If the 'family of belonging' is to have primacy, what does this mean for the European child who has been beaten by its parents, its most likely 'family of belonging'? Under what conditions can the interest of that child be 'pursued' outside the context of the 'family of belonging'?" (1989, p 237).

While there are some complexities in defining 'the family' for an individual FGC, there is an expectation that the members of the wider family will be involved in the decision-making process. It could be argued, however, that the approach may become undermining or disempowering if the child or adults at the centre of the situation do not see the involvement of other family members as legitimate or, indeed, welcome. The 'inclusive' assumptions underpinning the FGC approach may not be shared by all family groups. In such a case, the involvement of the wider family against the expressed wishes of the natural parents represents, potentially at least, another form of social control which could damage family relations further. While certain family members have a legal right to attend, definitions are broad and precisely who constitutes 'family' in this widest sense has been described as a legal minefield (Atkin, 1989)

Furthermore, in so far as the 'terms and conditions' of the FGC are stipulated by the professionals or the coordinators, the family control over the process is importantly limited. Potentially at least the process remains open to professional manipulation and the actual influence of the families on the decision-making process may be seen to extend only as far as the professionals are prepared to enable it to do so. On the other hand, the model does provide legal scope for the family collectively to influence the process. Section 26(1) of the CYPFA states that the family may regulate its procedure in such a manner as it sees fit. There is no prescription, however, over which part(s) of the family may have a greater or less say over the process, not even when the outcome of the meeting may have particular implications for one part of the family, such as the natural parents or the child.

In addition to the above dilemmas, there may be inherent and yet unresolved tensions between the principle of family decision making and the other objectives of the legislation. For example, Section 13(f) of the CYPFA is unequivocal about the principle that, where a child or young person is removed from his or her family, *hapu* and *iwi*, "wherever practicable", s/he should be "... returned to and protected from harm with that family" (1989 CYPFA, Section 13(f)). Clearly this assumes that the return of children to their families, wherever possible, is the appropriate outcome of the family meeting. The stated intention to give decision making back to the family is thus qualified by the expectation that they will make certain kinds of decisions about the child's care. Should the decisions made by families not be those desired, the potential for professionals subsequently to reject these decisions or undermine them by withholding the necessary support and resources is introduced.

Much debate also centres on the role of the 'independent' coordinators within the FGC and the extent to which their practice is regulated, and potentially restricted, by the Department of Social Welfare. Some have argued that the early vision of the coordinators' role, in which their legitimacy derived from the community, has shifted to one more formally based on State legitimacy – away from the communities they were originally intended to serve:

> **The philosophy shaping the co-ordinator role has changed: the concerns about power sharing, suspicion of 'professionals' and involvement of family/*whanau*, *hapu* and *iwi* expressed during the legislation formation have been replaced by a statement about operating within the bureaucracy. (Cleaver, 1995, p 10)**

The situation has now been reached, Cleaver argues, where coordinators are viewed as just another arm of the State: "... as merely another version of the professional social worker working from a bureaucratic power-base of a monocultural state organisation" (Cleaver, 1995, p 10).

Central to this issue, and to that of the operation of family group conferences more generally, is the broader political shift in attitudes towards the public sector that took place within New Zealand and other industrially developed societies towards the end of the 20th century. Under the influence of New Right approaches to the welfare state, the general thrust has been towards reducing the cost of public sector services. Such a context, it is argued, has served to constrain the independence of the coordinator and restrict the potential of the family group conference to develop meaningful 'partnerships' with the families involved: "New Right accounting practices and strait jacketing of social work delivery has significantly undermined the empowering and resourcing thrust of the CYPF Act, which itself was the product of a different set of economic trends" (Cameron and Wilson-Salt, 1995, p 19).

Conclusion

The specific forces that shaped the development of FGCs in New Zealand have been described here as unique to that country, but the more general themes underpinning the legislation can be seen to be common to contemporary child welfare and protection discourse in many other national jurisdictions. The critical difference in the New Zealand context, however, is the centrality of family group conferencing to the primary legislation. While there may be other child legislative contexts that seek to involve families and increase the informality and accessibility of decision making (such as the Children's Hearing System in Scotland), none have given families the central role that they occupy in the New Zealand legislation.

The prescriptiveness of the legislation, however, and the requirement to use the FGC approach within a specific framework, constitutes both the strength and the potential weakness of the approach. The prescription ensures that all families facing child protection/welfare concerns have a right to make decisions in law, and in practice this occurs more than in any other jurisdictions. The CYPFA aimed to ensure that FGCs would be implemented as a legislative change, rather than a change in the practice of social workers and, as such, could not be degraded to other forms of professionally-driven decision making.

The legislative requirement, however, also had a more negative side. The 'proceduralisation' of the principles of family empowerment has meant that the approach is to be imposed on all families, regardless of their particular needs and wishes. There are questions about the applicability of the approach to all families and whether the assumptions by which it is underpinned effectively shift responsibility too far away from the State and on to the family in question. There are also concerns about the extent to which professionals perceive the approach as a disembodied 'technique' or 'method', rather than as a set of principles based on the commitment to work more collaboratively with the families involved. The role of the coordinators is crucial here and many have questioned the tendency increasingly to draw their ranks from Department of Social Welfare staff, subject to the managerial and resource constraints of that Department. The implications of this move for the independence of the coordinators and for the operation of the family group decision making more generally will need further debate and scrutiny.

Fundamentally the FGC approach will only be effective if it operates within a wider set of services sufficient to enable families to make real choices and decisions. The extent to which this is the case, however, is intimately affected by the characteristics of the broader political and economic context within which social services departments operate. Unfortunately, the signs in New Zealand are not encouraging, with a reduced public sector under pressure from the effects of increasing social inequality. Within such a context it is possible that the operation of FGCs may serve to increase the burden being shouldered by families and their wider communities, without providing the necessary support and resources to enable them effectively to so do. In the following chapters we assess this and other central issues surrounding the FGC approach in the light of the research evidence from New Zealand and elsewhere. First, however, we turn to the development of the FGC approach in the UK context.

FOUR

Empowering professionals?

I am acutely aware of how people are sometimes disempowered
in their contact with social workers and lawyers and health care
workers, because we see ourselves as the professionals. The reverse
should be true – our role should be to make them feel more
capable of exercising control over their lives. (Boateng, 1997,
p 2)

Introduction

As this statement by the Health Minister in charge of children's services
implies, a major challenge to welfare professionals is to reverse the
prevalence of paternalistic approaches and find more effective ways of
working in partnership. As discussed in Chapter Two, the 1989 Children
Act set an agenda for more participatory approaches in child welfare
without providing for their format. The growing interest in family group
conferences in the UK can be seen in part to derive from a desire to find
effective ways of engaging with families which reflect the broad principles
of the legislation. This chapter will look at the development of FGCs in
the UK and discuss the implications for childcare social workers. It will
argue that, despite the fact that they appear to reflect the core principles
of the Children Act, FGCs have proved difficult to implement. The chapter
will consider some of the reasons why this is the case.

The evolution of FGCs in the UK

Family group conferences are relatively new in the UK and their influence
on the policy, practice and thinking of childcare organisations is just
beginning. It is far from clear how they will operate most effectively
under the 1989 Children Act (England & Wales), the 1995 Children
(Scotland) Act, or the 1995 Children's Order in Northern Ireland. As
discussed in Chapter Three, FGCs in New Zealand were introduced

through radical legislation, whereas in the UK interest in the approach grew out of the desire to improve practice under existing legislation. The key difference therefore is that, in the UK, FGCs are a *practice,* rather than a *legal* construct. This has had critical implications for their development.

As Chapter Two described, the history of childcare social work has been built on changing assumptions about the responsibilities of the family and State in relation to the care and protection of children. Critically, any approach based on collaboration requires the development of a consensus about the amount of responsibility each can and should take in the decision-making process. It was argued that, for the spirit of partnership underpinning the Children Act to be realised, in which responsibility rested primarily with parents but could be shared with professionals, a "sea change" (Rowe, 1989, p 2) in professional attitudes about families would be needed. Attitudinal rather than legal change is thus seen as the route to the development of more collaborative approaches. Such approaches, however, have been thin on the ground. As Ryburn and Atherton observe: "Partnership has become the word symbol for good practice ... but its common and repeated usage belies the fact that in many respects it is an idea still in search of practice" (1996, p 16). In this context, family group conferences have been promoted as providing the ideal format for working in partnership that the Children Act failed to prescribe (Nixon and Taverner, 1993; Morris, 1994b).

Beginnings

In 1990, a group of New Zealand practitioners visited England and Wales to share ideas and provide training on FGCs. The Family Rights Group (FRG – an independent national charity working to improve the law and practice relating to families) supported this visit and undertook to promote the FGC approach in the UK by means of a series of training events, national newsletters and publications (FRG, 1993, 1994; Morris, 1994; Morris and Tunnard, 1996). The FRG, which had lobbied influentially on the Children Act, asserted "... the enormous potential the model offered for increasing partnership between professionals and families" (Morris, 1996, p 10). The charity established a national pilot group, comprising a small number of local authorities and a voluntary organisation, to offer support and advice to developing projects. The initial FGC project sites included Gwynedd in North Wales, Hampshire, Hereford and Worcester, Warwickshire, Wandsworth and St Basil's Young Homeless Project in

Birmingham. All were initiated by practitioners or managers and required considerable enthusiasm and determination on the part of key individuals to get them off the ground.

Since the establishment of the first national pilot group in 1992, the observation of practice experience (Morris, 1994; Morris and Tunnard, 1996; Nixon, 1998) and the publication of the first research evaluations in the UK (Thomas, 1994; Barker and Barker, 1995; Lupton et al, 1995; Rosen, 1995; Crow and Marsh, 1997; Lupton and Stevens, 1997) there has been a growing interest in FGCs. In practice, however, their development has been limited. While certain authorities have made a commitment to developing this approach (notably Hampshire, Gwynedd, Wandsworth, Essex, Haringay, Greenwich and Wiltshire) FGCs more generally remain fairly peripheral to mainstream practice and decision making (Nixon, 1998). Given the obvious interest in this approach it is interesting to consider the reasons for its relative under-utilisation.

Decision making

The FGC approach is predicated on the belief that generally families will make better decisions for their children than professionals. Philosophically this idea clashes, not with the general ethos of the Children Act, but with the specific policy and procedures subsequently implemented by local authorities in relation to child protection. Designed and dominated by state bureaucrats, prevailing decision-making formats are typically underpinned by the assumption of professional expertise. A number of commentators have argued the disabling effect of the idea of the professional as expert (Croft and Beresford, 1988; Holman, 1993; Ryburn, 1994a). Such an approach, they contend, can be seen to lock providers and users of services into separate and sometimes conflicting 'power positions'. Intervention becomes problem-focused and based on a 'deficit model' of families characterised by negative cultural stereotyping, assumptions of individual pathology and an inadequate knowledge base (Ahmed, 1990; Ryburn, 1994a; Parton et al, 1997). In so far as users enter into contact with social work agencies from an existing position of powerlessness, resulting from day-to-day experiences of poverty, discrimination and oppression, this can be reinforced by the experience of social care services that deny choice and limit self-determination (Braye and Preston Shoot, 1995).

In effect, the expert model has continued to occupy the gap left by the

Children Act when it failed to prescribe any mechanism to ensure that partnership was integral to social work practice. By eschewing the question of exactly how partnership would work, the Act may have reduced the likelihood that it would be achieved. As Ryburn argues:

> **The Children Act requires no comprehensive reassessment of the role of professionals in child care and protection, and it therefore leaves substantially intact a practice culture which is likely to depend on the expertise and judgments of professionals. (Ryburn, 1994c, p 7)**

The authority vested in the social work role stems both from legislated duties and powers and, to an extent, from social and judicial expectations about professionals' publicly mandated roles. It has been argued that not only are social workers expected to know what is best for others, but they practice in the belief that are required to do so (Ryburn, 1991c). Such a stance leaves little room for negotiation about the nature of the problems involved nor indeed about their solution (this is a theme to which we shall return later). The prevailing professional decision-making models are not designed to facilitate partnership, but to enable expedient professional decision making – the language, protocols, location and functions all being heavily professionally orientated. The result is that families become largely inconsequential to the decision making and have little or no influence over the outcomes (DHSS, 1985a; DoH, 1991c, 1995b; Thoburn et al, 1995; Bell, 1996). In the words of one parent:

> **"No we don't really contribute to the plans, we were told what was going to happen, not consulted. The ball was in the social worker's court. I wanted to cooperate with her but if I had not wanted to, I'd have to have because of my name being on the [child protection] register. We didn't have the option to tell them to go away, we never knew what our rights were." (quoted in Lewis, 1995, p 5)**

Despite the centrality of parental responsibility and the clear intention to share responsibility at the heavier end of the intervention scale, parents have often been treated with indifference in decision making and at worst excluded (Corby et al, 1996). Conversely, however, where parents were involved it appears that that better working relationships were established between families and professionals (Bell and Sinclair, 1993). Critically, however, it is the professionals who determine the nature and extent of family involvement and, as Cleaver and Freeman's (1995) study of parental perspectives in child protection suggests, there may have been little progress in this respect:

> To most parents it is apparent the professionals not only hold all the cards, but control the rules of the game. The child protection system sets the style and pace of the investigation, makes judgments based on undisclosed criteria and decides a course of action regardless of parents' views. (Cleaver and Freeman, 1995, p 85)

One of the key blocks to more inclusive approaches derives from current perceptions of the potential for conflicts of interest within the family and concern about the effect of family power imbalances on the decisions that are made. As we have argued, the lack of partnership work to date in the field of child protection in particular reflects the perception of a central tension between the interests of adults and those of children. If one approach to child protection work is to confront the behaviour of adults in relation to children, then the attempt to build consensus with a parent may not be a high priority. At worst 'partnership' could be seen as a collusive activity that fails to challenge the abusive and power-laden behavior of a parent. As Biss (1995) argues:

> The blanket promotion of partnership within child protection presumes that parental empowerment within the process will necessarily best serve the needs of children. Partnership is an undifferentiated concept that can disguise and reinforce the power of an abusive parent. Power relationships within the family can be allowed to operated unquestioned. Non-abusive parents and children who are already in a powerless position can have this reinforced. (Biss, 1995, pp 172-3)

It is easy to see how social workers with statutory responsibilities to protect children can see partnership as perpetuating, rather than changing, abusive behaviour. In the light of research evidence that nearly all children involved in child protection interventions live with their parent/s (DoH, 1995a), the NSPCC (1996) warned that calls for partnership could lead to a lack of child focus: "The focus on partnership with parents can operate to the exclusion of the child's perspective" (1996, p 4).

Against this, it can been argued that there is little evidence that children and young people are any more involved in 'non-partnership' approaches and are considerably less involved than they wish to be, frequently voicing resentment or anxiety about meetings that are adult dominated (Mittler, 1992; Farnfield, 1997). The 'distance' children experience from decision making is reinforced not only because of their lack of power in relation to adults, proponents of partnership argue, but also from the fact that those making the decisions are largely 'strangers' to them with legal control (potentially at least) over their lives. Others point out that the power of adults derives, not from the ability necessarily to make better decisions, but from the physical, socioeconomic, and legal control they have over children. Thus Ryburn (1991b) challenges the idea that adults necessarily know better than children, even when, or perhaps especially when, those same adults will not be the consumers of whatever decision is made.

Official messages continue to be equivocal about the rights of children to participate in the child protection process. Thus a close reading of the Department of Health's (1995c) *The challenge of partnership* reveals that, although affirming the right of children to participate in decision making, the government remains of the view that it is up to the professionals to determine the extent of that participation:

> **Children have a *right* to be involved in decisions which will affect their lives and to express their wishes and feelings about their future. Deciding upon the level and nature of their involvement and participation in the child protection process provides one of the most demanding challenges for professionals. (DoH, 1995c, p 16; our emphasis)**

Even within the Children Act, with its explicit emphasis on the rights of the child, the decision about whether and to what degree they are involved in decisions taken about them is seen to lie with the professionals. The promised "reconceptualisation of children as people in their own right", it seems, has yet to occur (Lyon and Parton, 1995, p 41). The dominant assumption remains that professionals know what children need, how much stress they can tolerate, what they should and should not hear. If the participation of children is to be improved, it is argued, it will require a change in the way that all adults perceive children:

> **Parents as well as professionals need to be encouraged to see that enhancing children's ability to participate is not a lessening of**

their own rights and responsibilities but is an essential part of treating the child as a person and not as an object of concern. (Schofield and Thoburn, 1996, p 18)

The introduction of FGCs as a means of improving the participation of children and their families is thus potentially beset with difficulties. Attempts to make the approach 'fit in' with the existing system may challenge, not complement, prevailing assumptions and day-to-day practice. There is a danger that FGCs may be used to meet professional and organisational goals rather than to extend user involvement and control. The decision to introduce FGCs, and with whom and in what situations the approach will be applied, remains with the professionals and their agencies. Such a perspective was reflected in the government's proposals for consultation on *Working together* (1998):

We believe that Family Group Conferences work best if families are given clear parameters within which decisions can be made, and if conferences are held at a time when there is clarity about the nature of the problem to be discussed. (DoH, 1998, p 48)

Unless FGCs *replace* other forms of decision making, there is a danger that they get lost amidst a raft of other professional meetings that dilute or alter the original family plans. Furthermore, in attempts to make the two systems coexist, professional decisions will be perceived as having the greater weight and may be more likely to be monitored than those made by families. In such a situation, it is easy to imagine how family decisions could be seen as only ideas or suggestions for the professionals to use or ignore as they will. Conversely, of course, when the plans of professionals are not carried out by families, the latter may as a result be perceived as 'dysfunctional' uncooperative or 'uncaring' to their children (Rowe et al, 1984; Millham et al, 1986).

The key role of social services departments as gatekeepers of resources, it is argued, has led to a reduction in the autonomy of front-line practice. This may be seen to undermine the possibility of developing more flexible and creative responses to families' needs. If social workers are not enabled to negotiate and facilitate their work with families, the scope for FGC plans to influence the resources/services provided is likely to be greatly circumscribed. Furthermore, if value and emphasis is placed on tightly managing eligibility criteria, procedures and budgets, it is unlikely that social workers will be able easily to 'hand over' a planning process to family members whose needs and wishes will be unpredictable.

Flexibility or prescription

While the Children Act implicitly supports the FGC approach, unlike its New Zealand counterpart it provides no specific mandate for its practice. In the absence of legislative prescription, there is no consensus among families or professionals on the legitimacy of the extended family being involved in decision making. Furthermore, there is no agreement on exactly when, where, how often and with whom FGCs should be used. Whether they should be required for certain situations or offered to everyone is the subject of ongoing debate. To date, the use of FGCs in the UK has been hampered by a lack of resources, uncertain commitment to their practice and/or reluctance to embrace a new style of work.

As FGCs have stemmed from a practice base, rather than 'top-down' via central prescription, their use has inevitably been patchy and evolutionary. A central concern surrounding their implementation in the UK has been the need to build a consensus on the core principles and practices of FGCs while accepting local variations (Morris, 1996; Marsh and Crow, 1997). It has been noted elsewhere that social workers are vulnerable to interpreting the law in idiosyncratic and personal ways (Hallet and Birchall, 1992) and a family-centred approach such as FGCs, characterised by even less regulation and monitoring, is likely to be more susceptible to the whims of professionals. On the other hand, standardising methods would involve developing a procedural 'blue print' that would counter the commitment to run proceedings in a manner that suits the family. The tension between maintaining flexibility on the one hand and developing shared and equal standards of practice on the other, is obvious. The FGC attempts to address this dilemma through the role of the independent coordinator who works to broadly agreed operational principles but who is advised by the family in setting the particular style of their FGC. In this way each FGC is unique and the standards, to some extent at least, are set by the family themselves, while some uniformity of practice is maintained across the country.

The development of a family group conference approach within a context where social workers appear to be increasingly pushed towards more coercive and controlling approaches is highly problematic. The ascendancy of child protection work which, as we have argued, is increasingly conservative and reactive in nature (Parton, 1995, p 6) has meant attention is paid to complying with procedures that tend to restrict and prescribe practice rather than promote open and flexible ways of working with families. As the procedures are typically built on models that have been developed in response to social work 'mistakes' or things 'going wrong' they are framed negatively and defensively. In doing so they limit creative thinking and practices and concern themselves with processes rather than need. As Dingwall et al (1995) have argued:

> **The impact of proceeduralism and legalism is to shift the focus of attention in a child protection case from taking the *right* decision to taking a *defensible* decision. (Dingwall et al, 1995, p 251; original emphasis)**

In particular, a more proceduralised way of working places real limits on the possibilities of user influence and choice. The lack of flexibility resulting from over-reliance on procedures can serve to marginalise families and deskill both them and the professionals. For social workers operating in a climate of back watching and blame, taking risks could mean being disciplined or even losing their jobs (Christopherson, 1988). At the same time, paradoxically, it is argued that the growth of administrative complexity has increased the likelihood of social workers making procedural mistakes (Parton, 1997).

A major concern for FGC implementation groups across the UK has been to establish procedures that effectively make the link between FGCs and more established decision-making processes like planning meetings, statutory reviews and child protection conferences. Much attention has been paid to the relationships between the two (see for example, Smith and Hennessy, 1998) but this appears beset with problems. Firstly, the transplantation of FGCs into current systems has tended to antagonise rather than complement existing processes and procedures. Working in specific procedural and administrative contexts, there is a tendency for social workers to see FGCs as another 'technique' to use 'on' families, rather than representing a set of principles and values that could frame their agencies' practice. Moreover, with limited access or exposure to this approach, it is likely that FGCs will be used by social workers only when more established methods have failed. Secondly, the coexistence of FGC and traditional approaches can result in considerable confusion. While both are planning fora, they are based on contradictory assumptions and practices. With the former, for example, family members are strongly encouraged and enabled to become involved, whereas the latter have systematically limited family participation. Such a situation is likely to be confusing for families and professionals alike in so far as it gives quite different messages about who should routinely participate in planning.

At the beginning of the work in the UK, it was hoped that FGCs would have an effect on established systems and ways of working: "... have a broader impact on some of the culture, practice and thinking throughout the range of agencies involved in child care" (Nixon and Taverner, 1993, p 3). However, there seems little evidence to suggest that change is occurring and FGCs continue to occupy only the margins of policy and practice. One solution would be to prescribe FGCs for all child welfare problems. The problem here, however, is that, in spite of its ambition to be more family orientated, it may well be that a number of families simply do not welcome the FGC approach. Either through reluctance to involve the wider family or a lack of confidence in their own ability to plan, it may be that some families prefer the professionals to make the decisions. To impose FGCs on reluctant families would be to undermine the essential 'partnership' spirit of the approach.

The FGC approach attempts to manage the tension between compulsory intervention and family choice through the role of the independent FGC coordinator. In negotiating the arrangements for decision making the coordinator mediates between statutory agencies and families. As Fraser and Norton (1996) explain:

> **By negotiating decisions on seemingly practical matters the coordinator begins the process of balancing the rights and responsibilities of the state, the community, the child or young person and the family group. (Fraser and Norton, 1996, p 38)**

It is the coordinator who will have to establish the balance between professional participation and family control. This balance will also relate to the inclusion of certain family members against the objections of others. Whereas in New Zealand the mandate for inclusion of the wider family stems explicitly from law, in the UK it derives more implicitly from the legislative requirement to promote family connections and support and achieve the best outcome for the child. In New Zealand as much as the UK, however, the interpretation of these laws can focus on the objectives of professionals:

> **It is *policy* to seek participation of the wider family in spite of the**

parents' objections. This is done on the basis that the children have the right of access to a relative whether parents like it or not, particularly when they may not be able to continue to be cared for by their parents. (Wilcox et al, 1991, p 2; our emphasis)

This seems to reflect an implicit assumption that the parents' right to refuse a service extends only as far as is acceptable to professionals, or is contingent on them continuing to be able to exercise their caring responsibilities towards their children. On the other hand, from the child's viewpoint, it may be precisely the relative a parent wishes to exclude from a FGC that will bring vital information, confront a parent about his behaviour or even offer a solution to the problem. Seemingly distant uncles and aunts may become involved because of their relationship with the parent rather than the child, while at the same time may have a future relationship with that child (Maxwell and Morris, 1993). Nevertheless, the determination to include the wider family, in matters of conflict, potentially widens the net of informal social control. Morris et al (1996) argue that a distinction needs to be made between voluntary and compulsory interventions when we are looking at the use of FGCs:

... processes that make services voluntarily available must be distinguished from the use of statutory coercive power to ensure that children and families opt for what society considers to be in their best interests. It is the widening of nets of coercion that it is desirable to limit. (Morris et al, 1996, p 227)

The extent to which the FGC approach involves the imposition of new social work methods on people who may not want them is an important issue. Although, in principle, this is no different to the imposition of a child protection conference, the latter does not make explicit claims to 'empower' children and families. Such a situation highlights the paradox, discussed in Chapter One, of an attempt to enable families which involves professionals imposing a particular process on them. This appears to bring us unavoidably back to the assumptions about professionals 'knowing best' about what other people need. As Ivan Illich describes it: "Professional power is a specialised form of privilege to prescribe what is right for others and what they therefore need" (quoted in Wilcox et al,1991, p 1). If families do not see the FGC approach as legitimate or, indeed, welcome it may simply provide another experience of being dis-empowered. Not only has the State imposed a new structure upon them, but it has also attempted to define the nature and quality of their family relations. At its worst, this represents an intrusion into their family's life not only by the State but by the extended family/community as well.

A further disadvantage of FGCs becoming widely prescribed for all families is the inevitable bureaucratisation that will follow. The spirit of innovation and creativity that has come with practice in the UK may well be undermined by the administrative and procedural *modus operandi* that would develop out of the institutionalisation of FGCs in local authorities. It is unlikely in this context that the flexibility required to make each FGC as unique as each family group would be possible. A way of tackling this dilemma may be to place the independent coordinators outside the local authority to ensure that they have no organisational need to standardise the process. To do so, however, may be to render them vulnerable to fiscal cuts and/or marginal to the day-to-day work of the local authority and could have implications for the core principles of the FGC approach.

Information and assessment

> **Research can never produce an exact answer about the degree of risk of a particular placement for an individual child because of the interplay of factors which determine success or failure will be unique in each case. (DoH, 1991c, p 65)**

One of the major concerns facing social work today is the difficulty of achieving accurate assessments and, in particular, of improving the ability to identify and predict risk. In theory, at least, if social workers could produce better assessments, armed with knowledge of the latest research and skilled in contemporary assessment models, they could more accurately predict the possibility of child abuse. Assessment would thus provide a mechanism to avoid unwarranted intrusions into the privacy of most families at the same time as enabling more effective intervention in the lives of those children who need protection. However, as the above quotation implies, assessment is extremely complex and it is very difficult for social workers reliably to recognise, understand or predict child abuse/ abusive behavior (Parton et al, 1997). Parton et al (1997) provide a critique of the predominant 'disease model' which relies on an ostensibly scientific body of knowledge to identify the signs of child abuse. They argue that there has been little real progress in constructing a clear, reliable or agreed definition of child abuse. Consequently, the findings of specific research studies cannot be easily generalised to other contexts. This lack of definitional agreement means that the evidence informing assessment may be ambiguous or misleading. The dilemmas for practitioners in trying to understand the information they receive, it is argued, are considerable:

> **If researchers are unable to agree what constitutes child abuse it, potentially, puts policy makers and practitioners in an invidious position of trying to identify, prevent and treat a problem whose nature and magnitude remain undefined. (Parton et al, 1997, p 48)**

While there have been attempts made to identify factors that are predictive of child abuse (Finklehor, 1986; Greenland, 1987; Browne et al, 1989) there remains a need for more sophisticated and reliable research–based evidence to inform practice. Furthermore, it is arguable that the existing evidence may not be used very extensively. Munro (1988), for example, argues that social workers tend to use a personal and idiosyncratic approach rather than one which is informed by theory and research, and this has been a recurring theme of child abuse inquiries. Research into child protection, where perhaps the most structured and standardised form of decision making takes place, offers little reassurance that professionals can achieve a shared objectivity in their judgements. As mentioned in Chapter Two, Giller et al (1992) found little qualitative difference between those cases ending up on the child protection register and those which dropped off at an earlier stage. Furthermore, the child protection register, one of the most standardised organisational measures available to local authorities, is used inconsistently with enormous national and regional variations (DoH, 1995b) in spite of nationally accepted guidance and criteria. Gurrey (1997), in an overview of the number of children on the child protection register, highlighted the extent of the disparity: "The national average is that 32 children in 10,000 are on the register, yet this can vary from 9 in 10,000 in Kingston to 88 in 10,000 in Islington. You are 12 times more likely to registered for physical abuse in Bedfordshire than you are in Greewich" (1997, p 8).

We do not know, moreover, which statistic most accurately reflects the real levels of abuse or even whether a lower percentage of children on the register is an indicator of good or bad practice. Clearly the attempts of social workers to understand and quantify the problems of others is not an entirely dispassionate activity. Professionals will see the problems of others through the filters of their personal values and beliefs and through the framework and agendas of their organisations. Ryburn (1991c) argues that any claims to assessment providing rigorous objectivity should be treated with caution:

> **Every statement made in an assessment report by social workers is a least or much of a statement about that particular social worker, in the wider context of her or his role and agency, as it is a statement about those who are being assessed. (1991c, p 21)**

Given the limitations surrounding assessment processes, the extent to which families are involved in defining their problems would appear to be critical. The way families experience their problems may be very different from the way the professionals label them:

> **"My social worker came round and said my house was in a complete mess and what was I going to do about it. I didn't know that that was what neglect was." (a parent, quoted in Lewis, 1995, p 4)**

To enable families to participate in decisions that affect their lives, they may need to have a more substantive role in assessments. Without a role for families in defining their own problems and the causes, professional assessments will continue to dominate the planning process. Involving families in decision making may mean that responsibilities can be more evenly shared and understanding about the nature of the problem can be negotiated. The presence of family in decision-making forums, it could be argued, provides a powerful check on the value judgements and unexamined assumptions of professionals.

Smale and Tuson (1993) (and Smale, 1991) describe three models of assessment that are based on quite different assumptions about professional knowledge and expertise: the questioning model, the procedural model and the exchange model. These are all methods of assessment but, whereas the first two involve the assertion of professional and organisational control, the latter relies on notions of facilitation, negotiation and consensus. While the questioning and procedural models represent established practice, the exchange approach appears closer philosophically to the principles of the FGC approach.

The questioning model assumes that the worker will employ his/her knowledge and skill to form a judgement about the needs of others and the resources necessary to address them. The approach is relatively expedient for the professional and has advantages for the agency. Similarly, the procedural model attempts to describe people's needs through a professional/organisational perspective and it is the agency that frames the problems and solutions. Professionals typically gather information to establish the extent to which a client 'fits' predetermined criteria of eligibility. As Smale and Tuson (1993) describe it:

> **The agenda is set, not by the worker or the client, but by those who draw up the forms, and where the questions require specific answers about needs related to potential services, the process will be service driven rather needs driven. (Smale and Tuson, 1993, p 21)**

This model, it is argued, limits attempts at creative or negotiated solutions and not only restricts family participation, but also deskills the professionals and encourages a more 'administrative' approach to social care.

In contrast, the exchange model aims for greater user participation and attempts, at least, to give clients a greater say over the identification of their needs and the services required. Exchange is more complex, however; it takes longer and involves more people. There is a greater emphasis on problem solving rather than diagnosis or eligibility. Exchange places importance on:

> **... the process of problem solving; the ability to work towards a mutual understanding of 'the problem' with all the major actors. The process involves working with people to understand their differing perceptions and interests and to arrive at a compromise.... Instead of the worker making 'an assessment' and organising care and support for people, which carries the implicit assumption of control, the worker negotiates to get agreement about who should do what for whom. (Smale and Tuson, 1993, p 16)**

Despite the fact that the exchange model is closer to the spirit of the Children Act, it is the questioning and procedural models, these authors argue, that continue to dominate practice. Such models are based firmly on the assumption that the professionals know the right questions to ask the families. Yet families have knowledge about themselves that professionals are unlikely ever to obtain. As the DoH (1995c) has acknowledged:"Family members know more about their family than any professional can possibly know, they have an unique knowledge and understanding" (1995c, p 10). Current 'procedural' and 'questioning' models of assessment, however, not only forgo the possibility of obtaining this knowledge, but at the same time reinforce to families their lack of influence over the preoccupations of professionals. This is particularly evident in the field of child protection:

> **"If you try and challenge anyone's preconceptions about what's happening, then you get the feeling as though you are going to be seen as difficult and uncooperative and all of that. You're in a no win situation – double bind. If you say nothing you are sunk, if you challenge you are sunk." (a father, quoted in Lewis, 1995, p 5)**

The development of FGCs requires the adoption of a more exchange-based model of assessment, involving a different professional role in which the definition of problems, their resolution and management are shared with the families concerned. The reluctance of professionals to enable users to describe their own needs, however, has been well documented. Selwyn (1996), for example, analysed a cohort of adoption (Schedule II) reports about children's placement wishes. The research revealed that social workers described children's wishes in the 'third person' and did not represent their actual words at all. Fisher et al (1986) found that disagreement about the nature of the problems and the way to resolve them remained 'unexplored undercurrents' in the relationships between professionals and families, and Kelly (1990) highlighted how serious differences of perspective between parents and social workers were not addressed and hindered the pursuit of mutually agreed goals. Thus Lewis (1995) reports the words of one mother:

> **"No, we don't have a choice about anything, they decided. We wanted to be as a family but they were treating us as a separate thing. We told them we were trying to get a house to be a family but it didn't seem to sink in. As far as they were concerned, I was on my own with two babies being assessed." (quoted in Lewis, 1995, p 2)**

In practice the FGC approach should improve communication processes between families and professionals. FGCs must be conducted in the chosen language of the family (Morris, 1996; Kohar, 1994, 1996) and the use of any professional jargon or 'encoding' avoided (Nixon et al, 1996). The sharing of information and exchange of ideas is designed to act as a check on assumptions, mis-information and value judgements. Information, not only about assessments, but also concerning available services is crucial to effective operation of the FGC. Emphasis on services available at FGCs is likely to set the agenda for decision making; it may be difficult for families to make choices, if they have not used services before, or do not know the implications of such services (Willcocks et al, 1982). As Morrison (1988) argues, people want what they know rather than know what they want. The fact that information about services is a central precondition of professional power (Wagner Committee, 1988; Sinclair et al, 1990), however, may mean that its possession is difficult readily to relinquish.

Enabling families, enabling professionals

Much of the discourse about the inherent tensions in child welfare has focused on the conflict between the interests of the family and those of the State. The push for 'partnership' approaches has been founded on the need to ease the tension between these two diverse interests. Characteristically then, the early discourse on FGCs employed the notion of shifting power *between* the State and family rather than on considering their *shared responsibilities*. Historically, local authority departments with long-standing traditions of child rescue and securing 'permanency plans' for children, have tended to marginalise the role of families, supported in part by research which has repeatedly depicted the families of children in care as turbulent and fragmented (DoH, 1991c, p 44). However, as discussed in Chapter Two, replacing children's families rather than supplementing or supporting them, has had equally negative and often worse outcomes for children (Vernon and Fruin, 1986; Berridge and Cleaver, 1987; DoH, 1991c; Bullock et al, 1993; Utting, 1995). For the majority of children living at home with their families, moreover, the failure to work collaboratively will be at best a wasted opportunity to gain support for implementation and plans and, at worst, potentially increase the risk to children by driving a wedge between workers and clients (Thoburn et al, 1995, 1996). The reluctance of authorities to share responsibilities and control with families, it is argued, has underpinned some of the major deficits in practice and outcomes:

> **The greatest weakness of the traditional approach to permanency
> is that it was an attempt by professional to fix perfection. The
> Family Group Conference model is a reassertion of traditional
> social work skills of facilitation, meditation and enablement and
> it lies much closer to social workers' cardinal value of respect for
> persons. (Ryburn, 1994a, p 12)**

It would be easy, however, to reduce the problems around collaboration
to the attitudes of social workers (much like social workers are criticised
for reducing problems to the attitudes or behaviour of parents) rather
than to recognise the wider organisational, political and economic reasons
why participatory practice is limited. Participation, at the very least, needs
time and resources, flexibility and choice, commodities that are seen very
rarely in modern day childcare practice. The organisational blocks are
considerable. Not only do social workers find themselves operating in
ever decreasing fields, but the discretion they can exercise is increasingly
undermined by managerialist approaches to the work. The power to
control resources and shape policy directions are in the hands of those far
removed from the direct influence of service users or front-line workers
(Braye and Preston-Shoot, 1995). Typically the hierarchical organisations
to which they are primarily accountable exclude social workers from key
decisions. If social workers cannot be involved in or have influence over
the policy decisions they must ultimately implement, however, it is unlikely
that they in turn will value the involvement of service users.

Decision making in child welfare is undoubtedly a difficult and
demanding activity. As Cleaver and Freeman argue, it:

> **... requires the skill of Machiavelli, the wisdom of Solomon, the
> compassion of Augustine and the hide of the tax inspector.
> Making decisions proves to be something of a balancing act for
> professionals. Taking into account parental perspectives involves
> surrendering a degree of control to the powerless. (Cleaver and
> Freeman, 1995, p 19)**

While Cleaver and Freeman's quote suggests that professionals may need
to 'surrender' some of their control, however, for effective decision making,
it may be equally (or more) valid to describe the changes needed in terms
of increasing the amount of decision-making responsibility that is *shared*
within FGCs. *Giving* decision making to families may be seen to leave
professionals with something of a vacuum in terms of role or professional

status. Then answer perhaps is to understand and develop a different role that is closer to the spirit of the Children Act.

In many ways, its proponents argue (Ryburn, 1994a) the practice of FGCs may encourage a rediscovery of original social work values. The current erosion of professional autonomy has also adversely affected relationships with families. The increased political scrutiny and procedural complexity of social work practice has served to weaken the influence of those implementing as well as those 'consuming' the outcomes of decisions. The net effect may be the 'disempowerment' of social workers and families alike, with the high incidence of family alienation from the system being mirrored by growing levels of disaffection, 'burn-out' and absenteeism among social work staff. Thus Baldwin (1990) has highlighted the widespread sense of 'powerlessness' among residential childcare workers due to a perceived lack of influence on their organisations and their exclusion from the decisions surrounding the accommodation of a child in their care.

In contrast, the FGC approach attempts to generate a relationship between professionals and families based, as far as possible, on consensus and cooperation. In such a context there is no necessary reason why increasing the influence of families should occur at the expense of that of the professionals. It is possible to imagine a situation in which strengthening the role of families enhances, rather than erodes, the responsibilities of social workers and other professionals, not least by enabling decision making to draw on the different, but complementary, knowledge and experience of both sides of the partnership. In particular, by focusing on solutions rather than problems, the FGC may provide the opportunity for greater creativity and flexibility on the part of families and professionals alike. In the context of the wider financial and political constraints in which family decision making takes place, the commitment to shared responsibility and control may prove empowering for professionals as much as for families.

If we accept that the manner in which decisions are made will affect their outcomes, more inclusive approaches which attempt to build trust, improve communication and acknowledge different perspectives on problems and their resolution, are likely to improve the likelihood of successful implementation. As discussed in Chapter Six, families want professionals to understand their problems and listen to their ideas as much as professionals want families to appreciate their concerns and responsibilities. The aim is not to deny or minimise the risk, but to place it in its broader context. Given the complex nature of the problems faced by many families today, it is likely that an effective response will require a range of support and services from various agencies as well as from the family's wider community. Central to this effectiveness, as indicated in *Child protection: Messages from research* (DoH, 1995a) is the quality of the relationship between the family and its social worker. Developing better relationships with those with whom they work, moreover, may serve to improve the understanding and appreciation of the professional role on the part of the public more widely. Greater public confidence in social workers may in turn enhance the profession's own self-confidence and esteem.

Conclusion

This chapter has examined the implications of introducing a family decision-making approach to a context traditionally dominated by professionals. It has argued that legislation, research and policy have all espoused the importance of partnership principles but that, despite this, the notion of partnership has remained an idea 'in search of practice'. The current crisis of the social work profession, buffeted by volatile political and public expectations, has meant that practice has become increasingly defensive and conservative. Operating in a culture of blame and driven by the fear of making mistakes, the profession is unlikely to feel enabled to develop creative and innovative practice. The legal and managerial 'annexation' of social work practice has focused professional work on objectives of social control and resource rationing and engendered a proliferation of procedures which has undermined the control of all direct participants – social workers and family members alike. The net effect, it is argued, has been to disempower professionals both practically and intellectually, to: "Damage the capacity of the social work profession to think for itself" (Cooper, 1995, p 3).

In principle, FGCs appear to offer the opportunity to counter some of these more negative developments. Not only may they provide a more enabling, and possibly empowering, experience for the children and families involved, but they may also represent an opportunity for more traditional social work values and skills to reassert themselves, particularly amidst current calls for more positive forms of family support. Current government thinking, however, does not appear fully to embrace the partnership potential of the FGC approach. Thus the consultation document for the new *Working together* guidelines expresses doubts about the role of the FGCs in child protection and argues that "... decisions about whether to place a child on the child protection register must ultimately remain a matter for the professionals" (DoH, 1998, p 48). Given this political view, the research evidence on the strengths and weakness of the FGCs' approach relative to more traditional ways of working with children becomes particularly important if the approach is to move into mainstream practice. The next three chapters will examine the research evidence, from the UK and internationally, on the extent to which the FGC approach provides for more participatory and enabling ways of working with families and on its ability to ensure the care and protection of the children involved.

FIVE

International perspectives

Introduction

> Family group conferences reflect, in their philosophy and
> emphasis on the participation of families, young offenders and
> victims, cultural sensitivity and consensus decision-making and,
> in their practice, a capacity to be translated into diverse social
> contexts and jurisdictions. (Hudson et al, 1996, p 221)

Following their development in New Zealand, international interest in
family group conferences has grown rapidly. Although retaining some
common core components, the precise shape and nature of the FGC
approach has varied as it has been transplanted into different national
jurisdictions. There are also interesting international and intranational
variations in terms of the extent to which and ways in which the FGC
approach has been evaluated. While it cannot pretend to be exhaustive,
this chapter provides a brief overview of some of the major international
developments in the FGC approach, describing their main similarities
and differences. It goes on to examine the key findings of the available
research on the operation of FGCs and highlights the central issues and
debates emerging from this research. While the overview of the
development of the approach indicates the range of social problems and
issues with which FGCs are being used, the examination of the messages
from existing research focuses predominantly on its operation in the child
welfare context.

The international development of the FGC approach

Some of the earliest developments outside New Zealand occurred in the
United States where initiatives similar to the FGC model developed in a
number of different parts of the country. What is referred to as the family
group decision-making approach (FGDM) has been in use since the early
1990s in child welfare work (Graber et al, 1996) and is being practised in

around 10 states at the time of writing, although typically as pilot projects (Merkel-Holguin et al, 1997; Merkel-Holguin, 1996, 1998). While there are a number of different variants of FGDM, including the New Zealand FGC model itself, one of the most prevalent is the 'family unity meeting' – developed in Oregon around the same time as the FGCs in New Zealand and subsequently incorporating elements of the latter. This differs from the FGC insofar as the facilitator remains throughout the meeting (Graber et al, 1996) and there is no private planning time for families. Moreover, the underlying assumptions are very different. With the FGC approach, the wider family is seen as integral to the decision making. In the family unity model the involvement of the wider family is contingent on agreement by, and the needs of, the parents who are given the right of veto over the attendance of any family member (Merkel-Holguin, 1996).

In addition to the child welfare context, the family unity meeting is being used in work with chemically dependent parents, drug and alcohol prevention with school children and, as in New Zealand, in juvenile justice. Moves have been made to develop the model in situations of family violence, but only hesitantly, due to professional concerns about retaliations (Graber et al, 1996). Other types of family involvement include the family resource model which allows close family members to participate in decision making, but does not provide for the participation of members of the wider family group.

Although characterised by a range of approaches, the US developments in FGDM are united around a number of 'cornerstone principles', involving:"... family centred, family strengths-orientated, culturally sensitive and community-based practice" (Merkel-Holguin, 1998, p 18 – see also Immarigeon, 1996; Hardin, 1996; Printz-Winterfield, 1996). Despite its relative maturity, the development of FGDM remains patchy and on the margins, rather than in the mainstream, of US child welfare practice. As Printz-Winterfield argues:

> ... the impetus for utilising family group decision-making as a means of resolving issues of child abuse and neglect springs generally from outside the legal system ... implemented in selected cases and jurisdictions rather than as a formal part of state protection systems, casting it as a maverick innovation, rather than as an accepted addition to the repertoire of practice. (Printz-Winterfield, 1996, p 22)

In 1992, a religious family welfare agency in Victoria, Australia set out to develop the FGC approach in child protection planning meetings. Initially a two-year pilot project, it was subsequently extended in 1994, with funding from the Department of Health and Community Services, to cover two additional regions (urban and rural) and a new context: planning for the accommodation of children of mothers in prison (Swain, 1993; Ban and Swain, 1994a, 1994b; Ban, 1996). Other initiatives were also developing around the same time in Tasmania and Queensland. In Southern Australia family care meetings were established as part of the statutory care and protection process and a privately funded pilot project was set up by two non-governmental organisations in New South Wales (Ban, 1996). As in the US, the particular characteristics of the FGC approach in Australia vary across the country, but the Australian approach is distinctive from its New Zealand counterpart (and closer to the UK version) by its use in many cases of coordinators independent from the state (although as much by accident as design) and by the only limited extent of its statutory recognition (Ban, 1996; see also Wundersitz and Hetzel, 1996 on the use of family group conferencing with young offenders from aboriginal communities in South Australia).

In 1994 a family group decision-making demonstration project was set up in Newfoundland and Labrador, Canada, examining the use of FGDM in the context of family violence (typically violence by men against women and children in the home). Drawing on approaches developed by aboriginal people – such as 'reintegrative shaming', family preservation and community policing – and by feminists, the project was designed and supported by a coalition of community groups. Three very different communities, geographically and culturally, were involved in the project, each of which was considered historically suited to the FGDM approach: "The province has been orientated to consider models that affirm families and kindle community spirit" (Pennell and Burford, 1994, p 3). The project took referrals primarily from child welfare authorities and secondly from parole, youth community and probation services (Burford, 1994; Burford and Pennell, 1995; Pennell and Burford, 1996, 1997; see also Longclaws et al, 1996, on the use of family group conferences with young aboriginal offenders in Canada).

More recently the model has been developed elsewhere in Europe. Following pressure from over 1,000 grandmothers who felt that they were being overlooked as a potential resource for the family, the Swedish Association of Local Authorities established a two-year project in 1995 examining the operation of what were initially termed Family Advisory Forums (*Familijeradslag*). Ten local projects were initially selected to participate in the initiative, involving different types of communities dispersed across the country. The projects varied in terms of the kinds of families and problems involved. Some specifically targeted single parents or those needing income support; others extended the approach to groups such as adult drug and alcohol abusers (Lilja, 1997; Lidgren and Persson, 1997; Sundell et al, 1998). The first meetings, held in the early summer of 1996, built on the basic FGC model, but were "adjusted to meet Swedish circumstances" (Lidgren and Persson, 1997, p 18). The Swedish model is distinctive in being coordinated and researched nationally, under the management of the Swedish Board of Health and Welfare. The only financial support provided for this 'top-down' approach, however, is for the training of the individual project leaders (Sundell et al, 1988). The model is also unusual in its stated intention to recruit coordinators from a wide range of community sources and to avoid the use of full-time coordinators whom it was felt would become institutionalised (Lilja, 1997).

Interest in the model is also being shown in countries as diverse as South Africa, Israel, Singapore and Philippines (Hudson et al, 1996). In South Africa FGCs were piloted initially in youth justice, although subsequently extended to the child welfare context. The principle of family involvement had been long established in a range of community and family forums, such as the 'street committees' that emerged in the townships over the 1980s. These involved local people organising around social problems such as crime and violence in the face of the lack of interest from the authorities (Frank, 1998). The organic nature of such community structures also built on indigenous models of family and community decision making and the development of FGCs was largely targeted on contexts where family and community responsibilities had been eroded. As Branken and Batley (1998) explain:

> **An extremely important component of Family Group Conferences, if they are to have a long term impact on children's lives, is the need to rebuild the family support networks. [Where] the philosophy of *Ubuntu* [corporate responsibility and sharing] has been eroded ... we need to rebuild the spirit of *Ubuntu* ... it takes a whole village to raise a child. (Branken and Batley, 1998, p 89)**

The introduction of FGCs aimed to develop a new approach to work with young people in trouble with the law, one that sought resolution of conflict by means of family and community-based interventions. As in some parts of North America and Australia, the principle of family group conferencing has also been applied to work with children in some South African schools.

International research

Despite the growing interest in the FGC model, we would argue, its development has not always been underpinned by good quality, research-based evidence. Much of the available literature on the benefits of the approach is essentially promotional – designed to introduce the model to new audiences and to encourage its development in practice. Even in New Zealand, where FGCs have been in operation for the longest, evaluation has been limited in three respects: it has primarily focused on the adequacy of the statistical information collected by the Department of Social Welfare and concerned to identify and resolve any specific operational problems; it has almost exclusively centred on the perspectives of agencies and professionals rather than on those of the children and families involved and it has largely failed to follow through on the longer-term outcomes of the decisions being made. As Connolly argues, some of the good news about FGCs was initially based on slender evidence:

> ... although the early findings are encouraging, as yet there has been no research evidence to test the quality of Family Group Conference decisions. The quality and measure of success have hitherto been based largely on anecdotal information from workers involved in the process.... (Connolly, 1994, p 94)

Positive messages

Nevertheless, despite the above limitations, a body of more solid research evidence is beginning to accumulate from New Zealand and elsewhere, which can be seen to be delivering some reasonably consistent messages. The general thrust of this research is that FGCs are operating successfully, at least in terms of the process aims of the approach. Families generally appear to be willing to play an active part in making decisions about their children (Angus, 1991; Hassall and Maxwell, 1991) although Paterson and Harvey (1991) found that just under half of those invited to a FGC agreed to attend and Sundell et al (1998) puts the refusal rate in Sweden at 85%.

Once agreed, however, the overall number of family members attending FGCs is high compared with more traditional meetings (Thornton, 1993; Sundell et al, 1988) despite varying widely in many contexts (Swain, 1993; Pennell and Burford, 1996). The approach appears to be mobilising wider networks and relationships (Renouf et al, 1990; Paterson and Harvey, 1991) and fears that it would prove difficult to locate and 'reconstitute' dispersed family networks seem largely to have been unfounded (Hudson et al, 1996).

Overall, the FGC process seems to be viewed very positively by both families and professionals (Thornton, 1993; Burford and Pennell, 1995; Sundell et al, 1998) and as a considerable improvement on traditional approaches (Barbour, 1991; Thornton, 1993; Ban, 1996; Graber et al, 1996). There appears to be general agreement that the FGC approach serves to shift the focus from the problems in families to attempts to recognise and support their strengths (Hudson et al, 1996, p 223). In so doing, Barbour (1991) and others argue, there is 'intrinsic value' in the FGC process in so far as it may trigger a longer-term and more fundamental change in the ways in which families operate. Graber et al (1996) reveal that the attributes of family unity meetings seen to be of most value to the families themselves were the changed attitudes of the professionals: "... workers who listened, cared about them, believed in them, respected them, noticed their strengths, trusted them and didn't give up on them" (1996, p 183).

The evidence also suggests that FGCs appear generally to be operating as "... an effective decision-making process" (Angus, 1991, p 5) with agreement on the family plans being reached in over 90% of cases (Renouf et al, 1990; Paterson and Harvey, 1991; Hudson et al, 1996). In many cases, families are coming up with creative solutions, based on their private knowledge, that would not have occurred to, nor could have been provided by, the professionals involved (Barbour, 1991). The involvement of the wider family network appears to have increased the level and diversity of support available (Barbour, 1991; Hassall and Maxwell, 1991) and expanded the circle of those caring for the child (Graber et al, 1996). Pennell and Burford found that, although the overall volume of important social contacts surrounding the adults and young people was reduced subsequent to the family conference, the quality of support provided by the remaining contacts was enhanced. In terms of informational support, concrete support and (less so) emotional support, the overall level of support enjoyed by the family participants was closer after the conference to that experienced by other members of the community (Pennell and Burford, 1997).

In New Zealand at least the research suggests that the model may be achieving its objectives of diverting children from the courts and from State care (Maxwell and Robertson, 1991;Atkin, 1992). Research indicates that the FGCs are reducing the number of children subject to judicial decision making: in only 17% of all conferences held in New Zealand in 1990 was court action needed to determine or finalise the outcome (Maxwell and Robertson, 1991). There is also evidence that the number of children being cared for within the family may have increased (Thornton, 1993; Connolly, 1994) with "Fewer children ... living separate from their family or *whanau* than for many years" (Thornton, 1993, p 29). Thus Maxwell and Robertson (1991) found that, in just under two thirds of all care and protection cases, the child(ren) remained with original care givers (42%) or with the extended family (23%). Only just over one third (34%) was placed outside the family/*whanau*. The authors argue that this evidence suggests a "... substantial change" in the number of children being placed in State institutions (Maxwell and Robertson, 1991, p 15). The inconsistent nature of official record keeping, however, is such that it is not possible to compare these figures with outcomes for the years before the 1989 New Zealand legislation, and such exercises raise the central question, discussed in Chapter Seven, of the extent to which any observable changes can be attributed to the impact of a specific, and inevitably limited, intervention such as a family group conference. In the absence of any other method of intervention in New Zealand, moreover, it is impossible to ascertain the extent to which the changes identified would have occurred anyway.

Some largely operational difficulties are identified in the different national contexts in which the FGCs have been developed and many have resulted in subsequent adjustments to early practice. There are remaining questions, however, about how adequately the family plan is being recorded and whether sufficient detail is always provided to identify those responsible for implementing its various components (Paterson and Harvey, 1991). There is also some evidence that the subsequent monitoring of plans, to ensure that they are being carried out effectively and that the promised resources are forthcoming, is not always adequate (Renouf et al, 1990; Paterson and Harvey, 1991; Robertson, 1996). Pennell and Burford (1997) report the "inconsistent monitoring of plans" in the Newfoundland and Labrador demonstration project (1997, p 9) and Paterson (1993) reports that, of a sample of 157 FGC plans, under one quarter (24%) included a statement about monitoring. Inadequate monitoring and follow-up of the plans was the second most common problem identified by the professionals interviewed by Paterson and Harvey (1991) and was found to leave some families unclear about their responsibilities subsequent to the FGC (Robertson, 1996). The official review of the operation of the New Zealand childcare legislation recommended strengthening the process of monitoring and review of plans (Mason Report, 1992) and this was subsequently accepted and implemented by that country's Department of Social Welfare (Thornton, 1993).

Other, potentially problematic, operational issues also emerge from the literature. There are concerns about the time-scales involved, particularly in terms of the period between initial referral and the organisation of the FGC (Barbour, 1991; Thornton, 1993; Burford and Pennell, 1995; Ban, 1996). Paterson and Harvey (1991) found that just under two out of every 10 FGCs took more than two months to arrange. As Thornton argues, there is an inherent tension within the model between the requirement to maximise the number of family members attending and the need to hold the FGC as quickly as possible. Many emphasise the considerable responsibilities of the coordinators in gathering together the family group and ensuring the success of the meeting and Barbour, at least, considers that heavy reliance on the skills and commitment of the coordinators is the 'major flaw' in the FGC process (1991, p 21). There is evidence too, in countries other than New Zealand, of organisational resistance to the FGC approach. In Australia, for example, Ban (1996) discusses the problem of convincing some organisations of the cost-effectiveness of the FGC model and describes how the enthusiasm of some practitioners has been dampened by institutional resistance. Burford and Pennell echo some of these issues in the Canadian context and argue that more emphasis needs to be placed on training middle managers and ensuring the support of senior level staff (Burford, 1994). Such concerns notwithstanding, however, most reviews of the available research evidence (Thornton, 1993; Hudson et al, 1996; Levine, 1997) conclude that the overall verdict on the operation of FGCs is a positive one. Thornton, for example, argues:

> **The FGC must be considered a major part of the successes of the new legislation. Families are more involved than ever in making decisions and taking responsibility for their children. Fewer children are being separated from their family or *whanau* than for many years. (Thornton, 1993, p 29)**

Areas of concern

Despite supporting a generally optimistic view of the operation of FGCs, it is clear that the available research also contains some messages about areas of potentially more deep-seated uncertainty or concern. In particular, it is possible to identify five key areas within the literature on which the existing research is either silent or ambiguous: on the assessment of the extent to which the FGC approach achieves its objective of empowering the family members in the decision-making process; on whether the FGC process can deal adequately with family power imbalances; on the ways in which the potential tensions between different political expectations of the model are played out in specific contexts; on whether the model is applicable to all families and all situations; and, most importantly, on the extent to which the FGC approach is able to ensure that the best interests of the child are served, both during the meeting and in the longer term.

Enhancing family power

As we have seen in Chapter One, a central claim made by proponents of the FGC model is that it will effectively increase the power of the family group over decisions affecting the care of their children (Wilcox et al, 1991; Ryburn, 1994a; Hudson et al, 1996). As a model of shared decision making, Connolly contends, the FGC approach has "... challenged and extended our understanding of the roles family and worker can play in the area of child protection" (1994, p 99). Hudson et al argue that the evidence indicates that FGCs are able to give "effective voice" to the "traditionally disadvantaged" (1996, p 225). In particular, it is argued, the FGC increases the power of families by opening the actions and reasoning of professionals up to scrutiny (Angus, 1991). As well as increasing the clarity of professional concerns and the way in which they are communicated (Barbour, 1991) this can free the families from the feelings of dependency and helplessness which contribute to their powerlessness: "... what you witness is a metamorphosis of the family members from somewhat suspicious, sceptical and sometimes frightened or anxious participants to decision-makers in full flight" (Wilcox et al, 1991, p 5). By empowering family members, it is argued, the FGCs offer professionals a chance also to share the responsibility for decision making (Burford and Pennell, 1995). In the context of family violence, at least, there is evidence that some professionals expressed considerable relief at being able to so do: "I found it fruitful to meet so many family members and be able to form a more balanced picture of the situation. It was a real relief to find that the family and relatives took the matter seriously and accepted responsibility" (childcare worker, quoted in Lilja, 1997, p 3).

On the other hand there is also evidence that some professionals find the move to the role of information-giver difficult and are reluctant to cede control and responsibility to family members (Hudson et al, 1996; Ban, 1996). In New Zealand some professionals failed to comply with their statutory obligations in respect of the FGC process, with families not being given adequate notice about, nor sufficient say in, the timing and location of FGCs, and/or not being properly prepared for the meeting (Paterson and Harvey, 1991; Maxwell and Morris, 1993; Thornton, 1993). If families are to make informed decisions about the care of their child(ren) they must be given full information about the resources and help available. Concerns emerge from the New Zealand literature, however, about the extent to which the relevant professional 'information-givers' attend the Conferences (Paterson and Harvey, 1991) and about the quality of the information they provide once there (Mason Report, 1992; Maxwell and Morris, 1992). Interviews undertaken by Rimene (1993) with family members indicate that the use of professional jargon may, in some cases, have limited the quality of family decision making.

It is also clear from the literature that the perceived tension between family decision making and their statutory responsibilities has meant that some professionals have presented the family group with non negotiable 'bottom lines' (Ban, 1996). On the one hand, this may be necessary to prevent families making unrealistic plans that would not be supported by welfare agencies; on the other hand, it clearly constrains the extent of family control. In a few cases there is evidence of professionals attempting to take over the FGC proceedings and use the meeting to 'rubber stamp' their decisions (Hassell and Maxwell, 1991; Paterson and Harvey, 1991) and of professionals remaining (Thornton, 1993) or attempting to remain (Hardin, 1996) during the family-only session and in the formulation of the plan. It is also reported that many workers appear to be more comfortable with the individual casework situation than with large groups, particularly so, perhaps, where these may involve apparent loss of control to family members about whom the professionals know very little. As Walker (1996) reflects from the Maori experience: "Workers are generally uncomfortable with larger groups, especially where there is conflict" (1996, p 10).

The long drawn-out negotiations with families about the content of family plans which can occur (Burford and Pennell, 1995) also provide an opportunity for professionals further to influence the outcomes of the meetings. From the US, Hardin (1996) reports that some social workers have attempted to alter the written FGC plan. Even where they may not intend unduly to influence the outcomes, they may do so due to the tendency of some family members to defer to professionals. It may not be easy for those with a long history of State intervention in their lives, and particularly in the context of child protection or family violence, to challenge or disagree with professional opinions. There is evidence that many family participants remain keen to follow professional advice (Swain, 1993; Robertson, 1996; Graber et al, 1996). As Robertson (1996, p 53) argues, although the FGC process requires professionals to restrict themselves to an information-giving role, there is a 'fine line' between informing and influencing family decision making (also Swain, 1993). The report undertaken for the Office of the Commissioner for Children in New Zealand concluded that the FGC process was, potentially at least, susceptible to professional manipulation: "the new procedures are vulnerable to the actions of professionals, any of whom can readily take over, distort or destroy the FGC process" (Hassall and Maxwell, 1991, p 11).

The issue of professional influence is also relevant to the implementation and review of family plans. If professionals impose formal and elaborate arrangements for monitoring and reviewing plans, this may also serve to undermine the family's sense of self-determinacy. Inadequate monitoring of plans, however, may also prove problematic. If the decisions made by the families are not implemented, or allowed to fail, this will not enhance their sense of power or control. Evidence on the quality of monitoring and review, as we have seen, generally suggests an uneven and inconsistent picture. Moreover, as Hudson et al (1996) argue, the debate about whether professionals or the families should monitor plans is ongoing. Against the argument that family members will not honour the plans without external 'supervision', research indicates that professional monitoring may not be essential. In Oregon, for example, Graber et al (1996) report on the success of a shared responsibility for monitoring and other work suggests that families can (and possibly should) effectively monitor plans themselves. Thus the South African FGC pilots explicitly gave family members responsibility for the implementation of the plans, in order to enhance their sense of control: "By giving parents responsibility for reporting back on the progress with the plan, the parents are given back their role in parenting" (Branken and Batley, 1998, pp 100-1).

The clash of ideologies

As we argued in Chapter One, the idea of empowerment is politically and ideologically ambiguous. In particular, it may involve a central tension between the desire to promote greater family control on the one hand and the concern to ensure greater self-reliance on the other (Atkin, 1989; Barbour, 1991; Burford and Pennell, 1995; Lupton, 1998). As Barbour argues, this latter objective may be more pressing in times of financial austerity. Most of the countries in which FGCs have been developed, not least New Zealand, have been characterised by the reduction of welfare expenditure. There is evidence that in part the attractiveness of the FGC model to many policy makers derives from its low cost relative to residential alternatives (Barbour, 1991; Thornton, 1993) and there may be expectations that, by drawing more heavily on family support and resources, FGCs will reduce the volume of State support needed: "In the present climate of 'community care' and financial pressures, it was inevitable that moves would be made to make families responsible for their dependent members" (Barbour, 1991, p 21).

The tension between empowerment and enforced self-reliance is explicitly recognised in the formal report from the New Zealand Commissioner for Children: "The rhetoric of family responsibility can readily lead to the reduction of the support of the state sector which is essential to the well-being of many families" (Hassall and Maxwell, 1991, p 12). In particular, as Walker (1996) remarks from a Maori perspective, the desire to reduce State spending on welfare services sits uneasily with the commitment to family empowerment: "Pressures exist within child care agencies to exercise fiscal responsibility [cost cutting]. This ideologically driven agenda of not resourcing families to enable them to care for themselves undermines the principle of the empowerment of families" (1996, p 10).

There is evidence that funding for the FGCs is a major recurrent issue in all national contexts. Even in New Zealand there is concern that budget cuts may adversely affect the attendance of family members and participants from voluntary and community groups (Renouf et al, 1990; Strathern, 1991; Paterson and Harvey, 1991). In the Canadian context, Burford and Pennell similarly highlight the difficulties of securing interagency funding for families to attend (Burford and Pennell, 1995). As Burford and Pennell point out, a central issue here is the question of the extent to which the plans made by families are supported where necessary by State funding and resources. Again the available evidence is inconclusive. Thornton points out that in New Zealand over 30% of FGC plans involved no cost to or service from the state and in all FGCs the funding involved was well under the maximum limit (Thornton, 1993). She cites evidence of concern from some professionals that the "parsimonious control over budgets" (1993, p 27; Renouf et al, 1990) was undermining the resourcing of family plans. Rimene's (1993) research indicates that many families were not being adequately supported by the Department of Social Welfare and Roberston (1996) comments that in his view "it is probable" that some FGC decisions are being made in the basis of "... affordability rather than need" (1996, p 60). The reality in New Zealand, at least, is that it is not the FGC, but the Children and Young People's Service (CYPS) locality manager who determines what support and resources are provided to the family.

There are also questions about the extent to which FGCs represent a means for professionals and their agencies to 'off-load' problems onto families, placing expectations on them in so doing which are in excess of those they demand, or have achieved, themselves. Thus Burford and Pennell warn of a "fair degree of scepticism" on the part of families about "... social workers who are now in a position to insist on standards they could not achieve when the government was providing the service" (1995, p 50). It is clear too, as these and other authors have pointed out, that there is a potential alliance between the Centre Left interest in family empowerment and the concern of the political Right with the need to restore the authority of the family (Atkin, 1989). As Atkin argues, although the model has been promoted by those on the political Left and human rights groups, "... a policy of minimal state intervention and of family responsibility also is entirely consistent with right wing monetarist policies, which emphasise reduced public expenditure and greater individual and family responsibility" (1992, p 360). Precisely where the balance will lie between these very different political expectations of the model will vary from one county to another. More good quality research is needed to identify, within specific national and local contexts, precisely how these competing and potentially contradictory tendencies are being played out.

Applicability to all

Issues are also raised by the research literature about the extent to which the FGC approach will only work, or only work well, with certain families. Hudson et al (1996) argue that this concern is unfounded and that there is no relationship between the adequacy of family functioning and the likelihood of a successful outcome. Just the opposite: the evidence they suggest, "... casts new light on families that have previously been dismissed as 'incapable', 'disinterested' [sic] and 'dysfunctional'" (1996, p 223). Others appear to be less sure. There is some indication, in contexts where the model is not mandatory, that referrals to FGCs may be selective, involving only those families *judged by professionals* to have the necessary decision-making skills (Burford and Pennell, 1995; Ban, 1996). Even in New Zealand there is evidence that a small number of families were *perceived by practitioners* to be incapable of making sound decisions to safeguard their children (Paterson and Harvey, 1991).

On the other hand, there is also evidence of professionals referring more problematic and serious long-standing cases to FGCs (Lilja, 1997; Burford and Pennell, 1995). As Barbour remarks, this practice may serve to undermine the likelihood of the success of the FGC: "... targeting the FGC as an intervention of last resort puts limits on its effectiveness. Other forms of intervention will frequently already have been tried, and failed, complicating the situation the family is expected to resolve" (1991, p 20). In New Zealand, the FGC is employed largely after initial plans or services for the families have failed to improve the situation. Even where conscious effort has been made, as in Sweden, to introduce FGCs earlier in work with the family, the effect was the same: "... the selected families are mostly those which have been the subject of treatment for a long time" (Lilja, 1997, p 7). Lilja surmises that the reasons for this practice are either that the family members are reluctant to participate until the problem becomes serious and/or that professionals do not know how to achieve change and are looking to FGCs to provide a 'quick fix' to what are seen as fairly intractable problems.

For their part, it is clear that some families, in some circumstances, do not want to meet as a group and/or to take the decision regarding the care of the child(ren) (Ban, 1996; Sundell et al, 1998). In Sweden, as we have noted, Sundell found that some 85% of those offered a FGC refused, although data were not available at the time of writing on the reasons why they did so. Ban found that the main reasons given by families for their unwillingness, or refusal, to take part in the meeting were lack of time or a feeling that it was inappropriate for other (typically more distant) family members to get involved. Occasionally he found those resisting participation justified this by displacing the responsibility for the situation on to family members other than themselves (Ban, 1996). Burford and Pennell report that for some historically very dispersed families, the aim of reunification may prove practically unrealistic: "... the disintegration of their identities and genealogies is so complete that it cannot be aided by any kind of realignment of its members" (1995, p 48). It is interesting, given the question of the extent to which the FGC model will transplant to other cultural contexts to find that, in New Zealand, the coordinators reported that white (*pakeha*) families generally proved more reluctant to involve the wider family than those from Maori communities and that, as a result, their FGCs tended to comprise fewer members (Paterson and Harvey, 1991;Thornton, 1993). Even where the wider family group can be identified and reconstituted, it may not necessarily be able to engage in consensual decision making. Thus Barbour (1991) argues that the operation of the model is problematic to the extent that it assumes the existence of a cohesive family group which may not always be the case: "Some FGCs draw together a group of disparate individuals, connected by blood ties but effectively strangers to one another"(1991, p 19) and in these cases, she argues, it may be very difficult for the group members to work effectively together.

There are other concerns that certain situations may not be appropriate for family group conferencing. These in particular relate to situations marked by family violence, child sexual abuse, incest or contested custody (Barbour, 1991; Atkin, 1992; Connolly, 1994; Graber et al, 1996). Professionals in many national contexts have questioned the appropriateness of giving decisions about the care and accommodation of abused children to certain family members who may have been responsible for that abuse, or for failing to prevent its occurrence (Burford and Pennell, 1995; Graber et al, 1996; Robertson, 1996). Graber and colleagues, for example, report the concerns of professionals in Oregon about the use of the model with violent families "The prevailing belief is that victims of family violence, like victims of sexual abuse, would be placed at further risk of retaliatory abuse for exposing their abusers and would be reluctant to tell the whole story in front of their or the abuser's family" (Graber et al, 1996, p 189). Although finding that the operation of FGCs generally served to reduce the incidence of family violence, Pennell and Burford's outcome study reported that family conferences appeared to have had less success in situations where young people were abusing their mothers and where family relationships were "extremely turbulent" (1997, p 15). In addition, the families most likely to be subject to 'substantiated concerns' about ongoing abuse were those where the mother herself or her partner were the main abuser: "These families included some of the more chaotic families referred to the project" (1997, p 15). Nevertheless, the authors comment, the existence of such characteristics within a family should not be taken as a reason to exclude them from the approach; for many other similarly chaotic and turbulent families the conference was apparently successful.

Family power imbalances

A related concern to emerge from the literature is whether the FGC process, especially the family-only session, is susceptible to imbalances of power within family groups and thus to domination and distortion by more powerful members. In such a context there are questions about whether the voices and interests of less powerful members within the family – particularly women and children – are submerged. The key issue here is whether, if families are to be invited to make their own decisions, they should be allowed to do so in their own way, even if this means that the decision-making process is dominated by adult males. Hudson et al (1996) point out that traditional decision-making processes do nothing to challenge patriarchal attitudes and structures and argue that the concern that the FGC would replicate these structures has largely proved to be unfounded: "... fears raised by commentators about the disempowerment of women have not been supported by observers and researchers who note their active participation in the process in contrast with their non-participation in judicial processes" (1996, p 224). Burford and Pennell, however, report on one case where "their potential worst fear" was confirmed in that the male abuser used his power to ensure that the views of the child and the abused mother were not sufficiently represented (1995) and concede that, potentially at least, the abused person could continue to be caught in a 'conspiracy of silence' about future or undisclosed abuse.

A further concern within the literature is the extent to which the FGC itself, particularly the family-only session, will trigger hostility or even violence between the participants. Some degree of tension may be inevitable, given the difficult circumstances in which the family group is typically assembled. Reassembling the family group may in itself serve to uncover or reawaken previous conflicts (Paterson and Harvey, 1991; Barbour, 1991): "Bringing family members together can create a situation where conflict and unresolved issues within the family history are aroused" (Barbour, 1991, p 20). As many point out, in the absence of the coordinator or any other 'adjudicator' there is no formal mechanism for ensuring that everyone gets a fair chance to speak and that the family decision making is not dominated by one or two powerful individuals (Barbour, 1991; Atkin, 1992; Thornton, 1993).

Hudson et al (1996) argue that there is no evidence that left to themselves families will reproduce "... past patterns of conflict" (1996, p 223). Just the opposite, freeing them from the "heavy and present hand" of professionals, they suggest, is the only way in which they can begin to resolve and break away from previous negative forms of behaviour. Others contend that FGCs can be characterised by considerable family hostility (Barbour, 1991; Atkin, 1992) and Connolly considers that it is "not uncommon" for conferences to be divided by disputes between parents which affect the wider family group (1994, p 98). Paterson and Harvey report that the majority of coordinators had experienced some hostility or verbal abuse, and just over half felt that there had been at least one meeting in which the safety of the participants had been placed at risk (Paterson and Harvey, 1991). Again, more good quality information is needed, particularly on the experiences of family members themselves, before a balance of view can be reached on this question.

The interests of the child

The question about the extent to which the FGC ensures and prioritises the best interests of the child is one of the most fundamental questions raised by the research. As we have seen in Chapter Three, the FGC model involves a delicate balancing act between the rights and needs of the child and those of their family/*whanau*. The idea of the paramountcy of the child's interests as identifiable somehow in isolation from that of the family was criticised in New Zealand as mono-cultural and inappropriate to the aboriginal context. As Atkin points out, however, such a situation may be problematic for the non-Maori child for whom "... the concept of whanau as the 'family of belonging' has little meaning" (1989, p 237). Such a question must also apply to the development of the FGC approach in national contexts not characterised by the cultural traditions of Maori and Pacific Island communities. Even in the New Zealand context, concerns have been expressed about the possibility that the precedence given to the family group over the individual, may serve to undermine the paramountcy of the interests of the child (Atkin, 1989; Barbour, 1991; Connolly, 1994).

Paterson and Harvey's study (1991) indicates the existence of professional anxiety that, in some FGCs, the wishes of the family have taken precedence over the needs of the child. The authors argue that this is largely because decision making is viewed as the exclusive right of the family/*whanau* rather than that of all those entitled to attend the FGC, including a representative of the referral agency and the legal representative of the child. Paterson and Harvey also found that some agencies were concerned that children were not taking as much part in the decisions being made about them as they could. Graber et al, in the US context, report that professional staff expressed mixed views on the question of whether the FGC philosophy could compromise the safety of the children involved (1996, p 189).

As we have seen, many question whether the process of the FGC will increase the risk to the child or young person involved. Connolly, for example, asks whether, in a context where adults are denying the fact or extent of abuse, the child will be scapegoated within the FGC process (1994, p 98) and Barbour argues that the structure of the FGC "... disregards the family dynamics of sexual abuse" (1991, p 20). Against this, others contend that abused children are already at risk and the FGC is more likely to protect against additional abuse than to place them at further risk (Wilcox et al, 1991; Ryburn and Atherton, 1996). Abuse, it is argued, is perpetuated by individuals not families and it is precisely by 'opening up' the close family unit — by informing and involving members of the wider family group — that the FGC process is able to undermine the secrecy and intimacy on which abuse depends (Ryburn, 1993). The true facts of the abuse are more rather than less likely to emerge when the abuser is known to the family members (Burford and Pennell, 1995). Thorough assessment of this and other central questions is bedevilled by the lack of evidence on the views and experiences of the family members (particularly children and young people) and on the longer-term outcomes of the decisions made by the FGCs.

Longer-term outcomes

Generally there is little robust empirical evidence available internationally on what happens to families following a FGC. As Hudson et al (1996) conclude in their review of the evidence, the focus of much research has centred on issues of process and implementation and there is a need for studies which follow developments over time. The official review of the 1989 Act (the Mason Report, 1992) similarly marked up the lack of longitudinal investigation of the outcomes of FGCs. In particular, although there is indication that FGCs may be diverting children from State care, there is little sound evidence on the implications of so doing. Little is known about the quality of within-family care received by the children involved or about the extent to which families' decisions provide for any greater permanency of placement or whether children are "... merely drifting in family care instead of drifting in alternative care" (Connolly, 1994, p 95). There is evidence from New Zealand that professionals are divided in their view of whether primacy should be accorded to family/ *whanau* placements. While some were concerned that insufficient efforts were still being made to reunite children with their families, others marked up the continued need, with some children, for out-of-family placements (Paterson and Harvey, 1991). Hassall and Maxwell (1991) conclude that there is insufficient information on this crucial question: "Research is needed on the consequences of ensuring that children are more likely to remain with their families" (1991, p 7).

One of the few studies systematically to follow through the longer-term outcomes of FGCs and compare them with those from traditional meetings is the Newfoundland and Labrador study conducted by Pennell and Burford (1997). Their general conclusion is that, compared with those experiencing traditional meetings, those having family group meetings were better off in the longer term. In particular, they appeared less likely to experience continuing family violence: "According to children's protection services [CPS] records, some child and adult maltreatment remained, but overall it stopped or decreased" (1997, p 11). While child welfare workers felt that there were cases of children being abused or neglected following family group meetings, the extent to which their concerns were substantiated actually fell compared with the period before the meeting and the number of subsequent emergency visits and apprehensions declined. This contrasts with the situation following the traditional meetings in which the volume of substantiated concerns increased.

There was evidence too that, in addition to keeping the children safe, the quality of their lives and the quality (if not the level) of support they received from their important social contacts improved. This study also sheds some light on the important question of whether keeping children with their family or kin can be seen to compromise their safety in any way. Generally, the researchers concluded, this did not appear to be the case: "Given the overall reduction in substantiated abuse/neglect among the [FGC] project group, family group efforts to preserve or reunify family did not appear to be at the expense of children's safety" (Pennell and

Burford, 1997, p 13). As the authors of the study admit, however, the relatively small numbers involved and the non-random nature of the distribution between the FGC and the non-FGC cases means that caution may need to be exercised in respect of some of its findings. More work is needed to replicate this important study and assess the extent to which its findings are generalisable to other social work contexts and national jurisdictions.

Conclusion

In summary then it appears that, apart from some operational concerns about the time-scales involved and the mechanisms for review and monitoring, overall the evidence on the FGC process is generally very positive. It seems to be perceived, by both families and professional participants, as providing the potential at least, for the empowerment of families. It is clear, however, that relatively few studies have examined the experience of the process from the perspectives of the families involved and that there is need for more information on the extent to which those potentially vulnerable within the process perceive that they have played a full and equal part in the decision making. Questions may also remain about the extent to which the FGC approach can work with all kinds of families in all kinds of situations. Some of the optimism surrounding the approach appears still to be based on relatively slender empirical evidence. It is clear, moreover, to use the distinction drawn by Hudson et al (1996), that much more is known about the *process* of FGCs and their immediate *outputs,* than about their intermediate or longer-term *outcomes.* Central questions remain about the ability of the FGC approach to secure the safety and welfare of the children involved and, in particular, about the implications of the attempt to ensure that children are more likely to be cared for by members of their family group.

It is clear too that there is evidence of potentially more fundamental tensions or dilemmas underlying the approach, not least because of the different political assumptions and expectations about the 'empowerment' of families that underpin the development of FGCs. More research is needed on the particular balance that obtains, within specific contexts, between the enabling/empowering dimensions of the FGC and those that may be seen to be more coercing or controlling. In part this balance will be influenced by the extent to which professionals experience tensions between their statutory responsibilities and their commitment to family empowerment and find it difficult to cede their control over decision making to family members. In (possibly larger) part it will relate to the adequacy of the funding for FGCs and the extent to which the support and resources requested by families are ultimately forthcoming. If professionals resist sharing their power with families and/or if the financial underpinning of family decision making is inadequate, it is likely that the balance will tip away from the possibilities of family empowerment towards a less enlightened mixture of continued professional control and enforced self-reliance. It is to a more in-depth consideration of these central questions, in the context of the development of FGCs in England and Wales, that the subsequent chapters of the book now turn.

SIX

Empowerment in process?

Introduction

> It is important to be clear about what is not partnership. It is
> not equal power and it never can be, but it is about empowerment,
> about families having sufficient information to be able to
> understand and contribute to planning and have some influence
> over the outcome. (Jackson, 1994, p 15)

As we have seen, the proponents of the FGC model claim that it provides
a much better basis than traditional meetings for embodying the spirit of
partnership between professionals and families implicit in the 1989
Children Act. In comparison with traditional approaches, the FGC process,
it is argued, is more enabling of family participation and serves to increase
the involvement of families in the decision-making process, providing a
means for their greater empowerment (Wilcox et al, 1991; Jackson, 1993;
Ryburn and Atherton, 1996; Morris and Tunnard, 1996). As Jackson
emphasises, however, it is important to be explicit about what is meant by
'empowerment' here. In the child welfare context it is clearly impossible
for there to be a wholesale transfer of power and control to the families
involved. Rather, the basis for empowerment is seen to derive from an
approach which attempts to work with the strengths of family groups,
instead of focusing on their weakness and seeks to enable them to take
greater responsibility for the decisions made about their children.

As we have indicated, however, empowerment is a very slippery concept
to define and measure. In the specific case of the FGC it is clear that
there are at least two central (although related) dimensions to family
empowerment: that which derives from participation in the process itself
(*empowerment via participation*), from the experience of being able to make
decisions and have those decisions respected by professionals; and that
which comes from the impact or outcome of those decisions, from being
able to act upon the world to alter it for the better (*empowerment via
change*). The two dimensions are of course closely related: the empowering
effect of a successful outcome will in part derive from the family's collective

view of the extent to which it determined the content of the plan and, no matter how participatory the process, its potential for empowerment will be limited if the plans made by the families are ultimately unsuccessful. This chapter focuses on the evidence surrounding the first of these two dimensions: empowerment as participation; the rather less tractable question of empowerment via 'outcome' will be considered in the following two chapters.

In assessing the quality of the FGC process and its potential for the empowerment of those involved, the broad dimensions of 'contributing to planning' and 'influencing outcome' identified by Jackson (1994) will benefit from further refinement in relation to the different stages of the meeting. Operationalising these dimensions will involve consideration of the degree of family members' control over the initial arrangements for the FGC, including its composition, the adequacy of the information provided about the objectives of the conference and the extent to which family members are clear about the 'terms and conditions' of their involvement and that of other key participants. It will require investigation of whether the right professionals attend the meeting and provide appropriate and accessible information about their perception of the issues involved and the resources/support available. It will also involve examination of whether the process affords all involved an equal opportunity to speak and have their views respected, and the extent to which the family members, rather than the professionals, determine the final content of the plan.

Assessment of the empowerment potential of the FGC approach will also need to be undertaken in the context of the central issues raised by the international research literature, discussed in the last chapter. In respect of the FGC process, these involve the extent to which the family members' decision making is susceptible and subject to manipulation by the professionals involved. It will also require consideration of the central question of whether the FGC process, if empowering, is equally empowering of all family members, or whether it serves to empower only, or predominantly, those who are already relatively powerful within the family group. In examining these questions the chapter will draw on the available evidence from empirical research undertaken on the operation of the model in the England and Wales (Thomas, 1994; Barker and Barker, 1995; Lupton et al, 1995; Rosen, 1994; Crow and Marsh, 1997; Lupton and Stevens, 1997 and 1998; Smith, 1998; Smith and Hennessy, 1998; Simmonds et al, 1998).

The evidence base

A body of empirical evidence is now beginning to emerge on the operation of FGCs in England and Wales. In addition to the evaluations made of each of the four initial pilot sites in Hereford and Worcester (Thomas, 1994); Wandsworth, inner London (Rosen, 1994); Gwynedd, North Wales (Barker and Barker, 1995) and Winchester in Hampshire (Lupton et al, 1995; Lupton, 1998), data are also available on the operation of FGC initiatives in Essex (Smith, 1998; Smith and Hennessy, 1998) and Greenwich, inner London (Simmonds et al, 1998). Summary data on the characteristics of the four initial pilot FGCs are also available (Crow and Marsh, 1997) and follow-up evaluation of the families involved in the initial pilot FGCs is provided by Lupton and Stevens (1997 and 1998a, 1998b). These studies varied considerably in terms of the time and resources they had at their disposal and, consequently, in the scale and ambition of the research involved. Thomas in Hereford and Worcester, for example, had only a four-day consultancy in which to assess the model, whereas Crow and Marsh (1997) were funded for over two years by a national charitable foundation. Some, such as Essex were undertaken by in-house researchers (Smith, 1998) or those in quality assurance sections (Rosen, 1994), others were undertaken by academic-based researchers (Crow and Marsh, University of Sheffield and Thomas, University of Wales, Swansea). Yet others were conducted by independent researchers (Barker and Barker from MEDRA training and constancy services) or involved collaboration between academic and agency-based research staff (for example, Lupton from the University of Portsmouth and Stevens from Hampshire Social Services Department).

Although involving a range of methods and techniques, most of the studies employed a broadly 'pluralistic evaluative' design which surveyed, then compared and contrasted, the perspectives of key participants (Smith and Cantley, 1988). Interestingly, the various studies appear in many ways to be complementary, with the limitations and omissions of some being compensated for by others and providing between them a fairly comprehensive assessment of the FGC approach in practice. Apart from the national overview undertaken by Crow and Marsh, which describes the operational characteristics of all (80) FGCs held in the four initial pilots, the studies are mainly focused on the initial development of the approach in a particular site, with the number of FGCs being investigated ranging between seven (Barker and Barker, 1995) and 22 (Simmonds et al, 1998; Lupton et al, 1995). Lupton and Stevens' (1997) investigation, which covered the second year of the pilot's operation, comprised 72 FGCs in all, with in-depth longitudinal data being provided on half of the 26 conferences held in the first year. This study also provided some comparison of FGC process and outcome with those of traditional child protection conferences. Together the studies span the six years between 1993 and 1998.

Most of the studies (apart from Crow and Marsh, 1997 and Thomas, 1994) undertook in-depth or semi-structured interviews with the family members involved at or around the time of the FGC: Simmonds et al (1998) conducted individual interviews with 15 main carers (point in time not indicated), Barker and Barker (1995) with 28 family participants within four weeks of the FGC; Smith (1998) interviewed 26 family members (timing not indicated) with a further 83 completing questionnaires, and Lupton et al (1995) and Lupton and Stevens (1997) interviewed 103 family participants immediately post-FGC. Attempts to interview family members in Hereford and Worcester were frustrated by childcare social workers concerned about "... disturbing a situation which had settled down following a crisis" (Thomas, 1994, p 8). Smith (1998), Barker and Barker (1995) and Lupton and Stevens (1997) interviewed some of the children and young people involved, but the numbers were relatively small (6, 7 and 19 respectively). In addition to members of families participating, Rosen (1994) also interviewed individuals from four families who had refused the offer of a FGC. Both Rosen and Lupton et al (1995) followed up family members at a point subsequent to the FGC: Rosen with individual members of four families two to three months following the FGC and Lupton et al with 42 family group members at nine months post-FGC.

As well as collecting the views of family participants, all the studies, apart from Rosen, included interviews or discussions with social work professionals and/or the FGC coordinators. In most cases the professionals were those who had attended the relevant FGCs, but Crow and Marsh undertook telephone interviews with all social work staff in the participating teams, including (about half) those who had not attended a FGC. In addition to sending postal questionnaires to those attending the FGCs, Lupton et al conducted group discussions with all social workers in the childcare team in the pilot site, before and after the first year of implementation. All the initial pilot evaluations collected common baseline data on the operation of FGCs (subsequently aggregated by Crow and Marsh, 1997) and most analysed a range of documentary information (family plans/case file/minutes of relevant meetings). Researchers in the

Winchester site also attended and observed the FGCs researched in-depth and collected data on the decisions made at case allocation meetings (Lupton et al, 1995). The findings from these studies relevant to a consideration of the dimension of empowerment are described below, organised by the different stages of the FGC process.

Before the FGC

Who gets a FGC?

Clearly, the extent of family control over the FGC process is limited from the outset insofar as the initiative is service-provider led; although designated as a family meeting, the idea stems not from the families themselves but from the professionals concerned that they should be empowered to make their own decisions. In none of the FGCs studied had any families referred themselves for a FGC, although this is starting to happen now in the Hampshire site. In large part this is due not to a disinclination for the approach but to the general lack of public knowledge about the availability of the FGC option. The extent to which social workers/social services departments advertise the existence of FGCs, such that families can actively select the approach, will have an important bearing on the degree to which families develop an initial sense of ownership of the meeting.

There is evidence from the local studies, moreover, that professionals retain considerable control over whether and which families are offered the choice of a FGC. Although all the pilots involved child protection as well as family support and accommodation cases, most excluded, at least initially, what can be termed the 'heavier end' cases. Generally, the national overview of the initial pilots suggests that the FGC option appears to have been used more in situations where the child was considered at risk of neglect or emotional abuse than where there were concerns about physical or sexual abuse (Crow and Marsh, 1997). Most of the local pilots had decided against referring cases of sexual abuse, at least initially.

One of the local pilots which had specifically chosen to refer sexual abuse was inhibited by police reservations expressed about the relationship of the FGC approach to the criminal justice system. This initially resulted in a long list of cases to be excluded from a FGC, including those where extended family members were known to have previous criminal convictions unknown to the family, where holding a FGC could be seen to lead to violence, where there was *network/organised or multi-generational sexual abuse*, where a criminal investigation was continuing, where *persons were on police bail and/or a file had been forwarded to the Crown Prosecution Service*, where the child does not disclose the abuser, where the *abuse allegedly involved professionals* and where the "unbiased nature of the police or other agencies would be jeopardised" (Lupton et al, 1995). The fact that this list was more than halved after the pilot year had ended suggests that much of the professional anxiety may be seen to have been misplaced. Five categories of exclusion, however, remained (italicised above), plus the more general caveat about holding a FGC in any situation which could be seen (by professionals) to compromise the safety of the child and/or where the police and social services consider it "inappropriate" (Lupton and Stevens, 1997, p 12).

Clearly the potential tension between professionals' commitment to family empowerment and their sense of their statutory responsibilities is more acute in child protection situations, and greater use may be made of the FGC approach as confidence about its role in child protection grows. Most of the local authorities using the FGC approach are doing so as a supplement to, rather than substitute for, traditional child protection conferences (CPCs). One of the initial pilot sites, Gwynned in Wales, is, however, using FGCs as an alternative to CPCs, albeit after holding an initial meeting to decide whether an interim care plan is needed for the child. Another authority, Wiltshire, is considering a process of random allocation of cases to either a FGC or a traditional CPC. In this latter site, although fieldwork managers will have the discretion to refer back any case where professional staff have serious reservations about the use of a FGC they will have to make a written request for a traditional conference to the area manager. Such developments however, as we noted in Chapter Four, appeared to have been given official discouragement in the consultative document for the new *Working together* guidelines (DoH, 1998).

While there may be some indication that certain *types of situations* are less likely be referred to a FGC, the evidence about the (related) extent to which professionals are selective in terms of the *kinds of families* they consider suitable for a FGC is ambiguous. As we have seen, some concern is identifiable within the international literature about the amount of discretion employed by professionals in referring families to FGCs. Ban (1996), for example, reports that in Australia professionals were only referring those families which were seen to possess the right sort of decision-making skills. Marsh and Crow (1997) argue that there is no evidence that the families involved in the pilot FGCs were selected because they were seen to be 'easier' to work with. Just the opposite: they contend that the model tends to have been used, if anything, with more difficult cases and many professionals referred families to FGCs while having reservations about their ability to use the process effectively (Crow and Marsh, 1997). This finding was reinforced by Smith and Hennessy (1998). Thomas (1994) reports that, in one team at least, the FGC model was used where other attempts at working with the family had failed: "When we get stuck, I suppose ... sometimes we use it [FGC] proactively, but it tends to be, 'what else is there for us do?'" (research interview with childcare social worker, quoted in Thomas, 1994, p 5).

However, elsewhere in the UK research literature there is some evidence that the decision whether to refer to a FGC may have been taken on the basis of professional perceptions of the suitability of the family group (or its core members). Thus Thomas (1994) also reports that professionals appeared reluctant to refer to a FGC where there was clear antagonism on the part of key adults towards the child and/or with families seen to be violent. Elsewhere Marsh and Crow themselves report that FGCs were less likely to be offered to families with a "history of antagonistic involvement with social services" (1996, p 160) and those where, in the view of the professionals, there was no wider family network to invite (Marsh and Crow, 1996). Just over two out of every 10 professionals interviewed by Crow and Marsh, moreover, indicated that they would not use the FGC approach with families that were considered to be 'abusive' (1997, p 13).

Despite the origin of the FGC model as an attempt to develop more culturally sensitive work with Maori and Pacific Island communities, the available evidence suggests there may be an issue about its use with families from UK minority ethnic communities. Crow and Marsh indicate that nationally the proportion of children from these communities was 13%, but do not indicate the number of families involved. While this proportion is high for the UK overall, it must be remembered that children of such groups are greatly over-represented on the caseloads of social services and in the populations of residential homes (Rowe et al, 1989). Moreover, almost all of these children were located in just one of the inner London pilots. Smith (1998) in Essex reports the proportion of Black families involved to be roughly equal to their presence in the wider population and Simmonds et al (1998) in Greenwich notes that Black or dual heritage families comprised some 27% of the families having FGCs (but provides no indication of how this relates proportionately to the local population). Thomas (1994) records that all the children involved in the 11 FGCs in

Hereford and Worcester were white and Lupton and Stevens (1997) note that only one out of the total of 72 FGCs they investigated in Winchester, Hampshire involved a Black child and she was living with a white family at the time. While none of the research has analysed its findings systematically by the race of respondent (indeed in most cases the numbers involved are too small to sustain such an analysis), Crow and Marsh suggest that, while Black British, Afro-Caribbean and mixed heritage families appear no less likely to accept the FGC approach, there is 'some indication' that this is not the case with other groups: "... families with other origins may have found it more difficult to engage with the model" (1997, p 13). No further information is available, however, from this or other studies on the particular experience of families from minority ethnic groups.

Preparing families

The next stage in the process is introducing the idea of a FGC to the family concerned. Again, being adequately prepared for a situation, being clear about what and who is involved and why, is a central precondition for effective participation. Perhaps not surprisingly, while the great majority of families agreed to participate, the research suggests that some were initially rather suspicious about, or actively hostile to, the initial idea of a FGC (Rosen, 1994; Lupton et al, 1995; Simmonds et al, 1998). Barker and Barker report a feeling that the families were being made to "jump through hoops" to obtain support or resources and doubted that their family possessed the material or emotional resources to sort the problem out: "Social services didn't believe that the family couldn't help. They had to hear it for themselves. We had to prove our need for social services help" (family member, quoted in Barker and Barker, 1995, p 7). Lupton et al (1995) record that a minority of families saw it as just another 'new idea' being foisted on them by the social services department, and/or as a way of the social services department shifting the responsibility back onto them. Simmonds et al (1998) report that only a minority of those initially agreeing to a FGC thought it was a good idea; more than twice as many felt 'unsure' about the idea and two families agreed "... without being very keen on the idea at all" (1998, p 10). Five of the 10 carers who had discussed the idea with their wider family group found that the latter voiced "serious objections" (Simmonds et al, 1998).

No nationally aggregated data are available on the proportion of families referred for a FGC who declined to participate, nor on the reasons for their so doing. Lupton et al indicate that for three out of the total of 23 families referred in the pilot year (13%), a FGC did not proceed and Simmonds indicates that this was the case for around one quarter (24%) of the families; neither study, however, provides information on why this was the case. Rosen (1994) reports that four out of the 10 families she studied declined to participate. Interviews with two of these indicated that one felt the problem had already been resolved and the other that her family group was unsuitable for a FGC – a sentiment echoed by two of those who did agree and by some of those interviewed by Barker and Barker (1995): FGCs are for "... reasonably sensible people, who were able to work things out by talking and not for angry men who would come to them drunk" (child's mother, quoted in Rosen, 1994, p 5). While it appears that the great majority of those referred to a FGC agreed to the meeting, it is not clear how much choice they actually had about whether to participate in a FGC or not. As we have argued elsewhere (Lupton, 1998), families can refuse to be involved, and a few have done so, but many will appreciate the consequences of this action, either in terms of the likelihood of less 'empowering' forms of intervention being substituted and/or the possible loss of much needed help and support. In addition, because of the 'extended' nature of the family group involved in the FGCs, it is clear that refusal to participate, even on the part of very central family members, may not prevent the FGC being held.

Who is invited?

A further consideration in respect of FGCs as an empowering process concerns whether family members have control over the composition of the meeting. Do they or the coordinators actually decide who should attend? Overall, Crow and Marsh (1997) argue that nationally there is no evidence that coordinators excluded individuals against the wishes of others within the family group. The extent to which the opposite situation occurred – of coordinators refusing to exclude those not wanted by other family members – is, however, less clear-cut. While close family members are consulted by the coordinator, they do not have the final say over who attends. In particular they do not have the power to exclude other members of the family group; the power of veto rests ultimately with the coordinators and they are charged to use it sparingly. Unless very good reasons are given for their exclusion, the expectation is that all members of the extended family will attend. Families do retain some residual and largely negative power over this process, however, due to their private knowledge of who potentially comprises the 'extended family network'. Even if the coordinators wanted to contact some family members against the wishes of others, this could prove very difficult if those objecting chose to withhold the relevant information.

Overall, in exactly four out of every 10 of the pilot FGCs, at least one family member was excluded from the FGC (Crow and Marsh, 1997). Barker and Barker report that the process of deciding who to invite was the single issue most likely to cause divisions within the family group. No evidence is available nationally about the kinds of people excluded, or the reasons why, although Lupton et al (1995) and Barker and Barker (1995) examine this issue in two of the pilot sites. Lupton and her colleagues found that the majority of those excluded were male (typically natural or step-grandfathers, current or ex-partners of female participants) and that the main reasons for excluding were concerns about 'family tensions' of one kind or another. Some family members in their study and that conducted by Barker and Barker (1995) were anxious about the idea of including individuals with whom they had either little contact or poor relationships. A few were concerned about how certain individuals would behave and whether they would be capable of working cooperatively as a group. Some young people in particular were worried about the physical and emotional consequences of inviting particular individuals (mainly natural fathers):

> **Three young persons were initially very determined that their fathers should not be there. One said she was 'scared' of her father, another said that he would 'lie and bully' and the third had refused to see his father since they had had a physical fight, as a consequence of which, father and son were bringing charges of assault against one another. (Barker and Barker, 1995, p 15)**

In the majority of cases it appeared that the decision to exclude had been made by the coordinator in response to strong objections on the part of the child and/or her main carer. Barker and Barker report that the mothers of the child(ren) involved had a strong influence over who was invited: "Mothers commonly wish to exclude grandparents and other elderly relatives, because they wish to protect them from knowing the extent of the 'problem' and from feeling any responsibility to provide a solution" (1995, p 15). In a small number of cases in Lupton et al's study, certain members of the family threatened to boycott the meeting if those they disliked were invited. In only a minority of situations did it appear that the coordinators had prevailed over strong reservations held by the child or close family members. In one case two separate conferences were arranged to accommodate different 'warring' halves of a family group who would not sit in the same room, and in another the FGC was held (unsuccessfully) without the participation of the child's natural parents (Lupton et al, 1995). In Barker and Barker's study, all those teenage children who indicated that they did not want their natural fathers to attend were persuaded to change their minds by the coordinators. In the end, the evidence from the local pilot evaluations suggest that the great majority of those participating felt that the right family members had ultimately been invited and Barker and Barker at least argue that those who had been 'persuaded to agree' to certain family members attending felt 'immense relief' when they discovered that the problems they had anticipated had not materialised (1995, p 5).

Once the FGC and its composition had been agreed, the level of actual family participation was high, with a national average of just under six of every seven family members invited actually attending the meeting (Crow and Marsh, 1997, p 14). Simmonds et al (1998) comment on the large number of males attending, compared with the situation which typically obtains in CPCs. Smith reports that the high level of family participation was appreciated by professionals and family members alike, particularly the young people concerned: "I couldn't believe it when I walked into the room. All my family were there. Like they really cared for me" (research interview with young person, quoted in Smith, 1998, p 2). In those sites where feedback from families was obtained (Barker and Barker, 1995: Lupton et al, 1995; Rosen, 1994; Smith, 1998, Simmonds et al, 1998) the majority of family members invited to the FGC were positive about the idea of a family meeting, seeing it as a useful means of bringing people together to share ideas and offer help. Particular satisfaction was expressed about the fact that effort was made to hold FGCs at times that were convenient to the families themselves and in local community venues, rather than on social services' premises. This latter clearly helped to increase the sense of families' control over the process: "I think it was very good; it was held on neutral ground – everyone was on a par with everyone else [that was] a fair way to do it" (family member, quoted in Lupton et al, 1995, p 95).

In advance of the conference, coordinators put much time and effort into locating family members and explaining what was to happen. Most are contacted in person as well as by letter and/or telephone, and a pre-

FGC meeting may be arranged for a small number of families. This phase of the process is of great importance in ensuring that family members really understand the aims of the conference and the part that they and others are to play in it. As we have argued elsewhere, being clear about the 'terms and conditions' of involvement is a central precondition of effective user involvement (Lupton and Hall, 1993). Both Barker and Barker (1995) and Simmonds et al (1998) report that the majority of the family members interviewed felt that they had been prepared very well or 'well enough' for the meeting: "... they knew who would be there, why they were there and how the conference would be made up" (Barker and Barker, 1995, p 6). Lupton et al (1995), however, found that a sizeable minority had arrived at the meeting unsure about what was going to happen or what their role was to be. Well over one third of the family respondents in this study indicated that they felt the information provided in advance of the meeting could have been clearer: "... more information to all concerned could have been beneficial before the meeting as ... there were people there who were unaware of what was expected of them" (research interview with family member, quoted in Lupton, 1998, p 117).

The role of the professionals

As we have seen, the first stage of the FGC meeting involves the professionals giving information about their assessment of the case and the resources and support available from their agencies. The extent to which families feel in control of the decision making will depend on the quality and extent of this information, the clarity with which it is presented, and the degree to which the professionals are able or willing to separate out the 'facts' from their opinions, and/or to accept the potentially 'contested' nature of the problem. It will also depend on the right professionals attending and on their being in possession of the right information, but not in such numbers that they physically dominate the meeting.

Nationally it seems that the meetings have involved relatively small numbers of professionals: the ratio of family members to information-givers being on average 6:2, with professionals outnumbering family members in only two out of all the pilot FGCs (Crow and Marsh, 1997). Indeed, the evidence suggests that the problem may rather be, as in New Zealand, of getting the relevant professionals to attend the FGC and in convincing them of the merits of the FGC approach. Several of the professionals invited (all from agencies other than social services) in the pilot studied by Lupton et al (1995) failed to attend the FGC or to send a written report although, in contrast, Smith and Hennessy report a feeling on the part of professionals from non-social services departments that they were being excluded from the FGC approach. As the authors comment, it is important that the FGC approach recognises the interagency nature of child welfare interventions: "Some of the most critical comments came from workers outside Social Services suggesting that more attention needs to be focused on ensuring that collaborative working processes are not threatened by these workers feeling excluded and devalued" (Smith and Hennessy, 1998, p 45).

Many of the pilot studies identified concerns on the part of the professionals about the implications of greater family control over the decision-making process (Thomas, 1994; Lupton et al, 1995; Smith, 1998). Crow and Marsh report that, while well over a third saw the approach as a positive development of the principle of partnership, slightly more, four out of every 10, saw it as a threat to their professional power (Crow and Marsh, 1997). Thomas (1994) comments that such concerns may affect the decision about whether families should participate in a FGC:

> **It seemed to me as an outsider that, apart from the many ideological objections [to the FGC model], there were real concerns about loss of control over what might happen in a case, which lay behind the reluctance of some managers to [use] the model. It also seemed to me that staff who had used the model had similar inhibitions, and had been careful to select cases where such worries were of less significance.... (Thomas, 1994, p 12)**

Where there is evidence of the views of those professionals attending FGCs (Thomas, 1994; Barker and Barker, 1995; Lupton et al, 1995; Smith, 1998; Simmonds et al, 1998) it seems that the majority were comfortable with (if a bit anxious about) the role of information-giver. Thomas (1994, p 9) indeed reports a "... feeling of elation" on the part of some professionals at handing over responsibility to the families. Simmonds et al (1998) report that the great majority of the professionals involved felt that the purpose of the meeting had been set out well or "well enough". Smith (1998) and Lupton et al (1995) indicate that professionals had attempted to provide their reports in plain and accessible language: "You cut out all the professional jargon and say, this is how it is – what are you going to do about it?" (research interview with a social worker, quoted in Smith,

1998, p 4). There is evidence, however, that some, particularly, but not exclusively those from agencies other than social services departments, were disinclined to accord the FGC proceedings legitimacy, expressing in particular concerns about the confidentiality of the information to be discussed (Lupton et al, 1995; Smith, 1998). Despite assurances by the majority that they were clear about the distinctive nature of the information-giving role, moreover, exactly four out of every 10 professionals in Lupton et al's study revealed that they had communicated to the family group not just their assessment of the issues and details of available resources/support, but their view of what the outcome of the meeting should be. Moreover, even where they fell short of indicating what the precise outcomes should be, there is evidence in one site of professionals setting 'bottom lines' to the family decision making (Smith, 1998).

For their part, while family members generally thought that the right professionals came to the meetings, there was more variability in terms of their evaluation of the information they provided. Whereas Smith (1998) found that the majority of family members felt they had been provided with sufficient information on which to make their plan, this was the view of only just over half the family members interviewed by Lupton et al (1995). In the latter study, at least, many of the reports provided by the information-givers were seen to be too lengthy and/or too full of jargon to be really helpful to the families: "The information had no human side to it, it was all professional words" (interview with family member, quoted in Lupton et al, 1995, p 91). The main problem from these families' point of view was the tendency of some professionals to dwell on the problems rather than offer ideas about services and support. Generally they felt the information-giving sessions were too one-sided and they should be able to discuss or challenge the information as it was being provided: "The co-ordinators and the social worker wanted to stick to their report and if anyone intervened they wanted people to wait to the end when people might forget what they wanted to say. We wanted to discuss the reports and should have been able to discuss them as the points came up" (research interview with family member, quoted in Lupton et al, 1995). In particular, family members felt it would have been useful to have been given copies of the professionals' reports, preferably in advance of the meeting, so that they knew what to expect and could prepare their response. Barker and Barker found that family members particularly appreciated being given written material as a means of keeping the meeting focused; long verbal presentations by professionals were seen to make the family members "tense and nervous" (1995, p 8).

The family-only session

One of the key preconditions of a FGC, and an important physical manifestation of the attempt to afford family members greater control, is that the latter have an opportunity to discuss the issues and draw up their plans on their own, without the professionals. The available data suggest, however, that some families may have mixed feelings about the 'family-only stage'. Barker and Barker indicate that, despite many families finding it a distressing experience, they were in the main positive about the opportunity to discuss the issues without the professionals. The majority of those interviewed by Lupton et al (1995) indicated that they found it easier and more relaxing for the family group to talk on its own. Several commented that this was good for family members who would otherwise have been inhibited by the presence of professionals: "I don't think we would have come up with so much if the professionals had stayed. C never said anything until we were left on our own. He's really shy and he had some good ideas" (research interview with family member, quoted in Lupton et al, 1995, p 95).

Just under a quarter of those in this study, however, said that they did not feel the absence of professionals made any difference to the meeting, indicating that they would have said the same things whether the professionals were there or not. Others appreciated the family-only stage, but wanted to be able to call upon the professionals to assist them in their discussion if necessary. In principle, the professionals are supposed to remain available to the family throughout the FGC; in reality, pressures of work mean that most leave after the information-giving stage. The families found this did little to enhance their sense of being in control of the proceedings: "We had to keep coming out of the meeting to ask the professionals questions but they didn't hang around. We missed bits of the meeting by having to go out and find them" (research interview with family member, quoted in Lupton et al, 1995, p 92).

Both Barker and Barker (1995) and Lupton et al (1995), moreover, report a minority view from family members that the meeting would have been better if the professionals had remained throughout. In part this was because of a feeling that, if the professionals listened to the families' discussion, they would understand more about the problems they were facing. In part it was due to a view that the professional and/or the coordinator should remain as a detached observer to facilitate or arbitrate the family's discussions: "D didn't feel able to speak. You'd be more able to speak if you knew a mediator was there to control the conversation" (research interview with family member, quoted in Lupton et al, 1995, p 92). This latter was particularly seen to be necessary when those discussions got heated and/or were dominated by powerful family members. Over one quarter of the family members in this study and four out of every 10 in that of Simmonds et al (1998) indicated that they had experienced problems with the family-only session, as a result of family tensions or hostilities:"You can get the family going hammer and tongs at each other; a bit like that today" (research interview with family member, quoted in Lupton et al, 1995, p 93). Despite the pressure on some professionals (Barker and Barker, 1995) not to leave the family on its own, however, there were no recorded instances of the situation in New Zealand where the professionals had remained during the family discussion time (Renouf et al, 1990; Paterson and Harvey, 1991). There were, however, two cases where the coordinator had stayed with the family to facilitate the discussion, and Thomas (1994) found that in just under half the FGCs studied, the family group had chosen not to meet on its own.

Generally, however, the family members involved indicated that the FGC process was seen to be enabling of their active participation and gave them a sense of being in control of the decision-making process. In those studies which ascertained the views of family members (Barker and Barker, 1995; Lupton et al, 1995; Rosen, 1994; Smith, 1998; Simmonds et al, 1998), the majority indicated that they were satisfied, or very satisfied, with the process. Most participants felt that they had been listened to and that their opinions had been important some or all of the time: "The children have been listened to ... and we've been heard" (family member, quoted in Smith, 1998, p 5). Family members appreciated being given the responsibility for making the decisions about the child(ren):"Fantastic idea. It's the family that should have a say, not some government official" (family member, quoted in Lupton et al, 1995, p 94). Although falling short of explicitly articulating a sense of empowerment, many family participants stressed that the FGC was better than being told what to do by professionals: "... it's better than social services doing it themselves and then telling us what to do. When there was a case conference about me, I was the last person to know about it" (Lupton et al, 1995, p 95). For their part, the majority of professionals appeared to feel that the FGC process effectively gave more power and control to the families. Just under three quarters of the social workers interviewed across the initial pilot sites stated that they felt the FGC process "empowered" families (Crow and Marsh, 1997, p 22).

Empowerment for all?

The role of extended family members/significant others

One interesting question emerging from the international research literature concerns the extent to which the FGC process, if empowering, is empowering of all those who participate, or whether it advantages some individuals over others. One aspect of this issue (as yet insufficiently addressed in the existing literature) relates to the role of extended family members and significant others. Initial doubts were expressed in some of the local pilots about whether it would be possible or appropriate to identify and secure the participation of extended family members or significant others in the decision-making process (Lupton et al, 1995; Barker and Barker, 1995). Barker and Barker (1995) for example, identified a minority view on the part of some 'blood-tie' participants that the meeting should involve close family only, and a reciprocal concern on the part of less closely involved participants about their role: "In retrospect, some participants had very mixed feelings about the participation of 'friends', as 'friends' often offered the resources to resolve at least some of the issues under consideration, but this meant that they were also viewed as having 'power' or 'influence' over the decision-making" (1995, p 5).

The summary of the data from the initial pilot projects reveals considerable participation by extended family, friends, neighbours as well as natural and step-parents/guardians (Crow and Marsh, 1997). Few studies, however, have examined the experience of these more 'extended' members of the family group, not least because of the relatively small number of family member interviews generally undertaken. The Winchester study, however, did conduct sufficient family interviews (n=103) to enable examination of the data by the status of family members (Lupton and Stevens, 1997). Their findings indicate that extended family members were only slightly less likely to attend once invited than were those more closely involved in the current care of the child, and that they and significant others were the two groups most positive about being asked to join the meeting. In the event, the composition of the meetings was fairly evenly divided between close family members – parents, grandparents and siblings – and extended family members/significant others (Lupton et al, 1995).

As Roberston (1996) points out, however, there is an important difference between attending the FGC and being actively involved in, and influencing, the decisions being made. It may be the case that, although present, the contribution of those less closely involved with the child is seen to be less relevant or influential. Here the findings from the Winchester site are fairly clear. Although generally less positive about the extent or clarity of the initial information provided than other participants, extended family members were not markedly less likely to feel that they had sufficient opportunity to speak or to ask questions, and were slightly more likely than members of the immediate family to feel that they had been listened to and that their opinions were important. There was little difference between close and extended family members, moreover, on the question of whether all other members of the family group had appreciated their part in the meeting and had respected their views (Lupton and Stevens, 1997, 1998a).

Interestingly, the Winchester findings suggest that kinship ties may be more important than physical closeness to the child in terms of the nature and extent of participants' involvement in the FGC process. Thus comparison of the 'participation profiles' of extended family members with those of the 'significant others' attending the FGCs (friends, neighbours, advocates etc) reveals that more respect may have been given for the views and observations of 'significant others' (non-kin) but they may ultimately have had less influence on the decisions made than those of the extended family members (kin). 'Significant others' were among the participants most likely to feel able to ask questions and to be listened to and respected by others, but they were among those least likely to feel that their opinions were important. Extended family members, on the other hand, were more likely to share with those closer to the child a feeling that they were not always listened to, or have their views respected, by all of the family members all of the time, but they were more likely to feel that in the end their views had been important to the final decision made. Overall, the data suggest that the contribution of those from the wider family network is as central and influential in all key respects as that of the child's immediate family (Lupton and Stevens, 1997, 1998a).

Differences between the sexes

The other important question raised by the review of the international FGC literature concerns the ability of the model adequately to deal with family power imbalances. As we have seen, many commentators have questioned whether the FGC process, particularly the family-only session, enables all participants to get a fair hearing, regardless of their power and status within the family group (Atkin, 1989; Ban, 1993; Connolly, 1994).

While proponents of the model may argue, quite rightly, that such power imbalances are equally likely to characterise the traditional decision-making process, the existence of the family-only session within the FGC approach, where families are left to make decisions on their own, provides a more specific focus of concern in this respect. This raises a central dilemma within the FGC approach. If the commitment to family decision making is to be strong, then it must enable those families to make decisions in their own way; yet the normal manner of making decisions within a particular family could involve the dominance of one or more powerful individuals. Intervening in the way in which the family decision is reached, however, is not only likely to be difficult, given that it is undertaken in private, but may also be seen to undermine the central objectives of the FGC process. As we have argued in Chapter One, the quality of empowerment may be impaired if its terms and conditions are effectively controlled by professionals.

Consideration of the issue of gendered power relations was a central objective of the in-depth research undertaken by Lupton and Stevens (1997, 1998a, 1998b) and their comparison of the views of males (n=42) and females (n=50) at each stage of the FGC process reveals some interesting differences. In terms of the initial preparation before the conference, females were just as likely as males to find the information provided clear and sufficient, although slightly less positive about the timing and venue of the meetings and about the idea of participating in the meeting. In terms of the family-only stage, differences between the sexes were also discernible, although again not very extreme: women and girls felt equally positive about the family making the decision on its own, and generally were slightly more likely to feel that their opinions were important and listened to. Females were, however, also more likely to perceive that their views were not respected by all of the other family members present and to find the discussion more difficult without the professionals. Overall, female participants were only slightly less likely than the males to feel that their part in the process had been appreciated (Lupton and Stevens, 1997, 1998a).

The most striking differences between the sexes, however, were observable in terms of the information-giving session, where women and girls clearly felt much more inhibited (or perhaps were more prepared to admit to such feelings) than the males involved. These differences are interesting and indicate that *generally* it is the information-giving stage of the process, rather than the family-only session, that women and girls find difficult. This suggests that they are less concerned by dominant members of the family group than by the presence and reports of the professionals. This may be due to the tendency on the part of many professionals to blame the mother (implicitly or explicitly) – or for women to blame themselves/feel they are being blamed – for the problems which their children are experiencing. On the other hand, more females than males also felt that the family–only stage was more difficult without the presence of professionals; this may have been because they wanted an opportunity to question them further on the information provided and/ or challenge their opinions; it may, however, have been because they felt more secure or enabled with the professionals present. The fact that there was little observable difference between the sexes (or, indeed, the generations) in response to the question of whether any problems resulted in the family–only session as a result of the absence of professionals suggests that it is less likely to have been the latter reason (Lupton and Stevens, 1997, 1998a).

Participation of children and young people

The other central process issue identifiable in the international research literature concerns the possibility that the dominance of a few powerful individuals within the family group may serve to reduce the extent to which the decisions of the meeting reflect the best interests of the child (Atkin, 1989, 1991; Barbour, 1991; Tapp et al, 1992). As we have seen, Barker and Barker's study of one of the local FGC pilots found concerns expressed by several family members about the participation of certain individuals (particularly natural fathers) whom it was felt could bully or distress the young person concerned. They were particularly worried about what might happen in the family–only session, fearing that they and/or the child/young person would be unjustly blamed and that there would be an upsetting public scene (1995). Thomas similarly records the concern of many professionals that the voice of the child would be submerged in the presence of too many family members (1994).

To the extent that any decision-making meeting involves adults (strangers as well as family) discussing their lives, relationships and behaviour, most children and young people are likely to experience it as an uncomfortable and possibly distressing process. Farnfield's study (1997) of a small number of children attending CPCs provides evidence of considerable confusion and distress on the part of those concerned. Many said they felt guilty or as if they were in some way 'on trial'; others felt unhappy about being talked about as if they were not there. Shemmings' research (1996) highlighted the particular discomfort caused to children if adults disagreed or became angry with each other. As both authors conclude, securing the attendance of children is not enough: "The conclusion from listening to these children's views was that attendance on its own does not always achieve very much. In particular the children wanted to feel their presence was acknowledged by the conference and their views had been put over without interpretation or distortion by the professionals" (Farnfield, 1997, p 4).

Shemmings' (1996) study of 34 children involved in the child protection process (initial and review meetings) concluded that, despite the sensitive and innovative attempts on the part of the conference chairs to assist their participation, "quite a few" considered that their views had not always been sought and: "A number of children felt that, although they had been present physically, they had not really participated in the conference" (1996, p 37). Similarly, Thoburn et al (1995) concluded that, while children were more likely than their parents to be involved in decisions about the conduct of the investigation, none of the children involved were active participants in the initial conference stage. Again, although those over 10 years of age were found to be as likely as their parents to participate in the making of a protection plan, this still involved only about two out of every 10 young people. Overall they concluded, only around one quarter of the children involved could be seen to be participating or being 'partners' in a way appropriate to their age.

In contrast, the evidence from the pilot FGCs suggests that the children and young people involved not only attended in greater numbers, but, once there, appeared to participate more extensively. In contrast to the study by Thoburn et al (1995) who found that, in over 200 CPCs "There were few cases where the young people were present" (1995, p 232), summary data on all the initial pilots shows that almost all young people over the age of 10 years were invited to attend the FGC and only a very small number declined the invitation (Crow and Marsh, 1997). Lupton and Stevens (1997) provide some indication of the quality of that participation, although it should be noted the number of young respondents involved was limited (19 in all).

Overall, children and young people were no less likely than the adults to feel that the information provided in advance of the FGC was clear and sufficient, although a few highlighted the need for "... less adult words to make it more understandable", and that the venue and timing were suitable (Lupton et al, 1995, p 96). The young respondents were, however, markedly less positive initially than their adult counterparts about the idea of participating in the meeting. Once there, as we might expect, they generally found the information-giving session more difficult than did the adult members. While they were more likely than other participants to feel that they had the opportunity to speak, they were slightly less able to ask the questions they wanted and were more likely (second only to the immediate family members) to feel uncomfortable some or all of the time. In respect of the private family-only discussion, the children and young people were less clear about what they had to do but slightly more positive than the adult members about the idea of the family making a decision on its own. Markedly more than any other group, they indicated that they had found the discussion easier without the presence of professionals. Although slightly less so than the adult participants, the young participants generally felt that their opinion had been important and that others had listened to what they had to say. All of those who replied to the question felt that their part in the conference had been appreciated (Lupton and Stevens, 1997).

Conclusion

The available research evidence seems generally to support the claims that the FGC process encourages and enables active family participation in childcare decision making. The large majority of family members interviewed by researchers felt positive about the idea of holding a family meeting and considered that they had been adequately prepared for it. Once there, they clearly felt able to participate actively in the decision-making process: most indicated that there was sufficient opportunity to speak and to ask all the questions they wanted and that their opinions were generally listened to and respected by others, including the professionals. The opportunity to discuss the issues without the professionals present was generally welcomed and holding the meetings in 'neutral' venues was particularly appreciated. As far as the existing research has determined, the positive evaluation of the process was shared by the children and young people as much as the adults, by women as well as men and by more extended members of the family group/significant others as much as those more closely related to the child.

These experiences, moreover, are in sharp contrast with those of families involved in the traditional meetings. The study by Thoburn et al (1995) of parental participation in traditional CPCs, for example, found that under half the child's parents/carers felt that they had been given adequate information about the initial meeting and just under one quarter had actually attended. One third felt that their views had not been listened to and just under half that their views had carried no weight at all. The researchers concluded that, while the majority of parents/carers were consulted and involved in the process to some extent, only a small proportion could be considered as participating as partners and a minority were "... not involved, were manipulated or placated" (Thoburn et al, 1995, p 182). While there is clearly a need for a more controlled comparison of FGC and traditional approaches, the available evidence suggests that the FGC process does appear to enable a more effective partnership between professionals and families than do more traditional approaches and may provide the preconditions at least for the empowerment of family members.

Whether participating in a FGC represents an empowering process, however, will depend on the extent to which families not only participate in, but determine the nature of the decisions eventually made. As with their operation in other jurisdictions, the FGCs studied in England and Wales remain susceptible to professional/agency manipulation. Professionals retain the potential at least for control over the FGC process, not only by the initial decision about which families are offered the option of a FGC, but also by the manner in which they discharge the information-giving role within the meeting. Much will depend on the role of the coordinators and their ability (and inclination) to ensure that the possibilities for professional influence over family decision making are circumscribed. The independence of these key participants in the FGC process would thus seem to be a central precondition of family empowerment. In the end, however, no matter how much they are empowered by the decision-making process, the consolidation of family members' sense of control and self-determination requires that the decisions they make are respected and supported by the professionals and their agencies. This crucial question – of the outcome of family decisions – is considered in the final chapters of the book.

SEVEN

Assessing outcomes in child welfare

Martin Stevens

Introduction

As we have seen, there is now a growing body of research on the process and practice of FGCs. There is, however, much less robust evidence, as the next chapter will discuss, on the outcomes of the FGC approach. In part this is due to the relative immaturity of the development of the model in many national sites. In part, however, it is the result of the fact that the identification and measurement of outcomes is conceptually and methodologically difficult. Yet the focus on outcomes has been an increasingly important aspect of the debates surrounding social work/care generally, and child welfare and protection in particular, in the UK over the last two decades. This interest has been prompted by a range of factors, including concerns about the cost of services, a series of high profile child deaths and the growth of the consumer movement. As a result, Parker et al (1991) argue, the importance of outcome measures to researchers has become "self-evident" (1991, p 11).

Recent years have witnessed a move at central policy level to establish the 'evidence base' for social work practice with children and families. Thus, for example, in 1997 the Department of Health initiated (in collaboration with a consortium of local authorities in the South West region) the Centre for Evidence-Based Social Services (CEBSS) at the University of Exeter, whose remit is to promote the use of research-based evidence (MacDonald et al, 1992; Sheldon, 1994) in the development of social work practice. Local authorities across the country have also cooperated to fund 'Research in Practice', another initiative concerned to assess and disseminate more widely the results of child welfare research. Both these developments highlight the increased political importance placed on assessing and evaluating outcomes in child welfare and public social services generally, an enterprise supported by a growing number of academic/agency researchers (Parton, 1991; Parker et al, 1991; Thorpe, 1994; Farmer and Owen, 1995; Hill et al, 1996).

In this chapter we will start by examining the reasons for studying the impact or 'outcome' of social work interventions, and will consider some of the ways in which outcomes have been defined and evaluated in social care and child welfare. After a brief discussion of the concept of 'outcome', we will describe and critically assess the natural science approach to studying outcomes. The ways in which the outcomes of social phenomena, such as child welfare interventions, can be known will be compared with the investigation of 'outcome' (causality) in the physical world. We will go on to argue that there are fundamental differences between the ways in which the investigation of cause and effect can be undertaken in the natural and social worlds largely as a result of the role of human 'agency' in social outcomes.

Following this, we will briefly describe an alternative approach to the study of outcomes which arose partly as a result of the critique of the use of natural scientific methods in human studies. This, the 'interpretivist' or 'constructionist' approach (Guba and Lincoln, 1994), takes as its starting point the subjective meanings and experience of human actors involved in the phenomenon being studied. An attempt will be made to resolve the tensions between this approach and the 'empiricist' methods of the natural sciences, using the assessment of the 'empowerment' outcome of FGCs as an example. The idea of empowerment provides a good illustration of the difficulties of assessing cause and effect in real world context, not least because of the conceptual problems of defining the phenomenon being studied. While this discussion may appear to be of largely academic interest, we argue that its resolution has vitally important implications for practitioners, policy makers, researchers and, most importantly, for the children and families whose lives are subject to professional intervention.

Why study outcomes?

It is useful to begin by considering the fundamental question of why it is important to study outcomes. The answer to this may seem self-evident, but a brief look at the reasons for studying outcomes reveals much about the way in which they may be studied. A central reason is to link actions to objectives, thereby providing a means of evaluating and comparing the effect of different kinds of actions (Parker et al, 1991). In child welfare context, for example, evaluation of the effect of social work practice is necessary to assess the best means of making childcare decisions and the most appropriate type of intervention.

As Gibbons (1997) points out, however, the objectives of the childcare system and the problems it seeks to address are themselves by no means clear. If the objectives are not clear it is difficult effectively to evaluate the impact of the service or intervention. Different stakeholders may have distinctive objectives and expectations about outcomes, and therefore a variety of reasons for studying them. Motivations may, for example, be linked to the need to save money, or to make decisions about the best use of money. Practitioners may want to find the safest approach to child protection so that they can safeguard themselves from the negative consequences of child death. Families may want to know that the interventions they undergo have a good chance of resolving their problems. This creates a difficulty insofar as these different agendas will influence how outcomes are defined and how the relationship between the intervention and the outcome is postulated. For all these stakeholders, outcomes are a crucial issue, and it is thus very important to be clear about the confidence which can be placed in the results of outcome research, in order that it can be interpreted appropriately.

The idea of outcome

Many researchers have argued that the nature of the social world is such that it is almost impossible to identify the simple relationships between cause and effect that are characteristic of much natural scientific enquiry. In complex real world contexts such as child welfare, for example, it is argued that it may be more realistic to look for "patterns of benefit and loss" (Whitaker et al, quoted in DoH, 1991c, p 66; see also Parker et al, 1991 and Nocon and Qureshi, 1996) than to try and apply a uni-causal model (Frost, 1989). Hill et al (1996) for example, describe the uncertainty and unevenness of child welfare outcomes: "... the progress of children and families who have major difficulties may be complex with improvements and setbacks, depending on which aspects of development are considered" (1996, p 257). In the specific context of FGCs, it is clear that much work is needed to establish how the meeting, which happens at a particular time in the history of a child and a family, is connected with various states of affairs which occur much later.

To respond to the isues of the developmental nature of 'outcomes', many draw a distinction between the 'outputs' and 'outcomes' of a particular intervention. Outputs are then defined as those things which can be directly related to the intervention, such as the receipt of services or the production of a plan. Outcomes, on the other hand, tend to be linked to the impact on the service user or, in this case, the family (Nocon and Qureshi, 1996). In respect of FGCs, for example, a model of programme outcomes has been developed by Hudson et al (1996) characterised by a logical progression from 'inputs and resources', through tasks and activities to 'immediate results/outputs', 'immediate results/outcomes', 'intermediate results/outcomes' and 'ultimate results' and outcomes (see Chapter Eight for our adaptation of this framework). Other ways of analysing the concept of outcome have been suggested which also differentiate immediate, intermediate and ultimate or final stages in a developing process and between outputs and outcomes (Nocon and Qureshi, 1996). As these authors point out, however, these terms can be used in many different ways and the precise nature of the link between the programmes or interventions and the various features which are seen as outcomes (for example, child protected from abuse and neglect) is not typically examined by researchers.

The experimental approach

One approach to researching outcomes, which is attracting increasing interest in the social care setting, is the direct adoption of the methods of the natural sciences (typically experimental and survey designs). There is no reason, it is argued, why the outcomes of child welfare interventions cannot be treated in the same way as the outcomes of physical interventions. Those who advocate such an approach take the stance that the experimental design, which randomly allocates human subjects into experimental and control groups, and subjects them to quantifiable outcome measures, is unequivocally the 'gold standard' in all forms of scientific research:

> **There is no doubt that randomly-allocated equivalent group designs provide the most persuasive and potentially irrefutable evidence of effectiveness (or ineffectiveness) and such studies are essential. (MacDonald et al, 1992, p 618)**

Writing within the childcare context, Newman and Roberts (1997) similarly argue that outcomes can only be determined by the use of the methods of the natural sciences, in the form of randomised controlled trials, as far as this possible within the real world setting. Although Sheldon (a collaborator with MacDonald et al, 1992) concedes that, before the application of scientific methods can be possible, there is a need for "... developmental, illuminative and action research that seeks to draw lessons for practice as it proceeds" (1988, p 100), he too has no doubts that natural scientific methods are the final arbiter of 'what works' in social care, and that it is entirely possible to determine objective outcome measures and thence laws connecting them to interventions.

The same line is taken by Gibbons (1997), who claims that experimental methods would resolve the issue about whether the child protection approach was linked to a reduction in the number of episodes of repeated non-accidental child harming. She describes the type of experiment which would need to be carried out, with random allocation of referrals for child harm into groups which received or did not receive child protection plans, and then monitoring the number of episodes of repeated harm. While her advocacy of such an approach is tempered by recognition of the ethical considerations it would raise, the implication of her argument is clear that such an experiment, if it could be attempted, would provide robust causal explanation of the differences in child abuse rates. Such arguments, however, are problematic insofar as they can be seen to elevate the link between intervention and outcome to the status of a scientific law: the application of this type of intervention in these types of circumstance will produce this rate of child abuse cases, this number of looked after children and so on. While it would clearly be extremely expedient for political and policy purposes, such an approach is, we would argue, beset by many problems.

Outcomes and causality

One major problem with the incorporation of the natural scientific approaches to the human sciences derives from the extent to which they involve an oversimplified form of causal explanation. Outcomes are defined as the consequence of an intervention or service (Parker et al, 1991; Nocon and Qureshi, 1996) and, as such, are inescapably linked with the concept of causality. MacDonald et al's (1992) description of outcome research as being focused on the effectiveness of social work, makes this link explicit: effectiveness is defined as the ability to cause positive effects. The issue of cause and effect in social research is, however, a difficult one to resolve.

Causality can be seen as a concept which distinguishes the regularity with which night follows day (which is not a causal link) from the regularity of the behaviour of billiard balls (which is causally determined). In other words it enables us to distinguish predictive success from causal connection (Greenwood, 1988). Intuitively, it is possible to understand that the change in position and speed of the red billiard ball as it has been hit by the white is the effect or outcome of the collision. Given thorough knowledge of the speed of the white and the type of surface, and composition of the red ball (the pre-existing conditions), a clear causal chain may be established with a predictable outcome.

What can be known about this situation is provided by a description of what happened (the red ball moved at this speed, in this direction for this amount of time), plus the knowledge that this was the result of the red being hit by the white ball (notwithstanding the intention of the player). Thus the situation may be divided into *preconditions* (white ball moving towards the red at x metres per second, at y angle, on such a surface, etc), *event* (white strikes red) and *outcome* (red moves off at l metre per second at q angle). Repeated observations can establish that, given identical preconditions, the identical result will occur, within the limits of experimental error and allowing for microscopic influences, and that therefore prediction of the outcome becomes possible in any given case.

If we ignore the underlying philosophical debates about causality (Anscombe, 1975; Sosa, 1975), assessing the cause and effect relationships of simple events of this kind, within useful practical limits of accuracy, is relatively unproblematic (at least when dealing with objects of everyday size, travelling at relatively low speeds, to avoid the uncertainty of quantum effects and the problems of relativity). In more complicated physical systems (or 'multi-causal situations', Behi and Nolan, 1996, p 254), such as the weather, the situation is basically the same, except that it is much more difficult to apply the concept of causality in practice, due to the number of factors involved and the different ways in which they interact (Behi and Nolan, 1996). The same principle obtains, however, in that the events are causally linked, in the sense of there being a set of sufficient conditions which result in the identified effects (Greenwood, 1988). The events are, at this macro level, predictable, in principle if not in practice, to certain levels of accuracy, again determined by the probabilities introduced by quantum or relativity effects. Because both the cause and the effect can be described in a relatively unproblematic way, it is possible in principle to identify meaningful patterns.

In contrast to physical systems, however, causal chains in social situations such as child welfare are much more difficult to pinpoint, given that the identification of the problem, the intervention and the outcome are all problematic. In the physical example given above, tight description of the input (white ball moving towards the red at x metres per second, at y angle, on such a surface, etc) is essential for prediction of the outcome. Several authors (Thorpe, 1994; Parton, 1991, 1996), however, have pointed out that the socially constructed nature of the terms such as 'child abuse' means that it is not possible to have a single, objective description of the initial problem. For example, how would we define the problem in a situation where a child who has been behaving aggressively at school is excluded and the parents are at a loss to know what to do with her? Is the problem the behaviour of the child, the situation of the family (perhaps in poverty and isolated), the physical or mental condition of the of the parent, the operation of external threats (racial abuse in the neighbourhood/bullying in school) or the rules of the school? Clearly these are not mutually exclusive possibilities, but they show that there are a number of ways to describe the situation of families, and that the description chosen will be crucial in determining the type of intervention which is thought to be appropriate. Given the problem of establishing the precise preconditions of any situation in this way, explanation of the impact of prior events becomes difficult.

In addition to the fact that the preconditions are not easily identifiable, it is also the case that the intervention chosen may be difficult to delineate precisely (Smith and Cantley, 1988). One intervention, for example, may be regular visits to the child and family therapy service, if the family is lucky. What this actually involves in terms of an intervention or 'event' will be influenced by a range of factors, including the relationship between the child and the child guidance professional, the attitude of the parents to the intervention, the impact of being away from school and so on. In other words, the experience and meaning of the intervention will vary according to the perspective and values of the key persons involved. Respite care, as another example, may be perceived very differently by the child going unwillingly to a children's home for the weekend and by her parents who may enjoy a welcome break from the responsibilities of her care.

Furthermore, describing the outcome is also problematic. For example, changes which occur in the family situation can have many competing descriptions and evaluations, depending on the perspective of the people describing them. Lupton and Stevens (1997) for example, quote the case of a FGC outcome which involved the baby of a 16-year-old girl being adopted by her grandparents. As they argue, this may be perceived positively as a way of enabling the 16-year-old to grow towards independence and self-sufficiency, while ensuring the safety of her child, or more negatively, as the failure to keep a baby with her natural mother. In other words, the values and assumptions of the person who records/describes the situation intimately affects both the definition and evaluation of the outcome. These examples provide some indication of the difficulties of studying outcomes in child welfare. Not only is it not possible to identify a single criterion to measure the success of any particular intervention (Smith and Cantley, 1988) but any proposed criterion will be interpreted differently, according to the perspective of the viewer. In other words, the 'success' of a social intervention lies, in good part, in the eye of the beholder.

Some researchers have attempted to characterise outcomes in ways which acknowledge these difficulties, with the perspective of key participants being stressed as a central factor in the interpretation of all aspects of the situation (Parker et al, 1991; Farmer and Owen, 1995; Nocon and Qureshi, 1996). Others have tried to address further complexities surrounding the investigation of outcomes of child welfare such as the value-driven nature of child protection work (Thorpe, 1989; Parton, 1997). The importance of the level of generality of the outcome (whether to focus on the specific programme goals or on more general developmental outcomes) has also been examined (Parker et al, 1991; DoH, 1991c) as has the difficult question of the precise point at which an outcome can be considered to have occurred (Parker et al, 1991).

In most of these debates, two basic problems are being identified which influence the assessment of outcomes in different ways. The first problem is that child welfare situations are very complex, with large numbers of factors potentially influencing outcomes (Frost, 1989). The second area of difficulty is that of the role of human agency within such situations (Greenwood, 1988). While in principle the methods of the natural scientific approach can handle the problem of complexity as, for example, in meteorology, the issue of agency, we would suggest, is not so easily accommodated by the uncritical application of natural scientific methods.

Accounting for agency

The real dilemma highlighted here is how to account for the subjectively 'situated' nature of social interactions, including those of the research itself, while retaining the level of abstraction necessary to move from the description of the particular to the explanation of the general (Hammersley, 1989). One possible way through this dilemma is to consider whether the ideas of 'causality' and 'agency' are necessarily conflicting. Greenwood (1988), for example, stresses that the conflict is apparent rather than real and arises from a strict view of causality as being a set of sufficient conditions which make it inevitable that an event will occur at a particular time. He makes the point that in the physical world there are events for which there are *necessary* conditions (which make it possible for the event to occur) but not *sufficient* conditions. For example, some physical elements will emit beta particles and transmute to other elements only if they are of the requisite composition and structure. However, there is no set of sufficient conditions to make them do so at a particular time, due to the indeterminacy of quantum mechanics.

In an analogous way, Greenwood (1988) argues that subjective reasons can be seen as necessary but not sufficient conditions for human actions, and have to be taken into account as such when studying outcomes. When dealing with the outcomes of child welfare interventions, many of the typical events which are part of the outcome – episodes of abuse, violent behaviour of the child and so on – result from the actions of individual agents (Lupton and Stevens, 1997) and the impact of external factors on this situation has to be seen to operate in conjunction with such actions. For Greenwood, the role of the researcher is "to provide a theoretical account of how agents are enabled to determine their own actions for the sake of reasons" (1988, p 110). This echoes Blumer's argument that statistical approaches to cause and effect relationships ignore human agency: "... neglect the creative character of human interaction" (Hammersley, 1989, p 117). For Blumer, human action is not to be characterised in terms of response to stimuli (either external or internal, that is, sets of sufficient conditions), rather it is to be seen in terms of humans understanding the meanings of situations and conceiving of various possible courses of action (Hammersley, 1989). The only limited extent to which it is possible to objectify the actions and behaviour of social actors, it is argued, requires the development of different kinds of explanatory approaches from those applied to the natural world.

Subjectivist approaches

One response to the difficulties seen to be associated with natural scientific methods is to adopt an approach which takes as its starting point the problem of accounting for and understanding individual experience: a 'subjectivist' or 'interpretivist' approach (Hammersley, 1989; Guba, 1990;

Guba and Lincoln, 1994). This approach is based on different fundamental beliefs about the nature of the social world (ontology) and the ways in which we can know about it (epistemology) from those held by researchers adopting a natural science approach (Guba, 1990). With this approach, no independent existence can be ascribed to a situation over and above the relationships and meanings by which it is comprised (Shipman, 1988; Hammersley, 1989; Guba and Lincoln, 1994). The preconditions, the intervention and the outcome can only be seen as interpretations or constructions of a series of shared understandings, they have no independent existence. The aim of the researcher is thus to interpret and understand the subjective experience of those involved. From this position, any science of humanity has to be interpretative, because of the 'privileged' nature of the human subject as a 'self-interpreting animal' who is able to provide meaningful explanation for his/her actions via the use of language (Taylor, 1971; see Annells, 1996 and Schwandt, 1994 for more detailed discussion).

To those who argue this position, problems in child welfare are seen to reside in the interactions between the people involved, including both the subjects of professional intervention and the professionals themselves. By their efforts to describe and define the problem, social workers have an important influence on the situation in which they intervene. This description (as with those of the family members) will be mediated by their personal values and assumptions as well as by their relationship with the other actors involved. The definition of the social work problem is thus not something which can be seen to exist independently of that relationship. In the example discussed above of the child behaving aggressively in school, a researcher using the 'interpretivist' approach would be concerned to obtain an understanding of the meanings ascribed to the child's behaviour, and the different perspectives on the situation in which it occurs, rather than attempting to identify and isolate those factors seen to 'cause' the behaviour in question.

Because of the primacy that is accorded to the individual's subjective meanings, Guba and Lincoln (1994) and Hammersley (1989) acknowledge that this approach makes evaluating different interpretations of the world problematic. Ultimately, each subjective account is as valid as another and there is no way to differentiate between them. This makes it extremely difficult to apply the results of research beyond the immediate setting in which it was undertaken. Guba and Lincoln's response to this problem is to propose sets of criteria for the judgement of 'trustworthiness' (such as credibility) or 'authenticity' (such as fairness) of the results of research

(1994, p 114). All these authors, however, and Schwandt (1994), accept that the ability to move from the interpretations of individual actors in specific situations to a level of explanation that has more general applicability is difficult for a purely interpretivist approach. As Williams (1998) argues, however, the inability to make this move renders the research meaningless: "Assert that generalisation is impossible because of the variability between agents and the research can suggest nothing beyond itself" (1998, p 9).

A pragmatic resolution?

As we have argued, an experimental approach could, in principle, account for child welfare situations if the difficulties involved were merely a matter of complexity; that is, if the causal chains of factors affecting human behaviour could be studied in the same way as those, for example, influencing the weather. However, as we have discussed, there are more intractable problems in accounting for human agency and subjectivity which make it difficult to apply the experimental approach in the social world. It is this fundamental issue which lies behind the many critiques of the natural scientific approach, as identified by, for example, Guba and Lincoln (1994) and Thorpe (1994). The fact that human subjects make sense of their world, ascribe meanings and develop their own theoretical accounts presents a problem for the experimental approach (Hamersley, 1989; Trinder, 1996). As Guba and Lincoln argue, the preoccupation with the control and observation of sensory data inhibits the search, essential to the human sciences, for the meaning of those data:

> **... the notion that findings are created through the interaction of inquirer and phenomenon (which in the social sciences, is usually people) is often a more plausible description of the inquiry process than is the notion that findings are discovered through objective observation 'as they really are'. (Guba and Lincoln, 1994, p 107)**

Shipman (1988) argues that it is important to acknowledge the extent to which research using natural scientific approaches has highlighted important issues in public policy. He points to research within the context of the education system, for example, which has revealed the poverty of opportunity for children from poor backgrounds, and has led to some real changes in policy. Further, this research, he argues, was seen to carry policy weight precisely because it used the methods of natural science which enjoy considerable public legitimacy. He notes, however, as do many others, (Blumer, in Hammersley, 1989) the danger of reducing social research to statistically described relationships between variables, and the related difficulty of determinism which this tends to introduce (Shipman, 1988). Shipman also identifies a further problem with the 'reification' of socially constructed concepts and ideas like class, which are given "... a concrete almost god like nature" (1988, p 24), as if they were real entities with their own aims and defences.

One possible way forward through this apparent dichotomy of 'causality' versus 'meaning' is the approach of 'pluralistic evaluation', in which explanation is pursued via the use of multiple methods and perspectives, with clear understanding of their differing underpinnings. Smith and Cantley (1988) have argued for the development of this approach which enables a critical assessment of the limitations of the natural science approach without dismissing the possibility of quantification or use of experimental or survey methods: "... a qualitative account which identifies important factors for measurement is a necessary prerequisite to any attempt at the quantification of variables" (1988, p 126). Nocon and Qureshi (1996) make essentially the same point, describing how qualitative approaches can play a large role in determining the dimensions for quantification of outcomes in community care.

The obvious objection to the idea of methodological pluralism, however, is that it ignores the very real incompatibilities of the different epistemological 'stances' underpinning the empiricist and subjectivist approaches. This raises the question of the extent to which the use of particular methods or techniques implies a commitment to a particular set of assumptions about the nature of the world and the way in which it is known. How far, for example, does the use of experimental designs or structured questionnaires presuppose the adoption of a broadly empiricist epistemological approach? Many argue (Trinder, 1996; Bryman, 1998; Layder, 1998) that what can (only very crudely) be differentiated as 'quantitative' and 'qualitative' approaches are not mutually exclusive alternatives. Layder (1998), for example, contends that the world comprises many different aspects or 'domains' and that these can and should be 'known' in different ways, by different means. He advocates an approach which:

> **... encourages the idea of pursuing as many different analytical angles and making as many different methodological 'cuts' into the data as possible and feasible at any one time – including**

> qualitative and quantitative forms of analysis – since this provides a denser empirical coverage of the domains and their interpenetrations. (Layder, 1998, p 101)

Bryman (1998) argues that we can, and perhaps should, consider methods and techniques to be 'free-standing' rather than necessarily locked into a particular research tradition or standpoint and utilise them on the basis that they are appropriate to the problem being studied. The crucial question, he argues, "... is not whether there is an appropriate fit between epistemological position and method but whether there is an appropriate fit between the research problem and the method" (1998, p 14).

Assessing empowerment

We have described some of the problems associated with assessing the outcomes of child welfare interventions generally. There are, however, particular problems with the evaluation of FGC outcomes. As discussed in Chapter One and elsewhere (Lupton, 1998), the empowerment of family members is one of the explicit objectives of the approach. The idea of empowerment as an outcome, however, is especially problematic because of the non-specific and elusive nature of the concept. Not only is the definition of empowerment difficult to pin down but, as Baistow (1994/95) argues, the fact that empowerment does not occur at a specific moment but develops over time makes it even more difficult to evaluate. For Baistow, empowerment is assessed more appropriately by examining the individual experiences of people than by attempting to produce widely applicable measures which, she argues, thereby become less meaningful. This is because each person's need for and experience of empowerment must, by definition, be different.

Such a position raises the problem, which Baistow does not examine, of how, if at all, any more general understanding of empowerment can be possible. The difficulty can be seen to lie as Hallett (1987) points out, in the related problems of establishing the goals of empowerment, acknowledging the variation in the ways in which it can be operationalised, defining its, potentially multiple, criteria for success and establishing the necessary causal links. Moreover, as we have argued in Chapter One, empowerment does not occur in isolation, but is the product of a particular set of circumstances and a particular set of relationships. Analysis of the nature and extent of any empowerment outcome will have to be capable of apprehending the complex nature of these relationships and the fact that the phenomenon being studied is not easily demarcated from the context in which it occurs. The dearth of research on the outcomes of FGCs (and other childcare interventions) may, as we have argued, stem from the conceptual and methodological difficulties of assessing this complexity (Thornton, 1993; Robertson, 1996).

As we have seen, the question centres on the degree to which it is possible to make a judgement between different individual perspectives and subjective interpretations of the situation. Perspective is seen as crucial, as described by Parker et al (1991) and relevant to the question of causation, but it is not clear precisely how it can be applied in the case of an intervention such as a FGC. Many would argue the need to champion the family perspective as their general 'powerlessnes' means that their views and experiences are typically missing from any analysis of outcomes (Parton, 1996). Thus Hill et al (1996) point out, while many studies have looked at outcomes in child protection and care: "Only a few researchers have spoken directly with children and families" (1996, p 259).

Within the FGC approach it is clear that the perspectives of the family group members are seen to be central, but are the perspectives of all those involved equally important? What do we do if there are central differences in the perspectives of different key actors; should the perspectives of the 'closer' family members be seen as the most important? Is the view of the child to be seen as paramount? Clearly the family members' understanding of the situation is privileged: they are in possession of information which others will not know about the meanings of interventions. Thus the 16-year-old in the example quoted above, for example, would be able to describe how able she felt to look after the baby, and the impact on her life in a way which would be at some level difficult to challenge. Other perspectives on the situation, however, may highlight the importance of different aspects of the situation. The social worker involved, for example, may hold that it is more important that the baby continues to live with the girl, as the parent. If we are to understand, rather than simply describe, the reality we observe, we may have to make some judgement, at some level, about the relative weight to be given to contrasting perspectives.

Conclusion

In summary, it is clear that the evaluation of an intervention such as a FGC is beset by many difficulties. Typically, it may involve a problem or initial condition which is indeterminate due to its socially constructed nature; an intervention which may be perceived differently by all those involved (by each of the family members, the child(ren), the social worker and other professionals) and, following the FGC, outcomes which comprise a range of different strands (including inputs from professionals and possible changes in behaviour of the key participants) and whose nature may evolve over time. All of these stages of the FGC process are subject to the differing, and potentially conflicting, descriptions and interpretations of participants which makes it very difficult to establish a clear understanding of the particular or general impact of the FGC approach.

Clearly there will be some sort of relationship between the intervention and the changes which can be seen to have occurred subsequent to it. If a natural scientific or 'empiricist' approach is adopted, the changes post-intervention would be described by a detached and neutral observer (Johnson et al, 1984) who would attempt to link them statistically to the actions of social workers and/or other professionals. From the subjectivist position, however, this would be seen to miss the essential character of the situation in that the changes occurring only exist as intersubjective interpretations of the relationships between conscious, meaning-giving, human subjects. Thus it would only be possible to establish the extent and nature of any changes by examining in-depth the shared interpretations of individual experiences of specific events and relationships. The subjectivist position, however, is in danger of disappearing into a state of endless relativism, whereby it is unable to discriminate between the different individual accounts of participants, nor to move from the level of the particular to that of the general.

These are of course descriptions of two extreme positions which in their pure form are unlikely to describe any particular research approach. As Johnson et al (1984) argue, they should rather be thought of as broad research strategies which in their different ways are attempting to deal with the same set of tensions or 'persistent paradoxes': "... between fact and theory, freedom and determinism, structure and action, meaning and conditions, and so on" (Johnson et al, 1984, p 22). Actual researchers may tend to drift from one approach to another, developing a range of methodological 'coping strategies' in order that some form of social investigation can take place. Extreme adherence to one or other perspective may lead to a conclusion that no knowledge is possible.

Moreover, we have argued that, if the choice of research design does not necessarily presuppose a particular epistemological approach, there may be no reason for restricting an investigation to those methods and techniques typically associated with that approach. Just the opposite: it could be argued that establishing the precise nature of the relationship between intervention and subsequent events, drawing on the meanings of the subjective experiences of different stakeholders but attempting to establish regularities across a number of individual cases, will require the researchers to utilise as wide a range of methods and techniques as time and resources will allow.

We shall see in the next chapter that the research into the outcomes of FGCs is still at a fairly early, exploratory stage. In assessing the weight of available empirical evidence it is important to consider the implications of the particular designs and methods being employed. This requires us to identify whether the aims of the research are to establish causal laws between FGCs and certain types of results, and/or to illuminate the experiences of participants and/or, indeed, as Barnes (1993) describes, to align oneself with the aims of the promoters of FGCs and use the research to effect the desired change in policy and so on. It may well be that researchers have more than one of these aims and it is important that they have communicated them explicitly. All research involves a process of selection; both of the aspects of social reality being investigated and of the methods and techniques employed to uncover that reality. The central question is the appropriateness of the methods and designs so selected to the identified problem.

It is important, however, to maintain a certain level of humility about the limits of research. If it is accepted that it is possible to generalise meaningfully from the results of research, to some degree (and we would argue that it is possible), there can be a rational element to the development of policy and practice. Using research evidence can balance the other influences on policy decision making: resources, political expediency and clinical judgement. In the end, however, as the Department of Health report points out, even though there may be a wealth of research evidence which should not be ignored, "... it is also important to remember that research has to deal with generalities, whereas in child care decisions must be taken about individuals" (1991c, p 2). The real test of any research in the child welfare field is the contribution it can make to the quality of that individual decision making as well as to society's collective ability to provide care and protection for its children and young people.

EIGHT

Empowering outcomes?

Introduction

Chapter Six has established that the FGC process generally appears very enabling of family participation and represents, potentially at least, a means for greater partnership between the family members and the professionals. Effective participation in the process of decision making, however, is only one of the preconditions of user empowerment. No matter how potentially enabling the process, and accepting that this may itself be viewed as an "immediate output" (Hudson et al, 1996, p 15), the FGC will not serve to empower family members if the plans they make are not ultimately successful. While the experience of being involved may be empowering in itself, the quality or longevity of that empowerment will be impaired if those involved perceive that little has changed as a result and/or that their decisions have been undermined or ignored. Worse, such an experience may actively 'disempower' participants, reinforcing their perception of the limited extent of their control over events. Failure to protect a child or enhance his/her welfare may not only be profoundly disempowering for that child (or worse) but also for those who may feel that they have failed (possibly again) in their role as parents. Fear of plan failure was one of the main concerns expressed by the family members interviewed in one of the pilot studies (Lupton et al, 1995).

This chapter examines the available UK evidence on the outcomes of FGCs, again in the context of the key issues raised by the international literature. It begins by setting out the central objectives of the FGC approach using the framework devised by Hudson et al (1996) of a progression from 'immediate outputs' to 'ultimate outcomes'. The extent to which and ways in which these objectives can be seen to have been achieved is then examined and attempt is made to answer the central question of whether they, individually or in combination, appear to provide for the empowerment of those involved. Throughout the discussion, the nature of the existing research evidence on outcomes is described and the areas where additional research is needed are highlighted.

Evaluating outcomes

As we have argued in the previous chapter, the identification and evaluation of 'outcomes' in social life is notoriously difficult, not least in terms of establishing causality in the face of human agency. Yet it is clearly essential that we begin to grasp the nettle of 'what works' in childcare interventions, especially in the context of increased public scrutiny and reduced resources. This is particularly the case with a new initiative such as the FGC, which claims to represent the possibility of better outcomes for all those involved, both professionals and families, than are delivered by traditional ways of working. Developing the arguments of Nocon and Qureshi (1996) it is clear that the assessment of outcome must involve a number of interrelated stages or dimensions. The first stage is to establish what it is that is to be measured: the broad objectives or standards against which the actual performance of an intervention such as the FGC is ultimately to be evaluated. In the case of the FGC these must combine objectives intrinsic to the approach as well as those applicable to child welfare more generally (insofar as these are different).

Although generally underdeveloped in the literature, several studies have attempted to develop and utilise a range of different outcome measures in the child welfare context and these may offer a useful starting point. Farmer and Owen (1995), for example, employ three central dimensions of 'outcome' in child protection: whether the child has been protected; whether the child's welfare has been effectively enhanced; and whether the needs of the main carer have been met. These are broadly similar to those advanced by the Department of Health: promoting the child's welfare; partnership with parents/carers; effective strategic and individual planning (DoH, 1991c). Under the broad category of 'child's welfare' both differentiate 'protection from harm' from more general health and developmental issues, as do Parker et al (1991).

Such 'global' objectives are of limited use, however, in assessing the impact of interventions and need to be broken down or 'operationalised' into more specific and measurable dimensions. Thoburn et al (1995) refine the broadly desired outcomes of 'welfare' and 'protection' into a range of more measurable sub-dimensions: 'developmental progress'; 'emotional and behavioral problems'; 'settled nature of parenting arrangements'; 'positive parental contact'; and whether the protection plan is working as intended. In respect of the objective of 'partnership' these researchers utilise the definition put forward by the national FRG to identify some of the sub-dimensions of 'partnership': power shared; decisions made jointly; roles respected; rights to information, and so on.

In the specific context of FGCs, and acknowledging the need to identify different outcomes at different points in time, Hudson et al (1996) identify a number of levels or stages of outcome. The first level, that of the *immediate results/outputs*, captures the immediate impact of the FGC process in terms of the initial satisfaction of the families involved with the way the meeting was held, as well as the specific products of the meeting in terms of whether a plan was produced and monitoring/review arrangements established. The next tier, of *immediate results/outcomes*, reflects the post-meeting impact of the FGC in terms of family members' perceptions of the extent to which they are supported by the wider family group and whether these latter feel that their sense of responsibility towards the child has been enhanced as a result of the meeting.

Next comes the *intermediate outcome* of the extent to which the agreed plan was implemented and whether the child was retained within the extended family network or returned there from State care. Here, too, are the rather less easily definable dimensions of improved 'family functioning' and a strengthening of the overall 'motivation of the family to seek lasting solutions'. Finally, these authors identify two *ultimate outcomes* of the approach: the protection of children from abuse and neglect and the development of a "communal sense of responsibility" (1996, p 15). Interestingly, Hudson et al (1996) locate the outcome of 'empowerment' at the, relatively early, post-FGC stage. We would argue, however, that it should be seen as a component of the outcomes across all stages of the FGC from immediate results (empowerment through the successful resolution of the process) to ultimate outcomes (empowerment via the successful resolution of the family's problems).

Useful though these attempts are to establish the various central dimensions of desired outcome/output, it is clear that they are limited in two important ways. Although beginning the process of operationalising broad concepts such as 'participation' or 'empowerment' into measurable component parts, the identified dimensions vary considerably in terms of their level of conceptual operationalisation. This has important implications for the next stage of the process which is that of identifying *how* the individual dimensions of desired outcomes are to be measured. Thus, for example, while determining the means by which 'plan implementation' is to be assessed may be seen to be fairly straightforward, doing so for the rather less specific dimensions of 'family functioning' or 'enhanced sense of responsibility' may be considerably less so. Inevitably perhaps, given its slippery nature, the desired dimensions of empowerment typically achieve only very shadowy form.

Secondly, it is clear that the further we move from the broad objectives, such as 'child's welfare enhanced' to the more specific outcome measures, the more potentially contestable the identified dimensions become. Thus in Hudson et al (1996), one aspect of welfare is operationalised as "retained within the family network/returned from care", but many would argue that, in itself, such an outcome cannot be seen necessarily to ensure the welfare of the child; much will depend on the quality of the care provided within the family. Indeed it is possible that the achievement of this outcome may be directly in contradiction with that of another intermediate outcome objective, that of 'family functioning improved' or, indeed, with the desired 'ultimate result' of 'protection from abuse and neglect'. As we have argued, there are different and equally legitimate views of what constitutes a successful outcome and much will depend on which view is taken to underpin the development of outcome measures. In respect of empowerment, for example, Nocon and Qureshi (1996) point out:

> ... agreement on the importance of a broad area such as empowerment may turn out to be illusory when consideration is given to what specific observations should be made to measure this. Staff may feel the freedom to chose furniture and fittings constitutes empowerment whereas users may have in mind the right to chose staff. (Nocon and Qureshi, 1996, p 13)

This brings us to the third important limitation of the desired objectives and their associated measures; they have, by and large, been generated by academics and/or professionals, rather than, and often without consultation with, the people most closely affected by the intervention – the children and families themselves. Although Farmer and Owen, as we have indicated, did attempt to establish what those involved in CPCs saw as important events and issues, it is not clear how, if at all, these subjective evaluations were related to the measures eventually used to judge the success or otherwise of the intervention. Much more work is required by researchers to ensure that the agreed outcome measures reflect the values and experiences of the children and families themselves.

Despite these important limitations, to which we shall return at the end of the book, we have drawn on the studies outlined above to produce the following list of FGC outcome measures which we will use to structure the discussion of the available evidence and, as importantly, to identify gaps in existing research-based information.

FGC outcome measures

Immediate results/outputs
- Adequate and sustainable plan produced.
- Monitoring and review arrangements agreed.
- Empowerment via successful resolution of process.

Immediate results/outcomes
- Culture recognised and respected.
- Family support mobilised.
- Partnership between family and professionals.
- Empowerment via enhanced sense of responsibility.

Intermediate results/outcomes
- Plan implemented.
- Child retained within/returned to family network.
- Family motivated to seek lasting solutions.
- Empowerment via improved family functioning/strengthened relationships.

Ultimate results/outcomes
- Child(ren) protected from abuse and neglect.
- Child(ren)'s welfare promoted and enhanced.
- Communal sense of responsibility promoted.
- Needs of main parent/carer met.
- Empowerment via successful resolution of problem.

Source: adapted from Hudson et al (1996)

In what follows, the evidence on outcomes will be described and assessed for each of the broad dimensions identified above, based on the UK research available at the time of writing. The relevant studies have been described in detail in Chapter Six, but it is useful to differentiate here those (the majority) which focus predominantly on immediate outputs/ outcomes of the FGC such as whether a plan was produced (Barker and Barker, 1995; Smith, 1998; Thomas, 1994), those which provide some information on more intermediate outcomes, such as the extent to which the plan was implemented (Simmonds et al, 1998; Rosen, 1994), and those which also attempt to provide some information on longer-term, more 'ultimate' outcomes (Lupton et al, 1995; Lupton and Stevens, 1997; Crow and Marsh, 1997).

Immediate results/outputs

Hudson et al (1996) argue that, following the various activities and tasks comprising the FGC itself, the first subsequent stage of the meeting is that of its *immediate results/outputs*, among which they list the "satisfaction of the participants" with both process and outcome and the production of an "adequate and sustainable plan" (1996, p 10). The methods used to assess these two dimensions appear to be reasonably straightforward: questionnaires/interviews with the family and professional participants and information recorded (by the coordinators) on whether a plan was produced by the family group and agreed by the professionals/agencies. As we have already indicated there is now considerable accumulated evidence of the satisfaction of family participants with the FGC process (Barker and Barker, 1995; Lupton et al, 1995; Rosen, 1995; Crow and Marsh, 1997; Smith, 1998), with those who were in a position to do so comparing the process favourably with that of traditional meetings (Lupton et al, 1995).

The large majority (77 or 96%) of the 80 UK pilot FGCs also produced a plan with which most family participants were initially satisfied (Crow and Marsh, 1997). Where there is evidence of the views of the children involved (Lupton and Stevens, 1997) they appeared to have been slightly less happy with the plan than the adults but the majority nevertheless indicated that they too were satisfied with the final decisions made. Crow and Marsh report that interviews undertaken with childcare social workers, and other professionals across the pilot sites, indicated that they were 'generally impressed' with the plans produced by the family meetings, although more in-depth investigation in one of the pilot sites revealed that just under half the social workers actually involved in the FGCs (11 out of 24) expressed mixed feelings about (9), or dissatisfaction with (2), the plan produced (Lupton et al, 1995). Nevertheless, as Crow and Marsh point out, the fact that the majority of the plans were ultimately approved by the agencies involved (see below), suggests that they were broadly viewed as adequate in the sense that they were not seen to place the child at risk of significant harm.

Agreement of plans

As in New Zealand, the great majority of the plans made by the families in the UK pilot sites were subsequently agreed by the referring agencies. Crow and Marsh report that, of the 80 FGCs held in the first wave of the UK pilots, the majority 74 (93%) produced a plan which was subsequently agreed by the agencies, including 11 which were taken back to a CPC or the court and ratified "without difficulty" (1997, p 16). In one case the plan was rejected by the parents of the child (who had not attended the FGC), but in no case was the plan agreed by the family subsequently "rejected outright" by the agency (1997, p 16). Simmonds et al (1998) report that only one of the 22 plans from the FGCs they studied was rejected by the social services department. Lupton and Stevens' study of 72 FGCs held over two years in one pilot site similarly found few family plans that were not finally agreed and in almost all cases this was due to their rejection by other family members (mainly the child concerned). Only two cases were not agreed by the social services department, both of which involved care proceedings.

More detailed investigation of the available evidence, however, suggests that the findings in respect of 'agreement of plans' may not be as clear cut as they appear and, in particular, may be a fairly ambiguous indicator of family empowerment. This is so for two reasons: firstly, it is not evident to what extent, if at all, the plan agreed by the family was influenced by the professionals at the time of the meeting; and secondly, the term 'plan agreed' is itself extremely unclear.

As we have seen, there is considerable evidence from New Zealand of professionals using the FGC process to 'rubber stamp' their decisions about what the plans should contain (Hassall and Maxwell, 1991; Paterson and Harvey, 1991). The available evidence from the UK on this issue is limited and equivocal in its conclusions. Few studies paid this issue any explicit attention, although it was a feature of the non-participant observation made of FGCs by Lupton and her colleagues in one of the pilot sites. Their findings were mixed: on the one hand, in the estimation of the researchers present, the family group appeared to exercise considerable control over the content of the plan in the majority of cases, although inevitably some members were more influential than others; on the other hand, as we have seen, there was evidence of a significant minority of professionals attempting to encourage a particular outcome (Lupton et al, 1995).

Moreover, it is the case that the professionals retain considerable influence over the outcome of the FGC in terms of the information they provide to families about services and resources. Although the independent coordinator may attempt to ensure that all available resources are explored, they may lack a sufficiently intimate knowledge of the agencies in question to perform this task effectively. The family members, of course, are in even less of a position to judge how adequately all the possibilities have been covered. In this context it is interesting to note the findings of Lupton et al (1995) that, while all the professionals involved recognised that their role was to provide information about their assessment of the problem, just under half did not see it as providing information about the help they or their agencies could provide.

Despite its key role as an indicator of the success of the FGC approach, moreover, it is evident that the status of 'plan agreed' is not a straightforward one and varies according to local differences in both the FGC process and the recording practices of coordinators. The available evidence suggests that, rather than a fixed event, the agreement of plans should be viewed as a process which may have a number of different stages in between that of the initial 'plan agreed by family group' and the final 'plan implemented as agreed'. Firstly, although it is clear that the coordinator's record of 'plan agreed' should always mean that there is consensus on the part of family members, the situation varies across the country in terms of whether the professionals have remained or returned to the meeting also to agree the plan at this point. Although it is not universally, or possibly even predominantly, the case that "... all staff had agreed the plans at the end of the meeting itself" (Crow and Marsh, 1997, p 16) the national summary data on the level of plan agreement appear to be based on this assumption.

Where this is not the case, it is not always evident at what point the professionals subsequently do provide agreement to the plan. Clearly there are at least two central stages to this process: firstly, agreement that the plan is not considered likely to leave/put the child at risk of significant harm and secondly, agreement to provide the resources and services requested in the plan. Furthermore, it is clear that, although social work professionals will be able to agree to their part, the elements of the plan that are the responsibility of other agencies may themselves subsequently have to be subject to a (potentially lengthy) process of negotiation. To the extent that crucial elements depend on the response of other agencies/ professional groups, it is difficult to see how meaningfully the plan can be recorded as 'agreed' by social services staff alone. Thus Smith reports on the frustration of some social workers about the time taken to agree the resources for the plan "... the only issue the conference raised for me was having to keep the family waiting whilst I sought agreement to resource the plan" (1998, p 3). Whatever the situation, it is clear that this, potentially drawn out, process of agreeing the plan may leave considerable room for professionals to influence its content. More detailed information on the 'agreement process' is necessary before we can begin to assess the extent to which the family retains control and 'ownership' of the plan as finally implemented.

Monitoring and review

Another 'immediate result/output' identified by Hudson et al (1996) is that 'monitoring and review reports' are completed covering plan completion and actions taken (1996, p 10). As we have seen, the lack of adequate monitoring and review was a major concern identified in the New Zealand research and the official review of the legislation recommended improved arrangements for this aspect of the FGC process (Mason Report, 1992). No aggregated information appears to be available on this issue for the operation of the UK pilots nationally, but there is some evidence on current practice available from two of the pilot sites (Barker and Barker, 1995; Lupton et al, 1995; Lupton and Stevens, 1997) as well as from a third, more recent, local study (Smith, 1988). Again, the practice in this respect in the UK context appears to be variable. In the initiatives evaluated by Barker and Barker and Smith, it appears that the families are routinely offered the opportunity for a review of the progress of the plan. Three of the families in the Barker and Barker study felt that there was no need for a follow-up meeting, apparently feeling "... empowered to call a meeting amongst themselves to discuss the same or any other issues in the further" (Barker and Barker, 1995, p 12).

No such formal monitoring and review process was in place in the third UK site although the researchers found that arrangements had been made for almost all of the 72 plans to be monitored (Lupton and Stevens, 1997). However, for only just over one third of these plans was it agreed that the monitoring should be undertaken by the social worker; in over one quarter of cases it was to be left to the families themselves to oversee the plan and negotiate it if necessary through changed circumstances (Lupton and Stevens, 1997). This situation may be difficult for the families and may serve to lessen their sense of control over the ultimate outcomes. While families may be well placed to identify any difficulty with the implementation of the plan at an early stage, they may be less well placed than the professionals to do anything about these warning signs, particularly if they are due to the non-delivery of plan components by agency staff. The absence of any formal review stage as part of the FGC process, moreover, may increase the likelihood that families are drawn back into more traditional forms of decision making as a result of plan failure.

Immediate results/outcome

The enhancement of the family's 'sense of responsibility' and the 'recognition and respect of culture' may be among the more difficult dimensions of outcome to operationalise and measure, but are clearly crucial to the objective of empowerment. As a result, it is perhaps not surprising to find that there is relatively little available UK data on either dimension. Interviews with family members in a number of the local pilot sites provide some, albeit indirect, indication of the families' and professionals' perceptions of this issue, largely through the unsolicited comments provided by individual family members. Thus Lupton et al provide some qualitative evidence that many family members felt that the FGC process had encouraged a greater sense of responsibility on the part of those in the wider family group: "[It's] good where families not living in the same area can get together for the good of the child" (family member, quoted in Lupton et al, 1995, p 93). Little systematic evidence, however, was collected in this study or any of the other pilot evaluations on this dimension of the impact of the FGC approach.

In respect of recognising and working with cultural difference we know that one of the initial pilots was established specifically to work with young black homeless people, but no evaluation of the experiences of those involved is available as we write. Barker and Barker's report on the operation of the approach in Wales similarly contains little information about whether and in what ways attempts were made to reflect the distinctive culture of Welsh families. However, they do record the perception of one of the participants that the family-only discussion was dominated by one female member who, it was felt, "... naturally took over because she was English and therefore more assertive: Saesneg ydi hi'de – ganddi fwy o geg" (1995, p 10). Despite their insistence that "The way that cultural diversity is, or is not, respected" is a major theme of their research (Marsh and Crow, 1996, p 154), there is little discussion of this issue in the findings of the first wave of national pilots (Crow and Marsh, 1997; Marsh and Crow, 1997). Insofar as the importance of recognising and respecting culture remains one of the central desired outcomes of the FGC approach, this is an area which would seem to warrant further research attention.

One of the assumptions underpinning the idea of the FGC is that solutions to family problems can be found from within the family itself, drawing on the resources and strengths of the wider family network. 'Mobilising family support' is thus identified as an important immediate result of the FGC. Generally, it appears that the FGC model is effectively stimulating family self-help. Marsh and Crow (1997) report that almost all the family plans made in the first wave pilots included some help or resources from within the family group. The type of help varied, but "was almost always of a practical nature" (1997, p 143). Relatives found paid work for older children, for example, help was given with family finance, neighbours baby-sat for parents and friends accompanied mothers to exercise classes (Lupton et al, 1995; Marsh and Crow,1997). Across the pilot sites, only five plans included no reference to support from within the family and many involved imaginative solutions to particular family problems that would not have been thought of and/or could not have been provided by health and social care agencies. As one social worker in one of the pilot sites commented: "... the plan was more daring than we would have adopted. Just shows how wrong we can be.... A traditional meeting would not have come up with this plan" (quoted in Lupton and Stevens, 1997, p 50). Smith (1998) also reports comments by professionals about the imaginative contents of the plans: "... social workers were both surprised and pleased by the creative use of family resources" (1998, p 3).

Comparison with the outcomes of initial CPCs over the same period in one of the pilot sites indicates that the family input was significantly higher in the FGC plans than in those produced by the CPCs (Lupton et al, 1995). On the other hand, in most cases the level of family input to the FGC plans was fairly modest and the plans varied considerably in terms of the balance that obtained between family and State support. Moreover, it is interesting that all FGC plans requested some level of input from the social services department, albeit that in some cases this was only a continuation of the general support provided by the child's social worker, and many also included requests for assistance from health and, to a lesser extent, education services. Comparison with the plans produced by CPCs held over the same period indicates that the FGC plans did not appear to result in significantly less support being requested from the social services department and appear to have had more resource consequences for other agencies, particularly health, than did the case conference plans. This pattern is confirmed by Marsh and Crow's analysis of the data from the national pilots, where comparison with the services requested in CPC plans revealed that FGC families requested slightly less resources from social services but slightly more from other agencies, again particularly health and education (Marsh and Crow, 1997), and by Smith and Hennessy (1998). On this evidence, it seems, FGCs may be encouraging the provision of family support as a supplement, rather than an alternative, to agency intervention.

The final dimension of the desired immediate outcomes is that of the development of a 'partnership between the families and the professionals' in the decision making. This is a difficult dimension to assess and, again, the available evidence is limited. Given that the idea of 'partnership' is typically promoted by policy makers, academics and professionals, it is perhaps not surprising to find that none of the in-depth interview data with families explicitly refer to the notion of working together with professionals. Many, however, did reflect in their comments a perception that greater control over the outcomes had been given to the families (Lupton et al, 1995) and Smith and Hennessy (1998) report a sense of 'ownership' of the plans on the part of some family members: "As I see it, we have been given one big chance. I am going to make sure it works and if it doesn't, it will be our fault" (a mother, quoted in Smith and Hennessy, 1998, p 95). For their part, and more attuned to the concept of partnership, the professionals involved generally viewed the model as representing a significant step toward this objective. Just under three quarters (74% or 43) of those surveyed by Marsh and Crow, for example, indicated that they felt the FGC approach served to 'empower' the families involved and over one third explicitly saw it as an 'aid to partnership' work.

The extent to which FGCs are seen to shift the balance of power between the families and the professionals is perhaps best reflected in the views of some 40% of the professional respondents who saw the FGC approach as a threat to their professional power (Crow and Marsh, 1997, p 23). This negative perception of the FGC approach reflects the fact that almost half of those interviewed had had no direct involvement in FGCs. As the more in-depth data from the local evaluations reveal, fears about potential loss of control are much more likely to be held by those who have not seen FGCs in action. Indeed such fears are likely to be a major reason for their reluctance to utilise the approach. As Thomas (1994) indicates, for some at least of those who used FGCs, the opportunity to share responsibility was viewed with some relief: "The sense that it wasn't 'with' us ... euphoric ... the sense that it was where it ought to be, not only where the responsibility was but where the resources to solve the problem were" (social worker, quoted in Thomas, 1995, p 9). Clearly there is something of a 'self-fulfilling prophecy' at work here, insofar as those who were most positive about the 'partnership' effects of the FGC tended to have had direct experience of the FGC approach. These staff, however, were more likely to have referred families to the FGC in the first place if they were already predisposed to partnership ways of working. As Marsh and Crow comment: "... it was their engagement with the principles of the model which affected their practice *and* led them to refer to the project, rather than it being the evidence of outcomes of the meeting which led to changes" (1997, p 162).

Intermediate results/outcomes

Family functioning improved

Again, there is generally very little good quality evidence on this dimension of desired outcome. Lupton et al (1995) report that the great majority of family members they interviewed (84%) felt that the FGC had had no effect at all on the relationships between the family members. Of the minority who indicated that the meeting had had an effect on these relationships, half indicated that this had been positive, with increased contact where there had been none before, and as many indicated that the impact had been negative. In two cases, extended family members blamed the FGC for the subsequent complete breakdown in their contact with the child in question. Barker and Barker (1995) found that the majority of their respondents felt that the FGC had had a positive impact on the relationships of the family group. At the very least, this meant that individuals who had not previously been speaking to each other were now doing so, including a father and son who, prior to the FGC, had refused to be under the same roof. Generally these authors argue, the FGC engendered 'unexpected outcomes' within the family group, including: "... more open discussion, new learning about the dynamics of family relationships and seeing the issue from a new perspective" (1995, p 12). More in-depth research is clearly needed on this issue before we can assess the extent to which it represents a central outcome of the FGC approach.

Plan implementation

One aspect of the FGC process over which the family members may ultimately have little control is that of ensuring that the agreed plan is put into practice. Apart from the components of the plan for which they are directly responsible, individual family members have only limited influence over the extent to which the resources and help promised by others are delivered. Professionals may, if they are unhappy with the plan, simply fail to comply with its recommendations; even if supportive of the plan, they may be frustrated subsequently by financial or other constraints within their agencies. The latter may be particularly the case when the objective of the FGC is family support rather than child protection. Yet effective implementation of the plan is essential to the desired 'sustainability' of the decisions made by the family group. As Robertson rather tartly observes: "Plans count for nothing if they are not carried out" (1996, p 57).

The available evidence is divided on this question. On the one hand, the evidence suggests considerable success in terms of implementation. Thus Rosen (1994) indicates that three out of the four families interviewed two to three months following their FGC felt that the plan was being carried out, and Barker and Barker (1995) report that five out the six family groups interviewed within four weeks of the FGC felt that the plan was being implemented. Marsh and Crow followed up the plans over a period of up to 12 months after the conference, focusing not on the individual component parts, but on the 'overall intent' of the plan. This was measured by the 'stability of the planned placement' and ascertained via telephone interviews with the social workers involved. On this measure, they concluded that the plan was successfully implemented in about 60% of 'accommodation' cases, and over 80% of the cases involving child protection and 'looked after' children (Marsh and Crow, 1997).

A more in-depth examination of the implementation of the plans undertaken by Lupton and Stevens (1997), however, found that less than half the component items in the FGC plans were actually implemented fully as agreed. Allowing for those elements which subsequently proved unnecessary or inappropriate due to changing family circumstances and those elements which were offered but not taken up by the family, they found that exactly one third of all component parts of the plan were not provided as agreed by the family or the agencies involved. Smith and Hennessy (1998) similarly report that some 60% of the families interviewed felt that only part of the resources identified in the plan had been delivered.

One explanation for non-delivery may be that these elements of the plan were in some way unrealistic. Investigation of the 'missing' components for which family members were responsible, however, suggests that they were unrealistic only insofar as they typically involved key family members – often the child or young person – agreeing to change their behaviour in some way (Lupton and Stevens, 1998a). The fact that many subsequently failed to do so reflects the findings of earlier research undertaken by these authors that, in the enthusiasm of the FGC, many may commit themselves to a course of action that they may subsequently, in the cold light of an ordinary day, feel unable or unwilling to deliver (Lupton et al, 1995). This finding is confirmed by Simmonds et al (1998).

Most of the professionals interviewed by Lupton and Stevens considered that the resources requested from various agencies by the families were eminently realistic. Indeed, several had anticipated that families would have asked for more than they did:

> **"I expected the family to request more resources from social services, however they actually requested less and even gave reasons why they didn't want certain services. The level of resources requested appeared realistic and didn't make the family too dependent on the [social services] department." (social worker, reported in Lupton, 1998, p 122)**

Such a view is echoed by Smith (1998), who reports that most social workers found the families' requests to be 'reasonable' (1998, p 3). Given this, it was not clear why the missing components were not ultimately provided. The agencies defaulting in this way were not generally the social services department but others such as health and education services who may accord varying levels of commitment (or perceived legitimacy) to the FGC approach. Lupton and Stevens' evidence suggests that the social services department met approximately half the total number of requests for support it received (and agreed) via the family plans. In many other cases the required service was provided, but did not prove successful or appropriate.

In a significant minority of cases, however, the promised help and resources simply did not materialise. Simmonds et al (1998) reports that, although they appreciated what was required of them, some social workers failed to respond "... they did not necessarily agree with [the plan] or indeed act upon it" (1998, p 17). Marsh and Crow (1997) similarly record one case in which the plan was not carried out at all, apparently due to the disinclination of the social workers to implement it, and Smith and Hennessy (1998) report that two of the 20 family members interviewed felt that the social services department had let them down by not providing the support they had asked for. In yet other cases, as we have seen, the professionals indicated that they had found it difficult to implement the family plans. (Smith, 1998; Simmonds et al, 1998). Rather surprisingly perhaps, Lupton et al (1995) found that the failure to provide 'agreed' support was not any less likely to occur in cases which had initially been designated as 'child protection' than in those which were defined as 'accommodation' or 'in need'. In a small minority of cases, therefore, it does appear that, as a result of agency inaction, some families were very much left to their own devices following the FGC.

Retention within the family network/diversion from care

One of the main claims made by proponents of the FGC model is that, by drawing more on the resources and strengths of the wider family group, it will serve to divert children from State care. Two of the key *intermediate results/outcomes* of the Hudson model are thus the extent to which children are "retained within the extended family network" or are "returned to [the] family from state care" (1996, p 15). The available evidence from New Zealand suggest that these outcomes are generally being achieved (Maxwell and Robertson, 1991; Thornton, 1993). Adequate assessment of the outcomes of FGCs, however, requires that comparison is made with those of traditional meetings. Interestingly, of course, the lack of any alternative to FGCs in New Zealand means that it is difficult to assess whether such changes would have occurred even without the introduction of FGCs, as a result of other factors such as the closure of State institutions and/or developments in professional attitudes and practice. The inconsistency of official record-keeping, moreover, is such that researchers are unable to compare the information on current outcomes with that for the years before the introduction of FGCs (Maxwell and Robertson, 1991). The fact that in the UK FGCs have yet to replace traditional meetings also presents problems for comparative analysis. Running the FGC model alongside traditional arrangements opens up the possibility that implicit or explicit choices are made to refer certain kinds of cases/families to one type of meeting rather than the other (see Chapter Six). It is also clear that any comparison will be affected by the different degree of experience of and enthusiasm for FGC/traditional approaches on the part of professionals and by the 'contamination' which occurs when some families experience traditional meetings as well as FGCs (Lupton and Stevens, 1997).

Nevertheless, two UK studies have attempted some, fairly rudimentary, comparison of the outcomes of FGC and traditional meetings. Marsh and Crow compared 35 'looked after' children who they were able to follow-up 12 months after the FGC. At the time of the follow-up, 13 (or 38%) of these had remained in care, while 22 (or 62%) had returned home. Comparisons with data on a similar number of 'looked after' children who did not have a FGC but who were expected to return home shows that the 'return' rate for the FGC children was very similar. Moreover, these authors argue, once home, the evidence suggests that the FGC children were more likely to remain there. The comparison also indicates that children returning from care were much more likely to go to live with other family members than with their natural parents (Crow and Marsh, 1997).

On the question of the diversion from State care, Crow and Marsh report the speculative view of the social workers they interviewed subsequent to the meeting that many of the FGC children would have 'probably or definitely' been looked after had they had a traditional meeting: "For more than a quarter of the children, the [FGC] process was thought to have possibly or probably kept them within family care rather than becoming looked after by the state" (Crow and Marsh, 1997, p 19). Comparison of the actual outcomes of FGCs and a matched sample of CPCs undertaken by Lupton and Stevens (1997), however, indicates that the reality may be slightly more complex. On the one hand, it does appear to indicate that children were more likely to be accommodated within the family network following a FGC than after a traditional meeting with less use being made of foster care placements. On the other hand, it also suggests that more use was made of non-family accommodation (including children's homes) following a FGC and that overall fewer children proportionately were living with the same family at the end of the year than was the case after a traditional meeting. Although there was little difference in the number of moves made, those made by children having FGCs were lengthier, resulting in their spending longer periods overall away from their original homes. Generally, therefore, while FGCs resulted in the use of family placements rather than foster care, overall the use of non-family placements was not reduced and the likelihood that the child would remain with the original family was lessened.

As Lupton and Stevens (1997) note, these differences are in part likely to be related to the fact that the FGCs more often than traditional meetings involved adolescents whose behaviour was perceived by the adults involved to be causing problems in the home, and whose move into other forms of accommodation may have been difficult to prevent. The success of the FGC may thus have been to secure other family placements for these youngsters rather than the use of foster care by strangers. In none of the available UK studies is the number of cases involved, nor the methods used, adequate to sustain robust comparison. More rigorous comparative studies are needed, involving much larger numbers and more carefully matched (or random) samples, before we can conclude with any certainty that FGCs are more or less likely to retain children within the family network or return them from State care. Moreover, as many have argued in the New Zealand context, the objective of maintaining children within the family may itself be ambiguous and may not unequivocally equate with the best interests of the child (Barbour, 1991; Worrall, 1994). Much will depend on the quality and permanence of that care and on the extent to which it is adequately supported by the agencies concerned. On these vital questions, even in New Zealand, the research evidence is insubstantial. As Robertson's review of the available research in that country concludes, the evidence "... begs the most important question: are family conference decisions meeting the care and protection needs of children and young people?" (1996, p 62). This brings us to the discussion of the final category of ultimate outcomes.

Ultimate results/outcomes

For Hudson et al, two of the *ultimate results* of the FGC approach are whether "children are protected from abuse and neglect" and their "welfare promoted and enhanced" (1996, p 15). As in New Zealand, however, the evidence from the UK on these vital issues is currently partial and inconclusive. The two main studies to have addressed this issue each reveals only a limited piece of the picture. Marsh and Crow approached the problem by examining three indicators: information on registration, the incidence of re-abuse rates and the professionals' perception of the extent to which the child(ren) had been protected. These data were collected and aggregated for 64 children via telephone interviews with social workers 12 months or so post-FGC. Lupton and Stevens examined the issue by using information from interviews with professionals and family members, combined with client file data, to chart the changing situation of families over a period of 18 months following the FGC. These family 'case histories' provided a more detailed analysis of the outcomes – of the patterns of gains and losses – than available to Marsh and Crow, but inevitably involved a fairly small number of cases (11). Both studies attempted some limited comparison with information on the outcomes of traditional conferences and both asked professionals to speculate on what they felt the outcome would have been had the family been subject to a traditional meeting. Although each has important limitations, in combination the findings of these two studies offer some insight into the outcomes from the initial pilot FGCs, albeit over the medium term.

While recognising the limitations of indicators such as registration and re-registration and re-abuse, Crow and Marsh report that some 57% of the FGC children originally registered had been de-registered by 12 months following the conference. Further, no children had been registered or re-registered during this period. This compares favourably, they argue, with Thoburn et al's (1995) data on the registration rates for children following a traditional CPC, where 82% remained on the register six months after the CPC. It would, of course, have been interesting to compare the two samples at the same point in time, given that, as the authors acknowledge, the FGC children had effectively twice as long to come off the register and it is likely that there were significant differences in the case profiles of the two groups. Nevertheless this finding, combined with a 're-abuse' rate following a FGC of around 6% compared with between a quarter and one third child protection cases generally (DoH, 1995a), suggests that children are comparatively well protected by the plans made in the FGCs. These data are supported by the more subjective opinions of the social workers interviewed who considered that over two thirds of the children were better protected following the FGC and a further third felt that they were equally well protected. None thought that the plans produced by the FGC would have left the children involved less well protected than before (Crow and Marsh, 1997).

Lupton and Stevens provide some evidence on the views of family members as to the overall 'success' or otherwise of the plan in addressing the problems identified at the FGC. The relatively small number still participating by the 18-month follow-up (18 individuals from six families) means that the findings here need to be treated with caution, but they indicate that, taken together with the views of professionals, slightly more of the FGCs were seen by those involved to have been successful, or successful in parts, than were seen to have been unsuccessful. The professionals were more likely to have mixed views on the success or otherwise of the plans than the family members who tended to be more polarised in their judgements. Relating these subsequent assessments of 'success' to initial perceptions of the plan, it is interesting to note that those plans with which the professionals had formerly been less satisfied were more likely to have subsequently been considered unsuccessful (by both professionals and family members) than those with which the professionals had initially indicated their satisfaction. It is also the case, however, that many of the plans about which the professionals initially had mixed views, and a small number of those with which they had been dissatisfied, were subsequently considered by both them and the family members to have been wholly or partly successful (Lupton et al, 1995).

To complement the participants' views of the FGC outcomes, Lupton and her colleagues also made an assessment of the success of the plan, based on two criteria of whether the child's welfare had been enhanced and whether the child had been protected, utilising case file as well as interview data. Their aim was to assess the extent to which any identified change could be seen to be attributable directly or indirectly to the intervention of the FGC. They also differentiated between the impact of the actual plan produced and that of the FGC process; in some cases the plan itself may not have proved successful, but the 'unintended outcomes' of the process itself may have served to improve the family's situation.

Interestingly the researcher assessment was more likely to be positive than that of either the professional or the family members involved. Of the 11 detailed case histories, the researchers' assessment (made independently but argued and agreed jointly) was that a clear link could be established between the FGC and the situation of the family some 18 months after the conference in just over half of the cases. In four cases this link was wholly attributable to the FGC and in two cases it was partially so. In two cases they judged that the plan had had a positive impact and in another case that the FGC process itself (as opposed to the plan) had been a positive intervention. In a further case the outcome (mixed) was seen partially to be linked to the FGC plan. In only two cases, therefore, did it appear that the plan had a negative impact on the family situation; in one case this was considered to have been wholly influenced by the plan and in another to have been partially so influenced. In neither case, however, was the negative outcome such that the child was placed on the 'at risk' register following a FGC although in a small number of cases a follow-up child protection meeting had been held. In the majority of the other cases studied, changes in the child's situation subsequent to the FGC resulted from events/actions unrelated to the plan produced and which could not have easily been anticipated/affected by the decisions of the meeting.

Conclusion

The aim of this chapter has been to assess the available evidence concerning the 'empowering' nature of FGC outcomes. This has proved difficult due to the uneven and equivocal nature of the current 'evidence-base'. Existing research is limited on a number of the key identified dimensions of empowerment and almost entirely absent on others. We know a little about the level of the families' satisfaction with the plans produced, for example, but less about the specific ways in which or extent to which the decisions made affected their lives. While there are some limited data on the immediate impact of the FGC on family relationships, the UK evidence is silent on the potential for empowerment via improved family functioning and/or through the recognition and support of the family's culture.

In terms of those dimensions where the evidence is more substantial, the general picture is mixed. Examining the different outcome stages from immediate results to ultimate outcomes, we can see a complex picture in which the opportunities for family empowerment are in many cases matched by the possibilities of professional/agency manipulation. In terms of empowerment via the successful resolution of the process, for example (production and agreement of plans and monitoring arrangements), the high level of apparent agreement of the plans by social services agencies would seem to indicate a considerable willingness to respect family decision making. The (potentially) long drawn-out nature of the 'agreement process', however, particularly if it involves agencies other than social services, can enable professionals to reassert control over the contents of plans should they wish to do so. The uneven nature of the arrangements for monitoring and review, moreover, which in a minority of cases were left to the family group to discharge, may have mixed implications for the families' sense of empowerment. While some may welcome the opportunity for this area of responsibility, and may be in the best position to identify areas of potential difficulty or breakdown at an early stage, others may perceive they are not as well placed as the professionals to ensure that the identified components of the plan (particularly those from professional/agencies) are in place and may experience a stronger (and disempowering) sense of failure if the implementation of the plan is ultimately unsuccessful.

In terms of empowerment via greater family responsibility for outcomes (decision making in partnership with professionals and the implementation of agreed plans) the evidence is also limited. Although we know quite a lot about the families' views of the enabling nature of the process, there is very little explicit data on their overall assessment about whether they felt they, rather than the professionals, determined the final decisions of the meetings. We do know that the majority of professionals saw the FGC as a means, potentially at least, of enhancing family control over decisions. Some clearly found this threatening, fearing that greater family self-determination would serve to reduce the extent of professional responsibility and control. On the whole these latter tended to be the professionals who had least experience of FGCs. Others, predominantly those who had used the approach, appeared to appreciate the mutual benefits of sharing the responsibility for decision making with the wider family group.

On the objective of mobilising family support, there is more information: FGCs are clearly stimulating family self-help, drawing more on resources from family groups than traditional meetings and, in many cases, producing innovative and resourceful plans that the professionals would have been unlikely to conceive. The families' plans are also, however, building in support and resources from statutory agencies. A key dimension in terms of the potential for empowerment via successful resolution of the problem is thus the extent to which the support and resources requested (from both families and professionals) are actually provided. The available evidence indicates that, while in the main the families' plans are being implemented in full, or in large part, in a minority of cases the promised support and resources are not forthcoming. More information is needed on the reasons why, and implications of, the shortfall in plan components. Although the available evidence suggests that it is generally the family members themselves who default on offers of help, it also reveals situations in which the professionals/agencies (particularly those other than social services departments) have failed to deliver the identified support. As we have argued elsewhere, this is a crucial issue for the empowerment of those involved:

> **If families use their enhanced power to ask for resources that statutory agencies are not able or unwilling to provide, then this will represent a real test of the extent to which the development**

> **of [FGCs] is ultimately more about the reduction of state resources than the transfer of power to family members. (Lupton, 1998, p 126)**

On the 'ultimate outcomes' of the FGC decision making, the available evidence is extremely limited. What research has been undertaken provides a relatively positive view of the outcomes of the FGC on the part of key participants which, where comparison was possible with the outcomes of traditional meetings, appeared to be only marginally less effective in addressing the identified problem. Early indication from the few studies examining medium-term outcomes is that the plans produced by the FGCs seem no less likely than those from traditional meetings to ensure the safety of the child(ren) involved. Much less is known, however, about the extent to which and ways in which the FGC decisions serve to enhance the health and welfare of the child more generally, and almost nothing is known about its impact on the needs of the main carer of the child. On all three of these central outcome dimensions, and on that of the promotion of a communal sense of responsibility, more robust information is clearly needed. This has to be based on the outcomes of much larger numbers of FGCs and on more systematic and controlled comparison with those from traditional meetings over a longer period of time if it is effectively to establish that the FGC approach is able to ensure the care and protection of the children involved in the longer term.

NINE

Conclusion

As we explained in the introduction, we had several key objectives in writing this book. The first was to examine the nature and meaning of the idea of 'empowerment' in the child welfare context, using the operation of family group conferences (FGCs) as an illustration; the second was to assess the extent to which and ways in which the FGC approach represents a vehicle for the empowerment of the children and families involved. In examining these two questions the text has examined the findings from much of the available national and international research. A further objective of the book has thus been to evaluate the adequacy of the existing 'evidence-base' on the FGC approach and to identify areas where additional research is needed. Finally, the book is not intended as a purely academic discussion of the ideas and debates surrounding empowerment, nor just a researcher-eye view of the issues involved in the operationalisation and measurement of empowerment objectives. It set out to achieve both these things, but also to evaluate dispassionately the strengths and weaknesses of the FGC approach so that its current practice may be improved where necessary and lessons learned, where relevant, for other areas of work with children and families.

We began the book by discussing the politically and conceptually slippery concept of empowerment. Of particular importance to the assessment of an initiative such as the FGC is its ability to mean all things to all people, whatever their political standpoint. In the context of public sector rationalisation, it is important to note the ease with which the FGC rhetoric can resonate, on the one hand, with the commitment to greater user involvement and participation and, on the other, with the desire to reduce the extent of State support for families. More broadly, it is evident that the political promotion of the idea of empowerment contains regulatory as well as liberatory potential and we need to be clear, in specific contexts, where the particular balance between these two attributes actually lies. It is also evident that the notion of 'empowerment as professional practice' is surrounded by a range of dilemmas, not the least of which is the (self-contradictory) possibility of the unwilling participation of service users in professional-led empowerment initiatives. We have stressed, moreover, the importance of acknowledging the practical and political constraints over empowering practice in the context of social work in the 1990s, if the expectations of family members are not to be unrealistically raised and the enthusiasm of professionals committed to more empowering ways of working is not to be diminished.

Given its conceptual elusiveness, we argued, it is important for the broad objective of 'empowerment' to be broken down into more detailed and measurable component parts if the extent of its achievement is effectively to be assessed. In respect of FGCs we emphasised that, in addition to investigating the empowering potential of the FGC process (*empowerment via participation*), attention needs also to be paid to the extent to which greater empowerment via process is reinforced, or not undermined at least, by the outcomes of that process (*empowerment via change*). Following the framework devised by Hudson et al (1996), we argued that the assessment of FGC outcomes necessitates a developmental approach in which empowerment is seen potentially to result from any of a series of different stages of the approach, from the successful resolution of the process (immediate output), through an enhanced sense of responsibility (immediate outcome) and improved family functioning/relationships (intermediate outcome) to the successful resolution of the problem (ultimate outcome).

In terms of the available research it is clear that the messages concerning the empowerment potential of the FGC process are fairly consistent. Generally, it seems that professionals and family members alike consider that the process is considerably more enabling of effective family participation than more traditional decision-making approaches. There is some limited evidence, moreover, that those who are typically among the least powerful members of families (children and women in particular) do not appear to find participation in the meeting any more difficult nor perceive that they are any less likely than other participants to have influenced the decisions made by the group. Insofar as their views have been ascertained, children and young people in particular seem to feel fairly positive about the FGC process and about the idea of their family group, rather than professionals, making the decisions about their care. There is no evidence that those more distant from the child and their parent/main carer feel less closely involved in, or influential over, the FGC process. In the light of the research indicating the very limited extent of family participation in traditional meetings, FGCs appear to perform significantly better in terms of both the central dimensions of effective involvement identified by Jackson (1994) – "contribution to planning" and "influence over outcome" – and would seem to provide the basis at least for empowerment via participation.

Despite this generally positive picture, there is evidence both in England and Wales and in other national jurisdictions of some professional manipulation of the FGC process. Although this may typically fall short of workers remaining during the family-only session or insisting on a particular plan, professionals retain the potential for control in a range of ways: via the initial decision about who is eligible for a FGC, by the manner in which they discharge their information-giving role, by the establishment of bottom lines to family decision making and by the fairly ingrained inclination of some families to defer to professional advice and opinion. There is some evidence, nationally and internationally, of families not being adequately prepared for the meeting, of dissatisfaction with the length and complexity of some of the professional reports and of the unwillingness of professionals to enter into debate about their definitions of the problem. On the other hand, there is evidence that some family members were anxious about meeting without the professionals being there and there is need for further research on the effect of family power imbalances on the quality of the discussions held in the family-only session. In the light of the concerns expressed in the international literature about the extent to which the FGC approach pays insufficient attention to the power dynamics of child abuse, moreover, the relatively scant empirical evidence about the operation of the process, particularly the family-only stage, across the full range of child protection cases must remain a central concern.

The available evidence on the FGC process is considerably more extensive than that on its outcomes. We have argued that the empowerment potential of the FGC process will be undermined or lost if the decisions made by the family group are not implemented or prove ultimately unsuccessful. In this context, the research findings from both the UK and internationally are more ambiguous. While the fact that the great majority of FGC plans are agreed, at least 'in principle', by the professionals suggests that the objective of family decision making is being respected, the lengthy process of securing the support and resources requested is susceptible to considerable manipulation. Although the plans made by the families in general appear to have been considered successful, or successful in parts, more often than not, there is evidence of some concern about the adequacy of procedures for monitoring and review and about how fully the plans are being implemented. The fact that not all the components of family plans subsequently materialise provides particular cause for concern. On the whole, those plans have not generally proved to be unrealistic and have drawn on a range of types and sources of family/community support. The family groups, however, have not thereby held back from requesting resources and support from statutory agencies. This situation highlights a core dilemma at the heart of the FGC approach: fully to empower family members to make decisions about their children requires that maximum relevant resources are identified and provided by statutory agencies; the cold financial climate in which these agencies currently operate, however, provides them with strong incentives to strengthen the gate-keeping role of their professional staff.

One of the main messages to emerge from the national and international literature concerns the uncertainties surrounding the longer-term impact of the decisions made by FGCs on the safety and welfare of the child. The international research, particularly that from New Zealand, appears to indicate that FGCs are generally meeting the objective of diverting children from State care. The evidence from England and Wales, however, is more equivocal on this question; while there is some indication that FGCs were perceived by professionals to have diverted a significant minority of children from State care, there is also evidence that the impact of FGCs may have been to substitute family placement for foster care by strangers, rather than reduce overall the volume of children being 'looked after' by the State. Whatever the reality on this issue, there is a need for careful scrutiny of the consequences of more children being accommodated within their family network. While evidence from England and Wales suggests that FGCs may be no less likely than traditional methods to ensure the safety of the children involved (at least in the reasonably short term), less evidence is available about the longer-term impact of the approach on the more general physical and emotional welfare of the child(ren) involved.

The assessment of the strengths and weakness of the FGC approach relative to those of more traditional ways of working is bedevilled by the methodological difficulties of making the necessary comparative evaluations. While the length of time the FGC approach has been in operation in New Zealand provides the opportunity for the thoroughgoing assessment of both process and outcome, the lack of any alternative approach to child welfare decision making in that country makes full evaluation difficult. Comparison with the outcomes of pre-FGC decision making is problematic insofar as we cannot ascertain with any certainty whether any identified changes (such as reduced numbers of children entering State children's homes) would have occurred even without the introduction of FGCs, due to the operation of other factors (such as a general policy of deinstitutionalisation). Comparison in many other jurisdictions, including England and Wales, however, has not been assisted by the fact that the model is typically used to complement, rather than substitute for, traditional approaches. The running of the two approaches alongside each other within single authorities, childcare teams and even individual families, means that comparative assessment is hampered by considerable 'contamination' between the two approaches. Many families having a FGC also experience more traditional types of meeting/ways of working, including CPCs. In addition, it is clear that comparative evaluation has been hindered by the fact that, in some sites, the use of FGCs may have been restricted to certain kinds of families and certain kinds of situations. Effective assessment of the relative strengths and weaknesses of the FGC approach, particularly in respect of child protection, would require a much clearer demarcation between FGC and traditional approaches, ideally involving the random distribution of families across the full spectrum of child welfare/protection situations, than has been possible in England and Wales to date.

We have argued that our interest in the research evidence surrounding the operation of FGCs is not purely academic but is designed to draw out the implications of the research for the future development of the FGC approach and, hopefully, for more empowering ways of working with children and families more generally. In this respect it is interesting to consider why, despite the generally positive messages from the available research about its relative strengths, the FGC approach has not really flourished outside the New Zealand context. One possible reason is the lack of legal mandate for the approach in other national jurisdictions. While definitions of empowerment vary, a common literal description is 'legally to authorise' and it is significant that FGCs originated as a legal, rather than a 'good practice' construct. Via the FGC approach the New Zealand legislation sought to provide legal authorisation for family involvement and decision making. Despite the continued and growing interest in the FGC approach, however, there has been no comparable legislative change in other national jurisdictions. Without legal sanction for the decisions and outcomes of FGCs the process remains inescapably contingent on the agreement of professionals and their agencies.

The lack of a statutory mandate for FGCs, and the variety of ways the model has subsequently been developed, inevitably raises questions about the extent to which the original integrity of the approach has been maintained. In particular, there are many unresolved questions about whether and how FGCs are able to coexist with more traditional approaches which rely predominantly on professional decision making. The attempt to introduce the FGC approach in the UK, for example, has revealed some fundamental conflicts between, on the one hand, the desire to deliver speedy, consistent and safe professional decision making and, on the other, the aim of giving families more influence over decisions, which can be perceived as time-consuming, potentially inconsistent and unpredictable. While there still needs to be a debate in the UK on the precise nature of the key aims and principles of the FGC approach, it is clear that it cannot simply be viewed as another 'technique' or 'method' to be used on families. Although the principles underpinning the FGC approach have been discussed positively in the social work literature, and are present implicitly within the primary legislation, they have proved notoriously difficult to put into practice. The lack of other methods for developing these shared principles, moreover, has meant that FGCs inevitably sit uneasily within existing organisational and professional cultures. The result is that the FGC approach has typically been 'bolted on' to existing practice, remaining marginal to the core business of social services departments' work with children and families.

While professional interests played some part in the development of the New Zealand childcare legislation, the essential political momentum for change in that country came from Maori community groups concerned to replace the professionally-led model (child protection teams) with one that was more 'natural' and family orientated (FGCs). Although there remain questions about its implemention by professionals who retain control over structures, priorities and resources, the original 'bottom-up' nature of the FGC approach remains significant. In England and Wales, by contrast, the development of FGC practice and thinking has been almost exclusively professionally led. Given the clear and explicit intention within the FGC approach to involve families more extensively, it is ironic that the momentum for and development of FGCs has largely excluded service users. While the UK research has, to a certain extent, enabled the voice of users to be heard, and there has been some, limited, involvement of users in the training of professionals, there have been no significant attempts to date to involve children and families in the planning and design of FGC services. The vast majority of existing research, moreover, has focused on the views of professionals and/or on issues of implementation. As a result, more is known about the extent to which FGCs fit the needs and requirements of social services agencies – the cost of FGCs, the number of children in care/on the register, the number of professionals involved, the hours spent by coordinators and so on – than about how well they respond to the needs of the individual families involved.

One major potential area of resistance to the FGC approach in the UK and elsewhere has been the attitudes of professionals. As Cooper (1995) has argued, the increased 'proceduralisation' of social work over the last two decades has adversely affected its professional self-confidence. In the face of their own collective disempowerment, it may be difficult for professionals to embrace new ways of working which appear to reduce further their sphere of power and control. We have argued, however, that the practice of FGCs can be seen to reconfigure the relationship between families and professionals in ways that do not necessarily diminish the role of the latter. Rather than shifting power away from the professionals towards the families, it may be more appropriate to view the operation of FGCs as an attempt at greater 'power-sharing'. While the 'shares' may not be equal, the enhanced influence of the family on the decision-making process may ultimately prove to be more enabling of both professionals and families than more orthodox approaches. Better decisions are likely to result in a situation where both 'sides' of the relationship draw on their different, but complementary, sources of knowledge and experience and both exert influence over different spheres of responsibility. Moreover, as those closest to the problem, the family and front-line social workers who respectively 'consume' and implement the decisions of the FGC, are likely to have a mutual interest in identifying workable solutions. Although their influence may be limited, families are not passive recipients of services but play a central role in negotiating the decisions and actions of professionals. To the extent that the FGC enables the 'coproduction' of the plan by the professionals and the key family members, the greater will be the likelihood of its successful implementation.

The initial hostility to the idea of FGCs in the UK largely focused on the extent to which they would work with families perceived to be too dysfunctional or dangerous to participate more extensively in decision making. A few years on, it appears that the major impediment to the development of the FGC approach is not the nature of the family groups and their ability to respond to the opportunity for greater responsibility, but the existence of organisational, political and professional resistance to new ways of working, especially in child protection. While we have argued the limitations of the existing research evidence underpinning the development of the FGC approach, it is clear that it is considerably more extensive, and generally more positive, than that surrounding the effectiveness of other childcare interventions. If politicians and professionals are serious about the importance of research-based practice, we would argue that the evidence amassed in this text should go some way to assuaging any remaining concerns about the operation of FGCs as a viable approach to work with children and families and should encourage its utilisation more widely as an approach which, potentially at least, provides for the empowerment of families and professionals alike.

Bibliography

Adams, R. (1990) *Self-help, social work and empowerment*, Basingstoke: BASW Macmillian.

ADSS (Association of Directors of Social Services) (1996) *Children still in need – Refocusing child protection in the context of children in need*, London: NCH Action for Children.

Ahmed, S. (1990) *Black perspectives in social work*, Birmingham: Venture Press.

Aldgate, J. (1976) 'The child in care and his parents,' *Adoption and Fostering*, vol 84, no 2, pp 29-40.

Allan, A. (1992) 'The Mason Report. A commentary', *Social Work Review*, vol 4, no 4, pp 19-22.

Allen, G. (1991) 'Family group conferences: a family lawyer perspective', in R. Wilcox, D. Smith, J. Moore, A. Hewitt, G. Allan, H. Walker, M. Ropata, L. Monu and T. Featherstone, *Family decision-making, family group conferences, practitioners' views*, Lower Hutt, New Zealand: Practitioners Publishing.

Angus, J. (1991) 'The Act: one year on. perspectives on the Children, Young Persons and their Families Act, 1989', *Social Work Review*, vol 3, no 4, pp 5-6.

Annells, M. (1996) 'hermeneutic phenomenology: philosophical perspectives and current use in nursing research', *Journal of Advanced Nursing*, vol 23, pp 705-13.

Anscombe, G.E.M. (1975) 'Casualty and determination', in E. Sosa (ed) *Causation and conditionals*, Oxford: Oxford University Press.

Atkin, W.R. (1989) 'New Zealand: children versus families – is there any conflict?', *Journal of Family Law*, vol 27, no 1, pp 231-42.

Atkin. W.R. (1991) 'New Zealand: let the family decide: the new approach to family problems', *Journal of Family Law*, vol 29, no 2, pp 387-92.

Atkin, W.R. (1992) 'New Zealand: families children and ethnicity', *Journal of Family Law*, vol 30, no 2, pp 357-66.

Audit Commission (1994) *Seen but not heard: Co-ordinating community child health and social services for children in need*, London: HMSO.

Bainham, A. (1990) *Children: The new law – the Children Act 1989*, Bristol: Jordan and Sons.

Baistow, K. (1994/95) 'Liberation and regulation? Some paradoxes of empowerment', *Critical Social Policy*, vol 42, issue 14, no 3, pp 34-46.

Baldwin, N. (1990) *The power to care in children's homes*, Aldershot: Gower.

Ball, C. (1996) 'The Children Act 1988: creating a framework for partnership work with families', in K. Morris and J. Tunnard (eds) *Family group conferences. Messages from UK research and practice*, London: FRG.

Ban, P. (1993) 'Family decision making – the model as practised in New Zealand and its relevance in Australia', *Australian Social Work*, vol 46, pp 23-30.

Ban, P. (1996) 'Implementing and evaluating family group conferences with children and families in Victoria, Australia', in J. Hudson, A. Morris, G. Maxwell and B. Galaway (eds) *Family group conferences: Perspectives on policy and practice*, Annadale, NSW, Australia: The Federation Press/Criminal Justice Press.

Ban, P. and Swain, P. (1994a) 'Family group conferences in Australia's first project within child protection', *Children Australia*, vol 19, no 3, pp 19-21.

Ban, P. and Swain, P. (1994b) 'Family group conferences: putting the "family" back into child protection', *Children Australia*, vol 19, no 4, pp 11-14.

Barbour, A. (1991) 'Family group conferences: context and consequence', *Social Work Review*, vol 3, no 4, pp 16-21.

Barker, I. and Peck, E. (1987) 'Thinking it through: theorectical perspectives', in I. Barker and E. Peck, *Power in strange places*, Good Practices in Mental Health, London: MWD.

Barker, S.O. and Barker, R. (1995) *A study of the experiences and perceptions of family and staff participants in family group conferences* (Cwlym Project), Porthaethwy Gwynedd: MEDRA Research Group.

Barn, R. (1993) 'Black and white care careers: a different reality', in P. Marsh and J. Triseliotis (eds) *Prevention and reunification in child care*, London:Batsford.

Barnes, M. (1993) 'Introducing new stakeholders – user and researcher interests in evaluative research: a discussion of methods used to evaluate the Birmingham Community Care Special Action Project', *Policy & Politics*, vol 21, no 1, pp 47–58

Behi, R. and Nolan, M. (1996) 'Causality and control: key to the experiment', *British Journal of Nursing*, vol 5, no 4, pp 252–5.

Bebbington, A. and Miles, J. (1989) 'The background of children who enter local authority care', *British Journal of Social Work*, vol 19, no 5, pp 349–68.

Biehal, N. and Sainsbury, E. (1991) 'From values to rights in social work', *British Journal of Social Work*, vol 21, pp 245–7.

Bell, M. (1996) 'An account of the experiences of 51 families involved in a initial child protection conference', *Child and Family Social Work*, vol 1, no 1, pp 43–56.

Bell. M. and Sinclair, I. (1993) *Parental involvement in initial child protection conferences*,York: Department of Social Policy and Social Work, University of York.

Beresford, P. (1993) 'A programme for change; current issues in user involvement and empowerment', in P. Beresford and T. Harding (eds) *A challenge for change. Practical experiences of building user-led services*, London: NISW.

Beresford, P. and Croft, S. (1993) *Citizen involvement. A practical guide for change*, London: Macmillan.

Berridge, D. and Cleaver, H. (1987) *Foster home breakdown*, Oxford: Blackwell.

Biss, D. (1995) 'Weighing up the limitations of partnership policies in child protection', *Child Abuse Review*, vol 4, pp 172–5.

Blaug, R. (1995) 'Distortion of the face to face: communicative reason and social work practice', *British Journal of Social Work*, vol 25, pp 423–39.

Boateng, P. (1997) 'Taking responsibility and giving control', *Children's Service News*, DoH, Issue 10, July.

Boushel, M. and Farmer, E. (1996) 'Work with families where children are at risk: control and/or empowerment?', in P. Parsloe (ed) *Pathways to empowerment*, Birmingham: Venture Press.

Boushel, M. and Lebacq, M. (1992) 'Towards empowerment in child protection work', *Children and Society*, vol 6, no 1, pp 38-50.

Brandon, D. (1990) Contribution to 'Soapbox', *Social Work Today*, 3 May, no 39.

Branken, N. and Batley , M. (1998) 'The family group conference pilot project at the Interministerial Conference on Young People at Risk', *Putting the wrong right, A practice research study and implementation manual*, South Africa, Cape Town: The Printing Press.

Braye, S. and Preston-Shoot, M. (1995) *Empowering practice in social care*, Buckingham: Open University Press.

Brenton, M. (1985) *The voluntary sector in British social services*, London: Longman.

Browne, K., Davis, C. and Stratton, P. (1989) *Early prediction and prevention of child abuse*, Chichester: Wiley.

Bryman, A. (1998) 'Quantitative and qualitative research strategies', in T. May and M. Williams (eds) *Knowing the social world*, Buckingham: Open University Press.

Bullock, R., Little, M. and Millham, S. (1993) *going home, the return of children separated from their families*, Aldershot: Dartmouth.

Burford, G. (1994) *A hitchhikers guide to family group conferences*, Unpublished.

Burford, G. and Pennell, J. (1995a) 'Family group decision making: an innovation in child and family welfare', in J. Hudson and B. Galaway (eds) *Child welfare in Canada: Research and policy implications*, Toronto, Canada: Thompson Educational Publications, pp 140-53.

Burford, G. and Pennell, J. (1995b) *Family group decision making project implementation report summary*, Newfoundland, Canada: Memorial University.

Cameron, S. and Wilson-Salt, A. (1995) Summary of the Report 'The experience of social workers working in the area of care and protection under the Children, Young Person and their Families Act (1989)', *Social Work Review*, vol 12, pp 19-21.

Cannan, C. (1994/95) 'Enterprise culture, professional socialisation and social work education in Britain', *Critical Social Policy*, issue 42, vol 14, no 3, Winter, pp 5-19.

Caton, A. (1990) *The care and protection provisions of the Children, Young Persons and their Families Act 1989 — Resource paper*, Wellington, New Zealand: Department of Social Welfare.

Christopherson, R.J. (1998) 'Social work students' perceptions of child abuse: an internal comparison and postmodern interpretation of its findings', *British Journal of Social Work*, vol 28, pp 57-72.

Clarke, J. (1996) 'Capturing the customer: consumerism and social welfare', *Working Papers on Managerialism & Social Policy*, Milton Keynes: Open University.

Clarke, M. and Stewart, J. (1992) 'Empowerment: a theme for the 1990s', *Local Government Studies*, vol 18, no 2, pp 18-26.

Cleaver, H. and Freeman, P. (1995) *Parental perspectives in cases of suspected child abuse*, London: HMSO.

Cleaver, N. (1995) 'Another arm of the bureaucracy?', *New Zealand Social Work Now*, no 1, July, pp 7-10.

Cliffe, D. and Berridge, D. (1991) *Closing children's homes : An end to residential care?*, London: NCB.

Colton, M., Drury, C. and Williams, M. (1995) *Staying together: Supporting families under the Children Act*, Aldershot: Ashgate.

Connolly, M. (1994) 'An Act of empowerment: the Children, Young Persons and their Families Act (1989)', *British Journal of Social Work*, vol 24, pp 87-100.

Cooper, A. (1994) 'In care or en famille? Child protection, the family and the state in France and England', *Social Work in Europe*, vol 1, no 1, pp 59-67.

Cooper, A. (1995) 'Scare in the community: Britain in a moral panic — child abuse Part 4', *Community Care*, August, pp 3-9.

Cooper, A., Hetherington, R., Baistow, K., Pitts, J. and Spriggs, A. (1995) *Positive child protection: A view from abroad*, Dorset: Russell House Publishing.

Corby, B., Millar, M. and Young, L. (1996) 'Parental participation in child protection work: rethinking the rhetoric', *Bristol Journal of Social Work*, vol 26, no 4, pp 475-92.

Corrigan, P. and Leonard, P. (1978) *Social work under capitalism*, Basingstoke: Macmillian.

Craig, G. and Mayo, M. (1995) *Community empowerment. A reader in participation and development*, London: Zed Books

Croft, S. and Beresford, P. (1988) 'Time to build trust between them and us', *Social Work Today*, 8 September, pp 16-17.

Crow, G. and Marsh, P. (1997) *Family group conferences, partnership and child welfare: A research report on four pilot projects in England and Wales*, Sheffield: University of Sheffield Partnership Research Programme.

Cultler, F. and Waine, B. (1994) *Managing the welfare state*, Oxford: Berg.

Dale, P., Davis, M., Morrison, T. and Waters, J. (1986) *Dangerous families*, London and New York, NY: Tavistock Publications.

Department of Social Welfare (1988) *Puao Te Ata Tu*, Ministerial Advisory Committee Report on a Maori Perspective for the Department of Social Welfare, Wellington: Government Printers.

Department of Social Welfare (1992) *Children, Young Persons and their Families Act, 1989: The government's response to the Report of the Ministerial Review Team*, Wellington, New Zealand: Department of Social Welfare.

DHSS (Department of Health and Social Security) (1985a) *Social work decisions in child care: Recent research findings and their implications*, London: HMSO.

DHSS (1985b) *Review of child care law: Report to ministers of an interdepartmental working party*, London: HMSO.

DHSS/Welsh Office (1988) *Working together: A guide to arrangements for inter-agency co-operation for the protection of children from abuse*, London: HMSO.

Dingwall, R., Eekelaar, J. and Murrary, T. (1995) *The protection of children: State intervention and family life*, 2nd edn, London: Avebury.

DoH (Department of Health) (1988) *Report of the Committee of Enquiry into the Care and Supervision Provided in Relation to Maria Colwell*, London HMSO.

DoH (1989) *An introduction to the Children Act (1989)*, London: HMSO.

DoH (1991a) *The Children Act 1989. Guidance and regulations*, vol 1, Court Orders, London: HMSO.

DoH (1991b) *Child abuse: A study of Inquiry Reports 1980-1989*, London: HMSO.

DoH (1991c) *Patterns and outcomes in child placement. Messages from current research and their implications*, London: HMSO.

DoH (1995a) *Child protection: Messages from research*, London: HMSO.

DoH (1995b) *Social work decisions in child care*, London: HMSO.

DoH (1995c) *The challenge of partnership*, London: HMSO.

DoH (1996) *Choice and opportunity*, Cm 3390, London: HMSO.

DoH (1998) *Working together to safeguard children: New government proposals for inter-agency co-operation*, Consultation Paper, London: DoH.

DoH/SSI (Social Services Inspectorate) (1991) *Practitioners' and managers' guide to care management and assessment*, London: HMSO.

Dominelli, L. (1996) 'De-professionalising social work: anti-oppressive practice, competencies and post-modernism', *British Journal of Social Work*, vol 26, pp 153-75.

Dominelli, L. and McLeod, E. (1989) *Feminist social work*, Basingstoke: Macmillan.

Eekelaar, J. (1991) 'Parental responsibility: state of nature or nature of the state?', *Journal of Social Welfare and Family Law*, issue 1, pp 37-50.

Farmer, E. and Owen, M. (1995) *Child protection: Private risks and public remedies*, London: HMSO.

Farnfield, S. (1997) *The involvement of children in child protection conferences – Summary of findings*, Unpublished Conference Presentation, University of Reading.

Finklehor, D.A. (1986) *Sourcebook on child sexual abuse*, London: Sage Publications.

Fischer, J. (1978) 'Does anything work?', *Journal of Social Science Research*, vol 1, pp 215-43.

Fisher, D., Marsh, P., Phillips, D. and Sainsbury, E. (1986) *In and out of care: The experiences of children, parents and social workers*, London: Batsford.

Fisher, M., Lukey, V. and Wilkings, P. (1989) 'Social work in partnership – issues in collaborative research', in M. Stein (ed) *Research into practice*, Proceedings of the 4th Annual JVC/BASW Conference, Birmingham: BASW.

Fox Harding, L. (1991) *Perspectives in child care and policy*, London: Longman.

Frank, C. (1988) 'Family group conferences in South Africa: an overview', Unpublished paper presented to the Second International Forum on Family Group Conferences, The Guildhall, Winchester, 15-16 September.

Fraser, S. and Norton, J. (1996) 'Family group conferencing in New Zealand child protection work', in J. Hudson, A. Morris, G. Maxwell and B. Galaway (eds) *Family group conferences: Perspectives on policy and practice*, Annadale, NSW: The Federation Press/Criminal Justice Press.

FRG (Family Rights Group) (1993) *The legal framework for family involvement in decision-making*, London: FRG.

FRG (1994) *Partnership, family and child care work*, London: FRG.

Frost, N. (1989) *The politics of child welfare: Inequality, power and change*, London: Harvester Wheatsheaf.

Fulcher, L. and Ainsworth, F. (1994) 'Child welfare abandoned? The ideology and economics of contemporary service reform in New Zealand', *Social Work Review*, vol 6, pp 2-13.

Gaylin, W., Glasser, I., Marcus, S. and Rothman, D. (1978) *Doing good: The limits of benevolence*, New York, NY: Pantheon Books.

Geddis, D. (1979) *Child abuse. Report of a national symposium held in Dunedin*, September, Dunedin, New Zealand: National Children's Health Research Foundation.

Geddis, D. (1993) 'A critical analysis of the family group conference', *Family Law Bulletin*, vol 3, no 11, pp 141-4.

Gibbons, J. (ed) (1992) *The Children Act 1989 and family support: Principles into practice*, London: HMSO.

Gibbons, J. (1997) 'Relating outcomes to objectives in child protection policy', in N. Parton (ed) *Child protection and family support: Tensions, contradictions and possibilities*, London: Routledge.

Gibbons, J., Conroy, S. and Bell, C. (1995) *Operating the child protection system*, London HMSO.

Giller, H., Gasrmley, C. and Willens, P. (1992) *The effectiveness of child protection procedures: An evaluation in four ACPC areas*, Cheshire: Social Information Systems.

Graber, L., Keys, T. and White, J. (1996) 'Family group decision-making in the United States: the case of Oregon', in J. Hudson, A. Morris, G. Maxwell and B. Galaway (eds) *Family group conferences: Perspectives on policy and practice*, Annadale, NSW, Australia: The Federation Press/Criminal Justice Press.

Green, D.G. (1987) *The New Right*, Brighton: Harvester Wheatsheaf.

Greenland, C. (1987) *Preventing CAN deaths: An international study of deaths due to child abuse and neglect*, London: Tavistock.

Greenwood, J.D. (1988) 'Agency, casualty, and meaning', *Journal for the Theory of Social Behaviour*, vol 18, no 1, pp 95-115.

Grimshaw, R. (1996) *Plans and review: Getting it right for young people*, London: NCB.

Guba, E.G. (1990) 'The alternative paradigm dialog', in E.G. Guba, *The Paradigm Dialog*, London: Sage Publications Ltd.

Guba, E.G. and Lincoln, Y.S. (1994) 'Competing paradigms in qualitative research', in N.K. Denzin and Y.S. Lincoln (1994) *Handbook of qualitative research*, London: Sage Publications Ltd.

Gulbenkien Foundation (1995) *Children and violence*, Report of the Commission on Children and Violence convened by the Gulbenkien Foundation, London: Gulbenkien Foundation.

Gurrey, M. (1997) 'The right message', *Community Care*, 4-10 September 1997.

Hallett, C. (1987) *Critical issues in participation*, Newcastle-upon-Tyne: Association of Community Workers.

Hallett, C. and Birchall, E. (1992) *Coordination and child protection: A review of the literature*, London: HMSO.

Hammersley, M. (1989) *The dilemma of qualitative method: Herbert Blumer and the Chicago tradition*, London: Routledge.

Hardin, M. (1996) *Family group conferences in child abuse and neglect cases – Learning the experience of New Zealand*, Washington, DC: American Bar Association Center on Children and the Law.

Harding, L. (1989) *The child's generation*, 2nd edn, Oxford: Blackwell and Robertson.

Hassall, I.B. (1996) 'Origin and development of family group conferences', in J. Hudson, A. Morris, G. Maxwell and B. Galaway (1996) *Family group conferences: Perspectives on policy and practice*, Australia: The Federation Press.

Hassall, I.B. and Maxwell, G.M. (1991) 'The family group conference', in G.M. Maxwell (ed) *An appraisal of the first year of the Children, Young Persons and their Families Act, 1989*, Wellington, New Zealand: Office of the Commissioner for Children.

Higgins, R. (1992) 'Room to consume?', *Social Work Today*, vol 23, no 28, pp 14-15.

Hill, M. and Aldgate, J. (eds) (1996) *Child welfare services: Developments in law policy, practice, research*, London: Jessica Kingsley Publishers Ltd.

Hill, M., Triseliotis, J., Borland, M., Lambert, L. (1996) 'Outcomes of social work interventions with young people', in M. Hill and J. Aldgate (eds) *Child welfare services: Developments in law policy, practice, research*, London: Jessica Kingsley Publishers Ltd, pp 255-68.

Holdsworth, L. (1991) *Empowerment social work with physically disabled people*, Social Work Monographs, Norwich: University of East Anglia.

Holman, B. (1993) 'Pulling together', *The Guardian*, 10 January.

Home Office (1960) *Report of the Committee on Children and Young People* (Inglesby Report), Cmnd 1191, London: HMSO.

Home Office, DoH (Department of Health), DES (Department of Education and Science), Welsh Office (1991) *Working together under the Children Act, 1989. A guide to arrangements for interagency co-operation for the protection of children from abuse*, London: HMSO.

Horne, D. (1990) 'Themes of helping, empowerment and participation', in J. Thoburn (ed) *Participation in practice: A reader*, Norwich: University of East Anglia.

Howe, D. (1994) 'Modernity, post-modernity and social work', *British Journal of Social Work*, vol 24, no 5, pp 513-32.

Hudson, J., Galaway, B., Morris, A. and Maxwell, G. (1996) *Family group conferences: Perspectives on policy and practice*, Annadale, NSW, Australia: The Federation Press/Criminal Justice Press.

Ignatieff, M. (1989) 'Citizenship and moral narcissism', *Political Quarterly*, vol 60, pp 63-74.

Immarigeon, R. (1996) 'Family group conferences in Canada and the United States: an overview', in J. Hudson, A. Morris, G. Maxwell and B. Galaway (eds) *Family group conferences: Perspectives on policy and practice*, Anndale NSW, Australia: The Federation Press/Criminal Justice Press.

Jack, G. (1997) 'An ecological approach to social work with children and families', *Child and Family Social Work*, vol 2, pp 109-20.

Jack, G. and Stepney, P. (1995) 'The Children Act 1989 – Protection or persecution? Family support in child protection in the 1990s', *Critical Social Policy*, issue 43, vol 15, no 1, pp 26-39.

Jackson, M. (1989) Unpublished paper, cited in R. Wilcox et al, *Family decision-making*, Lower Hutt: New Zealand: Practitioners' Publishing.

Jackson, M. (1994) '"I'm afraid": the voice of the family', in A. Buchanan (ed) *Partnership in practice: The Children Act 1989*, Aldershot: Avebury.

Johnson, T., Dandeker, C. and Ashworth, C. (1984) *The structure of social theory*. Basingstoke: Macmillan Education Ltd.

Jones, C. and Novak, T. (1993) 'Social work today'; *British Journal of Social Work*, vol 23, pp195-212.

Kaganas, F. (1993) 'Unequal silence in partnership with families', *Community Care Supplement*, 28 October, p 1.

Kelly, G. (1990) *Patterns of care*, Belfast: Belfast Department of Social Work, Queens University.

Kelly, L. (1991) 'Women's refuges: 20 years on', *Spare Rib*, vol 221, pp 32-5.

Kempson, E. (1996) *Life on a low income*, York: York Publishing Service for the Joseph Rowntree Foundation.

King, M. and Piper, C. (1990) *How the law thinks about children*, Aldershot: Gower.

King, M. and Trowell, J. (1992) *Children's welfare and the law. The limits of legal intervention*, London: Sage Publications.

Kohar, S. (1994) 'Improving services for black families in Warwickshire', in K. Morris (ed) *Family group conferences: A report commissioned by the Department of Health*, London: FRG.

Kohar, S. (1996) 'A black practitioner's perspective on family group conferences', in K. Morris and J. Tunnard (eds) *Family group conferences: Messages from UK practice and research*, London: FRG.

Kumar, V. (1993) *Poverty and Inequality in the UK. The Effects on Children*. London: NCB.

Langan, M. and Lee, P. (1989) *Radical social work*, London: Unwin Hyman.

Layder, D. (1998) 'The reality of social domains: implications for theory and methods', in T. May and M. Williams (eds) *Knowing the social world*, Buckingham: Open University Press.

Levine, M. (1997) 'The family group conference in the New Zealand Children, Young Persons and their Families Act of 1989: review and evaluation', Unpublished paper, State University of New York at Buffalo.

Lewis, A. (1995) *Family participation and child protection – Partnerships with parents in child and family support and protection – A practical approach*, London: NCB.

Lidgren, H. and Persson, L. (1997) *A comparative study of family group conferences in England and Sweden in the spirit of power, rights, democracy and responsibility*, Final paper for Comparative Social Policy Course, Lund, Sweden: School of Social Work, University of Lund.

Lilja, I. (1997) *The family group conference project in Sweden*, Svenska Kommonforbundet Swedish Association of Local Authorities, Unpublished paper presented to 'Family Group Conferences in Action: International Forum', Winchester, June.

London Borough of Brent (1985) *A child in trust: Report of the Panel of Inquiry investigating the circumstances surrounding the death of Jasmine Beckford*, London: London Borough of Brent.

London Borough of Greenwich (1987) *A child in mind: Protection of children in a responsible society: Report of the Commission of Inquiry into the death of Kimberly Carlile*, London: London Borough of Greenwich.

London Borough of Lambeth (1987) *Whose child? The Report of the Panel appointed to inquire into the death of Tyra Henry*, London: London Borough of Lambeth.

London Edinburgh Weekend Return Group (1979) *In and against the state*, London: Pluto Press.

Longclaws, L., Galaway, B. and Barkwell, L. (1996) 'Piloting family group conferences for young aboriginal offenders in Winnipeg, Canada', in J. Hudson, A Morris, G. Maxwell and B. Galaway (eds) *Family group conferences: Perspectives on policy and practice*, Annadale NSW, Australia: The Federation Press/Criminal Justice Press.

Lupton, C. (1985) *Moving out: The experiences of older teenagers leaving care*, Portsmouth: SSRIU, University of Portsmouth.

Lupton, C. (1998) 'User empowerment or family self-reliance? The family group conference model', *British Journal of Social Work*, vol 28, no 1, pp 107-28.

Lupton, C. and Hall, B. (1993) 'Beyond the rhetoric: from policy to practice in user involvement', *Research, Policy and Planning*, vol 10, no 2, pp 6-11.

Lupton, C. and Khan, P. (1998) 'The role of health professionals in the child protection process', *Journal on Interprofessional Care*, vol 12, no 2, pp 209-23.

Lupton, C. and Sheppard, C. (1999) 'Lost lessons? The experience of a time-limited home school support project', *Children and Society*, vol 13, pp 20-31.

Lupton, C. and Stevens, M. (1997) *Family outcomes: Following through on family group conferences*, Portsmouth: Social Services and Information Unit, University of Portsmouth.

Lupton, C. and Stevens, M. (1998a) 'Planning in partnership? Family group conferences in the UK', *International Journal of Child and Family Welfare*, vol 3, no 2, pp 135-49.

Lupton, C. and Stevens, M. (1998b) 'Family group conferences: the UK experience', *The Interdisciplinary Report on Children and Families at Risk*, vol 1, no 2, pp 21-31.

Lupton, C., Barnard, S. and Swall-Yarrington, M. (1995) *Family planning? An evaluation of the family group confernce model*, Portsmouth: SSRIU, University of Portsmouth.

Lupton, C., Barnard, S. and Swall-Yarrington, M. (1998) *Family planning? An evaluation of the family group conference model*, Portsmouth: Social Services Research Information Unit, University of Portsmouth.

Lupton, C., Peckham, S. and Taylor, P. (1998) *The management of public involvement in healthcare purchasing*, Buckingham: Open University Press.

Lyon, C. and Parton, N. (1995) 'Children's rights and the Children Act 1989', in B. Franklin (ed) *The handbook of children's rights: Comparative policy and practice*, London: Routledge.

MacDonald, G., Sheldon, B. and Gillespie, J. (1992) 'Contemporary studies of the effectiveness of social work', *British Journal of Social Work*, vol 22, no 6, pp 615-43.

McGloin, P. and Turnbull, A. (1987) 'Child abuse reviews – the impact of the parents', *Social Work Today*, vol 19, no 6, pp 16–17.

Marsh, P. (1990) 'Changing practice in child care – the Children Act 1989', *Adoption and Fostering*, vol 14, no 4, pp 27-30.

Marsh, P. and Crow, G. (1997) *Family group conferences in child welfare*, Oxford: Blackwells.

Marsh, P. and Crow, G. (1996) 'Family group conferences in child welfare services in England and Wales', in J. Hudson, A. Morris, G. Maxwell and B. Galaway (eds) *Family group conferences: Perspectives on policy and practice*, Annadale, NSW, Australia: The Federation Press/Criminal Justice Press.

Marsh, P. and Fisher, M. (1992) 'Do we measure up?', *Community Care*, 14 May, pp 18-19.

Mason Report (1992) Report of the Ministerial Review Team to the Minister of Social Welfare the Hon, Jenny Shipley. *Review of the Children, Young Persons and their Families Act*, February, vol 1, Wellington, New Zealand: Government Printer.

MAU (Maori Advisory Unit) (1985) *Report*, Wellington, New Zealand: Government Printing.

Mauthner, M. (1997) 'Methodological aspects of collecting data from children: lessons from three research projects', *Children and Society*, vol 11, pp 16-28.

Maxwell, G.M. (ed) (1991) *An appraisal of the first year of the Children, Young Persons and their Families Act, 1989*, Wellington, New Zealand: Office of the Commissioner for Children, Government Printers.

Maxwell, G.M. and Morris, A. (1992) 'The family group conference: a new paradigm for making decisions about children and young people', *Children Australia*, vol 17, no 4, pp 11-15.

Maxwell, G.M. and Morris, A. (1993) *Family group conferences: Key elements*, Paper presented to Mission of St James and St Johns: Melbourne, Australia, 10 June.

Maxwell, G.M. and Robertson, J.P. (1991) *Statistics on the first year of the Children, Young Persons and their Families Act, 1989*, Wellington: The Commissioner for Children.

Merkel-Holguin, L. (1996) 'Putting families back into the child protection partnership', *Protecting Children*, vol 12, no 3, pp 4-7.

Merkel-Hoguin, L. (1998) 'Family group decision-making: harnessing family commitment and responsibility for the protection of children', *Interdisciplinary Report on At Risk Children and Families*, vol 1, no 2, pp 17-18.

Merkel-Holguin, L., Printz-Winterfeld, A., Harper, C.J., Coburn, N.A. and Fluke, J.D. (1997) *Implications for children's services for the 21st century: Family group decision making and patch*, Englewood, CO: American Humane Association.

Millham, S., Bullock, R,. Hoise, K. and Hack, M. (1986) *Lost in care*, Aldershot: Gower.

Mitchell, G. (1989) 'Empowerment and opportunity', *Social Work Today*, 16 March, p 14.

Mittler, H. (1992) 'Crossing frontiers', *Community Care*, 12 November, pp 22-3.

Moore, J. (1987) *The welfare state: The way ahead*, London: Conservative Political Centre.

Morris, A., Maxwell, G., Hudson, J. and Galaway, B. (1996) 'Concluding thoughts', in J. Hudson, A. Morris, G. Maxwell and B. Galaway (eds) *Family group conferences: Perspectives on policy and practice*, Annadale, NSW, Australia: The Federation Press/Criminal Justice Press.

Morris, K. (1994) 'Family group conferences in the UK', in *Family group conferences: A report commissioned by the Department of Health*, London: FRG.

Morris, K. (1996) 'An introduction to family group conferences', in K. Morris and J. Tunnard *Family group conferences: Messages from UK practice and research*, London: FRG.

Morris, K. and Tunnard, J. (eds) (1996) *Family group conferences: Messages from UK practice and research*, London: FRG.

Morrison, C. (1988) 'Consumerism – lessons from community work', *Public Administration*, vol 66, Summer, pp 205-14.

Munro, E. (1998) 'Improving social workers' knowledge base in child protection work', *British Journal of Social Work*, vol 28, pp 89-105.

NCOPF (National Council for One Parent Families) (1982) *Against natural justice: A study of the procedures used by local authorities in tackling parental rights resolutions over children in voluntary care*, London: NCOPF.

Newman, T. (1993) 'Keeping in step', *Community Care Supplement*, 28 October, pp 1-8.

Newman, T. and Roberts, H. (1997) 'Assessing social work effectiveness in child practice: the contribution of randomized controlled trials', *Child Care Health and Development*, vol 23, no 4, pp 287-96.

NHSE (National Health Service Executive) (1996) *Patient partnership*, London: NHSE.

NISW (National Institute of Social Work) (1982) *Social workers: Their roles and tasks* (Barclay Report), London: Bedford Square Press.

Nixon, P. (1998) *Using family group conferences to re-focus family support*, Unpublished paper presented to the Second International Forum on Family Group Conferences, Winchester Guildhall, Hampshire, 15–16 September.

Nixon, P. and Taverner, P. (1993) 'Winchester project update', *Family Group Conferences Newsletter*, issue no 2, September, London: FRG.

Nixon, P., Taverner, P. and Wallace, F. (1996) 'Family group conferences in Hampshire', in K. Morris and J. Tunnard (eds) *Family group conferences: Messages from UK practice and research*, London: FRG.

Nocon, A. and Qureshi, H. (1996) *Outcomes of community care for users and carers*, Buckingham: Open University Press.

NSPCC (National Society for the Prevention of Cruelty to Children) (1996) *Messages from the NSPCC – A contribution to the refocusing debate*, London: NSPCC.

Oliver, M. (1990) *The politics of disablement*, Basingstoke: Macmillian.

ONS (Office for National Statistics) (1997) *Social focus on families* – Pullinger, J. and Summerfield, C., London: The Stationary Office.

Oppenheim, C. and Harper, L. (1996) *Poverty: The facts*, London: Child Poverty Action Group.

Ormrod, R. (1983) 'Child care law: a personal perspective', *Adoption and Fostering*, vol 7, no 4, pp 10-16.

Packman, J. (1993) 'From prevention to partnership: child welfare services across three decades', *Children and Society*, vol 7, no 2, pp 183-95.

Packman, J., Randall, J. and Jacques, N. (1986) *Who needs care?*, Oxford: Blackwell.

Page, R. (1992) 'Empowerment, oppression and beyond: coherent strategy? A reply to Ward and Mullender', *Critical Social Policy*, issue 35, vol 12, no 2, Autumn, pp 89-93.

Parker, R., Ward, H., Jackson, S., Aldgate, J. and Wedge, P. (1991) *Assessing outcomes in child care*, London: HMSO.

Parton, N. (1979) 'The natural history of child abuse: a study in social problem definition', *British Journal of Social Work*, vol 9, no 4, pp 431-51.

Parton, N. (1991) *Governing the family: Child care, child protection and State*, London: Macmillan.

Parton, N. (1994) 'Problematics of government, (post) modernity and social work', *British Journal of Social Work*, vol 24, pp 9-32.

Parton, N. (1995) *Child welfare and child protection: The need for a radical re-think*, Paper presented to National Children's Bureau, London: NCB.

Parton, N. (1996) 'Child protection, family support and social work: a critical appraisal of the Department of Health research studies in child protection', *Child and Family Social Work*, vol 1, pp 3-11.

Parton, N. (ed) (1997) *Child protection and family support: Tensions, contradictions and possibilities*, London: Routeledge.

Parton, N., Thorpe, D. and Wattam, C. (1997) *Child protection: Risk and moral order*, Basingstoke: Macmillan.

Paterson, K. (1993) 'Evaluating the organization of care and protection FGCs', *Social Work Review*, vol 5, no 4, pp 14-17.

Paterson, K. and Harvey, M. (1991) *An evaluation of the organisation and operation of care and protection family group conferences*, Wellington, New Zealand: Evaluation Unit, Department of Social Welfare.

Pennell, J. and Burford, G. (1994) 'Widening the circle: family group decision making', *Journal of Child and Youth Care*, vol 9, no 1, pp 1-11.

Pennell, J. and Burford, G. (1996) 'Attending to context: family group decision making in Canada', in J. Hudson, A. Morris, G. Maxwell and B. Galaway (eds) *Family group conferences: Perspectives in policy and practice*, Annadale, NSW, Australia: The Federation Press/Criminal Justice Press.

Pennell, J. and Burford, G. (1997) *Family group decision making project. Outcome summary report*, Newfoundland, Canada: Memorial University.

Phillipson, J. (1992) *Practising equality. Women, men and social work*, London: CCETSW.

Pilalis, J., Rev Tanielu Mamea and Opai, S. (1988) *Dangerous situations: The report of the Inquiry Team reporting on the circumstances of the death of a child*, Wellington, New Zealand: Government Printers.

Pinderhughes, E.B. (1983) 'Empowerment for our clients and for ourselves', *Social Casework*, June, vol 64, no 6, pp 331-8.

Plowden Report (1969) *Children and their primary schools*, Central Advisory Council for Education, London: HMSO.

Pollitt, C. (1990) *Managerialism and the public services: The Anglo-American experience*, Oxford: Basil Blackwell.

Printz-Winterfeld, A. (1996) 'Legal issues in implementing family group decision-making in the US', *Protecting Children*, vol 12, no 3, pp 22-6.

Prosser, H. (1978) 'Perspectives on foster care', London: NCB and NFER.

Race Equality Unit (1990) 'Black and white alliance', in NISW, *Race in child protection*, London: Race Equality Unit, National Institute for Social Work.

Rappaport, J. (1984) 'Studies in empowerment', *Prevention in Human Services*, vol 3, pp 1-7.

Rappaport, J. (1995) cited in *Networking Bulletin from the Cornell Empowerment project*, Ithaca, NY: Cornell University.

Renouf, J., Robb, G. and Wells, P. (1990) *Children, Young Persons and their Families Act, 1989: A report on its first year of operation*, Wellington, New Zealand: Department of Social Welfare.

Richardson, A. (1983) *Participation*, London: Routledge and Kegan Paul.

Rimene, S. (1993) 'The Children, Young Persons and their Families Act 1989, from a Maori Perspective', Unpublished MA Thesis, Wellington, New Zealand: Victoria University.

Robertson, J. (1996) 'Research on family group conferences in New Zealand', in J. Hudson, A. Morris, G. Maxwell and B. Galaway (eds) *Family group conferences: Perspectives on policy and practice*, Annadale, NSW, Australia: The Federation Press/Criminal Justice Press.

Rojeck, C., Peacock, G. and Collins, S. (1988) *Social work and received ideas*, London: Routledge.

Rosen, G. (1994) *A study of family views of Wandsworth's family group conferences*, Unpublished Research Report, London: Wandsworth Social Services Department.

Rowe, J., Hundleby, M. and Garnett, L. (1989) *Child care now: A survey of placement problems*, London: BAAF.

Rowe, J., Cain, H., Hundleby, M. and Keane, A. (1984) *Long term foster care*. London: Batsford.

Rowe, J. (1989) 'Chance of a lifetime', *Adoption and Fostering*, vol 13, no 3, pp 1-2.

Ryburn, M. (1991a) 'Making the Children Act work: professional attitudes and professional power', *Early Child Development and Care*, vol 75, pp 71-8.

Ryburn, M. (1991b) 'The Children Act – power and empowerment', *Adoption and Fostering*, vol 15, no 3, pp 10-15.

Ryburn, M. (1991c) 'The right of assessment', *Adoption and Fostering*, vol 15, no 1, pp 20-7.

Ryburn, M. (1993) 'A new model for family decision-making in child care and protection', *Early Child Development and Care*, vol 86, pp 1-10.

Ryburn, M. (1994a) 'Planning for children here and in New Zealand. A comparison of the legislation', in J. Tunnard (ed) *Family group conferences – A Report Commissioned by the Department of Health*, London: FRG.

Ryburn, M. (1994b) 'The use of an adversarial process in contested adoptions' in M. Ryburn (ed) *Contested adoptions: Research, law, policy and practice*, Aldershot: Gower/Arenas.

Ryburn, M. (1994c) 'Planning for children here and in New Zealand: a comparison of the legislation', in K. Morris (ed) *Family group conferences: A report commissioned by the Department of Health*, London: FRG.

Ryburn, M. and Atherton, C. (1996) 'Family group conferences: partnership in practice', *Adoption and Fostering*, vol 20, no 1, 16-23.

SACHR (Standing Advisory Commission on Human Rights) (1994) *Early childhood services – 19th report on the Standing Advisory Commission on Human Rights*, Report 1993-94, SACHR, London: HMSO.

Sainsbury, E. (ed) (1994) *Working with children in need: Studies in complexity and challenge*, London and Bristol, USA: Jessica Kingsley Publishers Ltd.

Schmitt, B.D. (1978) *Child protection team handbook*, New York, NY: STPM Press.

Schofield, G. and Thoburn, J. (1996) Child protection. The voice of the child in decision-making' No 3, *Participation and Consent*, London: Institute for Public Policy Research.

Schwandt, T.A. (1994) 'Constructivist, interpretivist approaches to human inquiry', in N.K. Denzin and Y.S. Lincoln (eds) *Handbook of qualitative research*, London: Sage Publications Ltd.

Secretary of State for Social Services (1974) *Report of the Committee of Inquiry into the care and supervision provided in relation to Maria Colwell*, London: HMSO.

Secretary of State for Social Services (1988) *Report of the Inquiry into Child Abuse in Cleveland*. Cmnd 412, London: HMSO.

Seebohm Report (1968) *Report of the Committee on local authority and applied personal social services*, Cmnd 3703, London: HMSO.

Seligman, M.E.P. (1972) 'Learned helplessness', *Annual Review of Medicine*, vol 23, pp 407-12.

Selwyn, J. (1996) 'Ascertaining children's wishes and feelings in relation to adoption', *Adoption and Fostering*, vol 20, no 3, pp 14-20.

Servian, R. (1996) *Perceptions of power*, Unpublished Masters Thesis, Bristol: University of Bristol.

Shakley, P. and Ryan, M. (1994) 'What is the role of the consumer of health care?', *Journal of Social Policy*, vol 23, no 4, pp 517-41.

Sheldon, B. (1988) 'Group controlled experiments in the evaluation of social work services', in J. Lishman (ed) *Research highlights in social work 8: Evaluation*, Aberdeen: Department of Social Work, University of Aberdeen.

Sheldon, B. (1994) 'Social work effectiveness rseaerch: implications for probation and juvenile justice services', *The Howard Journal*, vol 33, no 3, pp 218-32.

Shemmings, D. (1996) *Involving children in child protection conferences*, Social Work Monographs No 152, Norwich: University of East Anglia.

Shipman, M. (1988) *The limitations of social research*, Harlow: Longman Group Ltd.

Simmonds, J., Bull, H. and Martyn, H. (1998) *Family group conferences in Greenwich Social Services*, London: Goldsmiths' College.

Sinclair, R. (1984) *Decision-making in statutory reviews on children in care*, Aldershot: Gower.

Sinclair, R., Crosbie, D. and Vickery, A. (1990) 'Organisational influences on professional behaviour: factors affecting social work involvement in "schemes"', *Journal of Social Policy*, vol 19, no 3, pp 361-74.

Sinclair, R., Garnett, L. and Berridge, D. (1995) *Social work assessments*, London: NCB.

Skeffington Report, The (1969) *People and planning*, London: HMSO.

Smale, G. (1991) *Developing models of empowerment and practice theory*, Practice and Development Exchange, London: NISW.

Smale, G. and Tuson, G. (1993) *Empowerment, assessment, care management and the skilled worker*, London: HMSO.

Smith, C. (1997) 'Children's rights: have carers abandoned values?', *Children's Society*, vol 11, pp 3-15.

Smith, G. and Cantley, C. (1988) 'Pluralistic evaluation', in J. Lishman (ed) *Research highlights in social work 8: Evaluation*, Aberdeen: Department of Social Work, University of Aberdeen.

Smith, J.F. and Fawcett, S.B. (1991) 'Behaviour analysis of social action constructs: the case of empowerment', *Behaviour Change*, vol 8, no 1, pp 4-9.

Smith, L. (1998) *Essex Family Group Conference Project, Summary Report*, Essex County Council Social Services.

Smith, L. and Hennessy, J.(1998) *Making a difference. The Essex Family Group Conference Project*, Essex: Essex Social Services.

Social Services Committee (1984) *Children in care*, Cm 360, London: HMSO.

Sosa, E. (ed) (1975) *Causation and conditionals*, Oxford: Oxford University Press.

Stewart, J. and Walsh, K. (1992) 'Change in the management of public services', *Public Administration*, vol 70, Winter, pp 499-518.

Strathern, B. (1991) 'Implementation, a year on', *Social Work Review*, vol 3, no 4, pp 14-15.

Sundell, K., Haeggman, U. and Karlsson, U. (1998) *The Swedish family group conference study*, Unpublished paper, Stockholm: The Resource Administration for Schools and Social Services.

Swain, P. (1993) *Safe in our hands – The evaluation report of the family decision-making project*, Melbourne, Australia: Mission of St James and St Johns.

Swarup, N. (1992) *Equal voice: The service needs of black and minority ethnic communities*, Portsmouth: SSRIU, University of Portsmouth.

Tapp, P. (1990) 'Family group conferences on the Children, Young Persons and their Families Act 1989: an ineffective statute?', *New Zealand Recent Law Review*, vol 2, pp 82-8.

Tapp, P., Geddis, D. and Taylor, N. (1992) 'Protecting the family', in M. Hengham and B. Atkin (eds) *Family law policy in New Zealand*, Auckland, New Zealand: Oxford University Press.

Taylor, C. (1971) 'Interpretation and the sciences of man', *The Review of Metaphysics*, vol 25, no 1, pp 3-51.

Thoburn, J., Lewis, A. and Shemmings, D. (1995a) 'Family participation in child protection', *Child Abuse Review*, vol 4, p 161.

Thoburn, J., Lewis, A. and Shemmings, D. (1995b) *Paternalism or partnership? Family involvement in the child protection process*, London: HMSO.

Thoburn, J., Lewis, A. and Shemmings, D. (1996) 'Partnership-based practice in child protection work', in M. Hill and J. Aldgate (eds) *Child welfare services*, London: Jessica Kingsley, pp 132-43.

Thomas, N. (1994) *In the driving seat – A study of the family group meetings project in Hereford*, Swansea: Department of Social Policy and Applied Social Studies, University of Wales

Thornton, C. (1993) *Family group conferences – A literature review*, New Zealand: Practitioners Publishing CG Allen.

Thorpe, D. (1989) *Patterns of child protection intervention and service delivery: Report of the pilot project*, Research Report No 4, Crime Research Centre, Perth, Australia: University of Western Australia.

Thorpe, D. (1994) *Evaluating child protection*, Buckingham and Philadelphia: Open University Press.

Trinder, C. (1996) 'Social work research: the state of the art (or science)', *Child and Family Social Work*, vol 1, pp 223-42.

Triseliotis, J. (1980) 'Growing up in foster care and after', in J. Triseliotis (ed) *New developments in foster care and adoption*, London: Routledge and Kegan Paul.

Triseliotis, J., Burland, M., Hill, M. and Lambert, L. (1995) *Teenagers and the social work services*, London:HMSO.

Tunnard, J. (1991) 'Setting the scene for partnership in The Children Act 1989', *Working in partnership with families*, London: FRG.

Tunstill, J. (1997) 'Implementing the family support clauses of the 1989 Children Act: legislative, professional and organisational obstacles', in N. Parton (ed) *Child protection and family support – Tensions, contradictions and possibilities*, London: Routledge.

Utting, D. (1995) *Family and parenthood – supporting families, preventing breakdown*, York: Joseph Rowntree Foundation.

Vernon, J. and Fruin, D. (1986) *In care: A study of social work decision-making*, London: NCB.

Wagner Committee (1988) 'Residential care', *A positive choice – Report of the Independent Review of Residential Care*, chaired by Gillian Wagner, London: HMSO.

Walker, H. (1996) 'Whanau Hui. Family decision making and the family group conference: an indigenous Maori view', in American Humane Association, *Protecting children*, Englewood, CO: American Humane Association.

WARAG (Women's Anti Racist Action Group) (1984) *Institutional racism report to the Department of Social Welfare*, Wellington, New Zealand: Government Printer.

Ward, D. and Mullender, A. (1991) 'Empowerment and oppression: an indissoluble pairing for contemporary social work', *Critical Social Policy*, issue 32, pp 21-30.

Wedge, P. and Mantle, G. (1991) *Sibling groups and social work: A study of children referred for permanent family placement*, Aldershot: Avebury.

Wilcox, R., Smith, D., Moore, J., Hewitt, A., Allan, G., Walker, H., Ropata, M., Monu, L. and Featherstone, T. (1991) *Family Decision-Making. Family group conferences: Practitioners' views*, Lower Hutt, New Zealand: Practitioners' Publishing.

Willcocks, D., Pearce, S., Kellaher, L. and Ring, J. (1982) *The residential life of old people*. London: Surrey Research Unit, Polytechnic of North London.

Williams, F. (1992) 'Somewhere over the rainbow: universality and diversity in social policy', *Social Policy Review, 1991-92*, London: Social Policy Association.

Williams, M. (1998) 'The social world as knowable', in T. May and M. Williams (eds) *Knowing the social world*, Buckingham: Open University Press.

Worral, J. (1994) 'The CYPF Act and kinship care', Paper presented to the IYF Family Rights and Responsibilities Symposium, Wellington, New Zealand.

Wundersitz, J. and Hetzel, S. (1996) 'Family conferencing from young offenders: the South Australian experience', in J. Hudson, A. Morris, G. Maxwell and B. Galaway (eds) *Family group conferences: Perspectives on policy and practice*, Anndale, NSW. Australia: The Federation Press/Criminal Justice Press.

Index